THE WORLD OF PARA HANDY

a selection from the stories

by

Neil Munro

(Hugh Foulis)

With three previously uncollected stories

Introduced and Annotated

by

Brian D. Osborne

&

Ronald Armstrong

SEANACHAIDH PUBLISHING LTD
GREENOCK

Seanachaidh Publishing Ltd
14 William Street
Greenock PA15 1BT
Scotland

Graphic Design by: William Stewart D.A.

Printed by Holmes MacDougall Ltd, Edinburgh

ISBN 0 948963 65 4

FOREWORD

THE REMARKABLE endurance of the 'Para Handy' stories, which still attract a wide audience eighty years after their first appearance in the Glasgow Evening News, was testified to by the success of the Seanachaidh edition of the collected stories published in 1986. Apart from the continuing popularity of the stories, however, there are two reasons for suggesting that readers will find this volume useful.

Firstly we hope to rehabilitate some of Munro's literary reputation, once considerable and largely based on his historical novels, but we believe properly owing as much to these shorter pieces.

Along with the reading public's appetite for the West Highland tales goes a wider celebrity, amounting almost to notoriety, which owes much to the television adaptations of recent years. At any rate the man in the street has an image of Para Handy and a range of quotations and anecdote based on the character or its televised representation even if he has never read the stories. We are unaware of any other collection of Scots comic prose which enjoys such a lasting and secure place in the affections of the public.

Paradoxically, though, Munro's creation can be termed neglected, since hardly any critic has taken the stories seriously. The only Munro with an entry in Margaret Drabble's 'Oxford Companion to English Literature' is H.H. Munro ('Saki'). Furthermore Munro seems to have set the tone for the undervaluing of these stories by his publishing them under the pen-name of 'Hugh Foulis'.

As importantly, we feel that present day readers, while relishing the vivid and highly accessible comedy of character and dialogue, will appreciate the stories more fully with an understanding of the background and an explanation of the many specific references to contemporary people and events. These tales have a richly observed setting, rooted in time and place and the largely vanished Glasgow, Clyde and West Highland world of the Vital Spark needs and deserves describing and illustrating.

The explanatory notes, which accompany a selection of favourite stories, also look at such intriguing questions as: where was Para Handy born; what were his religious views; what did he think of international affairs; what did he do before captaining the Vital Spark?

Also included are three stories which have never before appeared in book form and which have been rescued from the pages of the 'Glasgow Evening News'.

PARA'S WORLD

No ONE surely, reads these stories for the social history, when there are so many other good reasons, yet a clear picture emerges of a lost world of West Highland villages bound together by the sea and the vessels on it. In late Victorian or Edwardian times (the period covered by the stories is roughly 1900-1918) these communities were enjoying a golden age of water transport. Along Munro's native Loch Fyneside alone there were seven piers and yet other places where a boat came out to meet the steamer.

A winter service was kept up but it was the holiday trade which made the steamers profitable. Munro's description of a typical July Saturday which appears in 'Wee Teeny' (a story not included in this collection) is worth quoting for its characteristically colourful account of a scene which could be repeated at any one of scores of piers from Craigendoran to Campbeltown.

'The last passenger steamer to sail that day from Ardrishaig was a trip from Rothesay. It was Glasgow Fair Saturday and Ardrishaig Quay was black with people. There was a marvellously stimulating odour of dulse, herring and shell-fish, for everybody carried away in a handkerchief a few samples of these marine products that are now the only sea-side souvenirs not made in Germany. The Vital Spark in ballast, Clydeward bound, lay inside the passenger steamer, ready to start when the latter had got under weigh, and Para Handy and his mate meanwhile sat on the fo'c'sle-head of 'the smertest boat in the tred' watching the frantic efforts of lady excursionists to get their husbands on the steamer before it was too late, and the deliberate efforts of the said husbands to slink away up the village again just for one more drink. Wildly the steamer hooted from her siren, fiercely clanged her bell, vociferously the Captain roared upon his bridge, people aboard yelled eagerly to friends ashore to hurry up, and the people ashore as eagerly demanded to know what all the hurry was about, and where the bleezes was Wull. Women loudly defied the purser to let the ship go away without their John, for he had paid his money for his ticket, and though he was only a working-man his money was as good as anybody else's; and John, on the quay, with his hat thrust back on his head, his thumbs in the armhole of his waistcoat and a red handkerchief full of dulse at his feet, gave a display of step-dancing that was responsible for a great deal of the congestion of traffic at the shore end of the gangway.'

This description, with its colour, vitality and shrewd observation could almost be from the 'Pickwick Papers.'

At the same time the gabbarts, and later the steam puffers, were attending to the more essential needs of these coastal communities. The puffer was generally thought of as a coal boat, but could also be pressed into carrying a tremendous variety of goods. If we are to believe her skipper the Vital Spark was suited to carrying 'nice genteel luggage for the shooting lodges' as did the doyenne of steamers, the 'Columba', but in practice the cargoes were more likely to be 'coals and whunstone, and oak bark, and timber, and trash like that.'. She did take a farmer's flitting on at least one occasion, though, the mixed cargo included everything ' from bird cages to cottage pianos'.

A life in the 'coastin' tred' was hard and dirty no doubt, but you might not suppose so from a quick glance at these stories. Para, Dougie and the rest of the crew, 'Brutain's hardy sons' each and every one, certainly are seen now and then battling against a gale but usually the picture is of a leisurely life—'we went into Greenock for some marmalade, and did we no' stay three days'. In harbour there was from time to time some conflict between the skipper and the crew. Para, with an eye to enhancing the ship's reputation as the 'smertest boat in the tred', would often wish some painting to be done, while the crew, if in funds, would rather go ashore and relax in a harbour-side inn.

When the crew were officially at ease, they would sit in the fo'c'sle, a small triangular space in the bows of the ship which acted as cabin, galley and mess-room for the four man crew, and tell a baur or two of: 'All the seas that lie between Bowling and Stornoway'

PARA'S PLACES

TURN TO the chapter 'Para in Print' to discover that Munro's stories, appearing as they did in an evening newspaper, were written with an eye to topical events and personalities; very much of their Time. They were, however, even more firmly rooted in a Sense of Place.

We have been unable to detect even a single reference to an imaginary loch, harbour or even a public house in all of the references which appear in our thirty eight selected stories.

Just how deep were Munro's knowledge and affection for 'Para's Places' we can guess from a glimpse of his 1907 publication 'The Clyde, River and Firth'. This popular account, perhaps rather overwritten to modern taste, gives a lyrical description of the river from its source to Ailsa Craig. A few extracts from its beautifully illustrated pages will provide an interesting commentary on the setting in which Munro placed the Captain and his crew. And firstly . . .

GLASGOW

'A mighty place for trade . . .; with a stern and arid Sabbath; and a preposterous early hour for the closing of public houses'

The crew of the Vital Spark seldom venture out of the relatively circumscribed area of the harbour and the housing areas nearby like Gorbals, Plantation & Finnieston.

On either side of

'a fairway of 620 feet at its widest and 362 at its narrowest point' . . . 'the harbour life slops over its actual precincts, and the neighbouring streets . . . bear a marine impress. Their tall "lands" of flats fed from a common stair are the homes of folk whose men are on the quays.'

In 'Dougie's Family' Munro informs us that the mate, and his wife and ten children, live up one of these common stairs in the Plantation area, and in the very next tenement lives Dan MacPhail and his family. Even the Captain goes to live in Glasgow after his marriage to the baker's little widow. At other times we hear of 'baals' and similar 'high jeenks' at presumably the Highlanders' Institute; a canary is purchased at the Bird Market; and of course the 'Highlandman's Umbrella' is used as a meeting place for exiles from the North. As Para says 'it's Gleska for gaiety, if you have the money'.

Neil Munro was a working journalist before anything else and his Glasgow and its river are seen from the perspective which comes from first-hand experience. Undoubtedly he haunted the ferries, lingered on the quays among sailors of all nations and gazed at the cargoes loading and unloading in the harbour of what was then the second city of the Empire.

Yet perhaps more than just a working journalist, even in the cub reporter days; a poet perhaps, a Conrad or an Orwell before his time? (Though not exactly 'Down and Out in Glasgow'). Examine this characteristic passage from 'The Clyde' and speculate.

> Nor even then can one rightly comprehend the harbour who has not brooded beside sheer-leg and crane-jib that are mightily moving enormous weights as if they had been toys; swallowed the coal-dust of the docks, dodged traction engines, eaten Irish stew for breakfast in the Sailors' Home, watched Geordie Geddes trawl for corpses, sat in the fo'c'sles of 'tramps', stood in a fog by the pilot on the bridge, heard the sorrows of a Shore Superintendent and the loyal lies of witnesses in a Board of Trade examination, who feel bound to 'stick by the owners' and swear their engines backed ten minutes before the accident; or sat on a cask in the Prince's Dock on peaceful Sabbath mornings when the shipping seemed asleep, or an unseen concertina played some sailor's jig for canticle.

Did the memory of the 'unseen concertina' provide an inspiration for our jaunty character Sunny Jim? It is a jig-tune he plays on his 'bonny wee melodeon' to accompany the dancing sausages in the story 'A New Cook' which first appeared a few months after the publication of 'The Clyde, River and Firth'.

THE UPPER RIVER

The stretch of the river from Bowling to Greenock features in several of the tales. Although never stated, the Vital Spark's home port would seem to have been Bowling, although she frequently called in at Greenock for orders and cargoes. Although the puffer design was based on the necessity to pass through the 70 foot locks on the Forth and Clyde Canal the 'Vital Spark' was an 'outside boat' and we have no record of the crew negotiating the Forth and Clyde Canal.

THE FIRTH OF CLYDE

The wider Firth was where the courses of the elegant passenger steamers of Messrs. Macbrayne and the railway companies crossed that of the workaday Vital Spark. The great fin de siècle holiday boom had led to the expansion of resorts such as Largs, Millport and Rothesay. Newer watering places had grown up alongside older communities and the steam puffer came into its own as a workhorse to bring in the building materials and fuel. Neil Munro described all this in his graceful commentary on the river, 'The Clyde, River and Firth'. In his fictional recreation of this world Para Handy is to be found ploughing all the waters of the estuary.

Down to ARRAN for example; Para has a wager with a Brodick man about a singing canary and returns with a 'cargo of grevel' to collect his bet. It is also in Arran that we first hear of Hurricane Jack, that larger than life character, 'as weel kent in Calcutta as if he wass in the Coocaddens', stealing 'wan smaal wee sheep' from the shore on the island's west coast at Catacol.

Elsewhere, at the head of LOCH LONG, the Arrochar midges are so fierce one night that they provoke the Captain to such hyperbole as to make 'Mudges' a favourite tale with anyone who has visited the West Coast in high summer.

LOCH FYNE

The Clyde's longest sea-loch is the real centre of Para Handy's world. About one half of the stories have a connection with this area and Para himself may have been born there. However, for a fuller discussion of this point, see the notes to 'In Search of a Wife'.

Go to Loch Fyne now and to the uninitiated it may seem like a sleepy backwater, but to the devoted readers of these tales almost every place has its delightful associations:

busy TARBERT—where Para met the spae-wife at the Fair and where he fell foul of the law for sounding the ship's whistle at 2.00 a.m.

romantic CAMPBELTOWN—scene of the Tar's wedding and where Para went to court the widow Crawford

And perhaps most magical of all, FURNACE—'where you don't need tickets for a baal as long as you ken the man at the door and taalk the Gaalic at him.'

You might follow the 'Royal Route' from the Clyde to Ardrishaig today, through the Crinan Canal and out into West Highland waters through the Dorus Mor, the 'Great Gate', sailing perhaps as far as Mull, where at Tobermory the enterprising crew sold tickets to look at the whale. There is indeed much charm in the descriptions of these more distant scenes; however in reading this book you must, above all, know your Loch Fyne as it was in the heyday of the herring fishing, that legendary time of 'high jeenks and big hauls; you werena very smert if you werena into both of them.'

   . . . many generations of Loch Fyneside men have followed a vocation which has much of the uncertainty of backing horses without so much amusement. Towns like Inveraray, Lochgilphead, and Tarbert grew up, as it were, round the fishing smacks that in old days ran into their bays for shelter, and Minard, Crarae, Lochgair, Castle Lachlan, Strachur, and other villages on either side of the Loch depend to some extent for their existence on the silver harvest of the sea

Munro: Clyde, River and Firth.

Crinan Canal *Argyll & Bute District Libraries*

THE HUMOUR OF 'PARA HANDY'

ALMOST ALL of the comic flavour of these stories is to be found in the dialogue rather than in the narrative, and no part of the dialogue is more important than Para Handy's own contribution. Into the mouth of his skipper Munro has put any amount of humorous anecdotes and reflections, so much so that some of the stories are virtually monologues. For example, although it may be a matter of taste, to many readers the semi-mythical Hurricane Jack as described by Para with a 'back on him like a shipping box' is preferable to the Jack who later makes a personal appearance in the stories.

Para's speech is of course given a fine exotic touch by the fact that he, and Dougie the Mate, have 'the Gaalic'. [No lover of these stories could, with the wealth of examples provided, commit the solecism of pronouncing Gaelic as 'Gaylic'!]

While there may be a touch of the stage Highlander about such 'Handyisms' as 'chust sublime' and 'high jeenks', that is really only another way of saying that the Captain is a larger-than-life character. He is an original, curiously reminiscent of a Dickensian character such as Sam Weller or one of Sir Walter Scott's Doric speakers. In a more far-fetched way Para also has a certain resemblance to 'the wily Odysseus', another sea-farer who roamed among sea-girt islands, had an adventure with sheep and who 'had rather a gallant way with the sex, generally said 'mem' to them all. . . .'

Para too, is no stranger to exaggeration, but more often it is an appreciative 'baur' of epic proportions about the mighty Hurricane Jack who

> . . . iss a man that can sail anything and go anywhere, and aalways be the perfect chentleman. A millionaire's yat or a washin-boyne—it's aal the same to Jeck . . . And never anything else but 'lastic sided boots, even in the coorsest weather. . . .

Much of the humour of the stories lies in the juxtaposition of the Highland characters, Para and Dougie, and the Lowland figures, The Tar, Sunny Jim and, particularly, Macphail the Engineer (who, despite his Highland surname, is a low country man, from Motherwell in industrial Lanarkshire.) Hugh MacDiarmid (C.M.Grieve) has written of the 'Caledonian antizyzygy'—the contrast or conflict between the two competing strains within the Scottish personality. In the tensions between the romantic, generous, imaginative Highland skipper and the thrawn, prosaic Lowland engineer we see a fine example of the contrast between the two races.

> 'Do you know the way it iss that steamboat enchineers is alwaays doon in the mooth like that? It's the want of nature. They never let themselves go. Poor duvvles, workin' away among their bits o' enchines, they never get the wind and sun aboot them right the same ass us seamen'.

Additional piquancy is given to the situation by Macphail, the severely practical engineer, having a none too secret passion for the most lurid penny novelettes.

A new dimension comes into the stories with the arrival of the Glaswegian Sunny Jim. As a replacement for The Tar, Davie Green, to give him his full name for once, is more than good value. He it is who devises the Tobermory whale exhibition and starts the persecution of the Captain after the death of the cockatoo in 'An Ocean Tragedy'—

> 'If it's no' murder, it's manslaughter; monkeys, cockatoos, and parrots a' come under the Act o' Parliament. A cockatoo's no' like a canary; it's able to speak the language and give an opeenion, and the man that wad kill a cockatoo wad kill a wean.'

The persecution or 'roasting' of Para by his crew is a most amusing example of a traditional kind of Scottish humour; something kindlier than satire and more subtle than ridicule. It may be descended from the ancient Scottish literary custom of 'flyting' as found in the poems of Dunbar and his contemporaries and survives to this day in the innocent sport found in every workplace of 'taking a loan of' someone and in its latest form 'winding someone up'. To wind a workmate up, as his shipmates do to Dougie in 'Dougie's Family' is to lead him on to make statements or commit indiscretions which will provide scope for innocent amusement.

Curiously enough Para Handy has not himself had many imitators, except perhaps in a coincidental way in Sean O'Casey's Captain Jack Boyle, who actually was 'only wanst on the watter, on an old collier from here to Liverpool.'

PARA IN PRINT

EVERY MONDAY 'The Looker-On' column in the Glasgow Evening News gave Neil Munro the chance to reflect on current events, to air his views or to entertain with a short story. On Monday 16th January 1905 a new and enduring character in Scottish fiction was launched on the public:

> 'A short, thick-set man, with a red beard, a hard round felt hat ridiculously out of harmony with a blue pilot jacket and trousers and a seaman's jersey. . . .'

in short, Para Handy, Master Mariner, had arrived.

At intervals of two or three weeks during 1905 and the early months of 1906 a further instalment in the saga of the Vital Spark and her crew appeared to brighten the Glaswegians' Mondays. How quickly Para and the Vital Spark became an accepted part of Glasgow life, of local folklore almost, may be judged from a cartoon which appeared in the News on 9th August 1905. Headlined 'The Next Tramway Extension' it was a comment on the recent gift of the Ardgoil Estate to the City of Glasgow and shows a Glasgow Corporation tramcar mounted on a ship named Vital Spark and headed down river to the new Argyllshire property. In less than eight months and after only 13 stories Munro's creation had so completely come to life that the Vital Spark had become a name that a cartoonist could use without explanation or sub-title.

By the Spring of 1906 William Blackwood & Sons were arranging for the publication of the first anthology of Para stories—twenty-two tales which originally appeared in the News and three stories 'Lodgers on a Houseboat', 'The Disappointment of Erchie's Niece' and 'Para Handy's Wedding', written especially for the book. Three News stories were not included in the anthology 'The Vital Spark and her Queer Crew' and have never appeared in book form until now. Quite why these three stories were dropped is not clear, though one, 'Para Handy at the Poll', published in January 1906, is clearly a topical reference to the General Election of that time, and might have been thought less appropriate for book publication.

One other News story from this period, 'The Maids of Bute', was held over and appeared in the second anthology 'In Highland Harbours with Para Handy, S.S. Vital Spark' in 1911. The final anthology 'Hurricane Jack of the Vital Spark' did not appear until 1923. The omnibus edition of the Para stories, the Erchie stories and the tales of Jimmy Swan (which was the first to formally link Munro, rather than 'Hugh Foulis', with these stories) appeared in 1931, the year after Munro's death.

The order of stories in the 1906 anthology bore little relationship to the original order of newspaper publication—except that 'Para Handy Master Mariner'—the first story in the book was also the first story to appear in the News. Some stories had obvious topicality, for example 'Three Dry Days', which is set in February, that odd month when as Dougie says '. . . the New Year's no' right bye, and the Gleska Fair's chust comin' on . . .' appeared on 5th February 1906 and its companion piece 'The Valentine That Misfired' came out on 19th February, as close to St. Valentine's Day as the schedule would allow.

Two of the extra stories written for the anthology would seem to have had particular aims. 'The Disappointment of Erchie's Niece' reintroduces the reader to Erchie Macpherson from the 'Erchie, My Droll Friend' series. Munro had published an anthology of Erchie stories in 1904 and this was perhaps an attempt to link the two sets of stories with benefit to the sales of both volumes.

Another of the new stories written for book publication, 'Para Handy's Wedding' is clearly an extremely appropriate way to round off the volume. It perhaps, in view of Munro's very limited interest in these humorous sketches, was also meant to end the career of Peter Macfarlane.

However like another contemporary writer, Sir Arthur Conan Doyle, who also considered that his historical novels were his most important work and his short stories of lesser worth, the character refused to be killed. Just as Holmes survived the Reichenbach Falls, so Para survives marriage to the Widow Crawford and to our delight continues to sail the west coast for many years.

If the newspaper publication of the stories had been an obvious success, so too was their appearance in book form. The News in its regular weekly book page, the 'In the Bookshop' column, noted on 12th April 1906

'Among the shilling books specially suited for reading on the Spring Holiday, I must note 'The Vital Spark' which is just being published by Messrs. Blackwood. It would seem that the success of Erchie has given the booksellers confidence in anything bearing the signature of 'Hugh Foulis', as the orders for 'The Vital Spark' are much larger than for the former book. London orders are particularly large. As most Glasgow people know, the sketches, which originally appeared in the 'News', of the exploits of Para Handy and his crew are intensely funny, without degenerating into caricature, and it is safe to predict a very large sale for the book when it is placed before the public.

After what must have been a long wait for admirers of Para the Vital Spark sailed again on 10th February 1908 when Sunny Jim appeared as 'A New Cook'. Over the next three years the bulk of the stories which were to feature in the second anthology 'In Highland Harbours with Para Handy, S.S. Vital Spark' appeared at irregular intervals in the News.

The return of Para was welcomed in an enthusiastic letter to the editor and after a few weeks Munro's two humorous series—Para and Erchie—were moved from the Monday 'Looker-On' spot to the Saturday edition with its week-end reading section. In the announcement of this change both series were, for the first time, announced as being written by Neil Munro. However by the end of the year Para was back as an irregular feature in the 'Looker-On' column.

Many of the stories of this period are very closely linked to and inspired by contemporary events and it would seem that Munro increasingly waited for the right moment before turning out a Para story. For example 'To Campbeltown by Sea' is set in a heat wave and published in July 1908 when Scotland was suffering a remarkable spell of heat and drought and 'Para Handy's Vote' relates to the General Election of December 1910. The collection which appeared in July 1911 was enthusiastically welcomed—the News reviewer noting 'they sparkle with a humour that is ever fresh'.

These 'minor pieces', which Munro turned out as part of his regular journalistic work and which he thought of so little worth, have been his most lasting works. They were transferred into successful television series which brought the Vital Spark and her crew to an audience far beyond Munro's Glasgow.

The omnibus edition reprinted regularly for twenty years, being replaced in Blackwood's list by a collection of the three volumes of the Para stories in 1955, the Erchie and Jimmy Swan stories going out of print at this time. A paperback edition of the Para Handy stories appeared from Pan in 1969 and the Seanachaidh edition of the complete Para stories in 1986. The historical novels, which Munro valued so highly, had by the 1980's all gone out of print.

NEIL MUNRO

'MY GOODNESS! . . . and you'll be writing things for the papers? Cot bless me!...and do you tell me you can be makin' a living off that? I'm not asking you, mind, hoo mich you'll be makin', don't tell me; not a cheep! not a cheep! But I'll wudger it's more than Maclean the munister.'

Neil Munro was born in Inveraray on Loch Fyneside, in the building known as Crombie's Land on June 3rd 1864. Generations of his family had lived and worked as farmers and shepherds at the village of Carnus, now disappeared, in Glen Aray—or so at least goes the version printed in all the standard sources.

In fact the truth is slightly different. Munro was in fact born on June 3rd 1863—exactly one year earlier than the 'official' date—the illegitimate son of Ann Munro, Kitchen Maid. There is no record of a marriage of this Ann Munro to the James Thompson Munro who was later represented as Neil Munro's father, e.g. on Neil's death certificate. The 1871 census returns for Inveraray record a family living in a one roomed dwelling at McVicar's Land, Ark Lane, consisting of Angus McArthur Munro, aged 66, formerly a crofter; his daughter, Agnes Munro, unmarried domestic servant aged 38 and Neil, his grandson, aged 7. (It is noteworthy that the correct date of birth had been supplied to the census enumerator.) It would thus seem that Munro, like his hero Para Handy, was '. . . brocht up wi' an auntie. . . .'

He attended the village school at High Balantyre and when he left school he was at the age of fourteen

'. . . insinuated, without any regard for my own desires, into a country lawyer's office, wherefrom I withdrew myself as soon as I arrived at years of discretion and revolt.' (The Brave Days)

The country lawyer's office was in fact the office of the Sheriff Clerk of Argyll and one may speculate as to the influence which placed a poor boy from a country school with no obvious family influence in such a sought after and prestigious post. During his five years there he countered the boredom of office routine by reading and developed his flair for writing by contributing short articles for local newspapers.

His youthful boredom was coupled with a realisation that the future for the small communities of Loch Fyneside was bleak. Years later in his 'The Clyde, River and Firth' he wrote:

In 1750 the Duke of Argyll could raise if necessary 10,000 men able to bear arms. The bulk of them must have been found between the shores of Loch Fyne and Loch Awe; single glens of Loch Fyne could turn out over two hundred swords; now they are desolate.

In May 1881 like many ambitious young men before him, and even more since, he took the sea-road south to Glasgow and, while learning shorthand, earned his living in the cashier's office of an ironmonger's shop in the Trongate. Before long however he found a post on a small local newspaper, spending ten years there before moving on to a newspaper of some significance, The Greenock Advertiser. He next worked for The Glasgow News where he remained until it closed, when he was offered a post with the much larger Glasgow Evening News. He soon became chief reporter as well as Art, Drama and Literary Critic and was made editor in 1918, a position which he held until his reluctant retirement in 1927.

While engaged on his journalistic work Munro began writing short stories, novels and poetry. His shorter work appeared.in a number of the flourishing literary periodicals of the period and a collection of stories 'The Lost Pibroch' was published by Blackwoods in 1896.

His early novels such as 'John Splendid' and 'Gillian the Dreamer' dealt mainly with what would today be described—rather deprecatingly—as a 'Celtic twilight' or romantic view of history. After 1903 he changed tack, abandoned history and attempted a more realistic style. The change did not suit some critics who saw him as a major writer of historical romance in the Scott and Stevenson tradition and did not think that his realistic novels matched up to works such as John MacDougall Hay's 'Gillespie' and other contemporary works of the realist 'anti-kailyard' school of Scottish fiction.

Two collections of essays and journalism were published after his death 'The Brave Days' and 'The Looker-On'. 'The Brave Days' being a series of autobiographical sketches he contributed to the News after his retirement, while the other collection gathered together some of the splendidly characteristic pieces from his literary journalism, some special reports and the regular 'Looker- On' column from earlier in the century.

Before the First World War he had in fact semi-retired from daily journalism to devote himself to his more serious writing but was recalled to edit the News in 1918. He moved in 1927 to a beautiful Regency villa in Helensburgh overlooking his beloved Firth of Clyde. He named the house 'Cromalt' after a stream in his native Inveraray.

On 27th December 1930 the Dumbartonshire local paper The Lennox Herald noted:

The death has occurred at his residence, 'Cromalt', of Mr Neil Munro, LL.D., the Scottish novelist and journalist. He was in his 67th year and had been in failing health for some time. Of a reticent and unassuming nature, he never sought public favour, but as long ago as 1908 he was honoured with the degree of LL.D by Glasgow University and, only two months ago, a similar compliment was paid him by Edinburgh University. He received the freedom of his native town of Inveraray in 1909.

His death attracted little notice although the novelist Hugh Walpole lamented the death of 'one of Scotland's few great novelists'. One of his great advocates was a friend and former News colleague, the novelist George Blake, who edited and introduced the two posthumous collections 'The Brave Days' and 'The Looker-On'. In his introduction to the former volume Blake speaks of Munro's reticent nature and of the contrast between his two personalities and two fields of writing—the Neil Munro of the novels and the 'Hugh Foulis' of the lighter writing and the journalism. There was also certainly an evident tension manifest in much of his work between the Glasgow journalist, working in a city which he knew well and loved deeply and the Highland exile, forever homesick for the Argyllshire of his childhood.

Munro was buried at Kilmalieu, in Inveraray, and there is a monument to him on a bleak hillside in Glen Aray, facing the vanished home of his ancestors.

ACKNOWLEDGEMENTS

THE AUTHORS are grateful to Graham Hopner of Dumbarton District Libraries for his help with Neil Munro's biography. Our thanks are also due to David Harvie for his contribution to this section and for other advice and encouragement and to Jessie MacLeod for her advice on matters Gaelic.

Most of the illustrations are from Argyll & Bute District Libraries Local Studies collection and our sincere thanks are due to Andrew Ewan, the District Librarian and his colleagues for their help and assistance.

CONTENTS

Stories from: "Hurricane Jack of the *Vital Spark*"

Previously Uncollected Stories

1 PARA HANDY, MASTER MARINER

A SHORT, thick-set man, with a red beard, a hard round felt hat, ridiculously out of harmony with a blue pilot jacket and trousers and a seaman's jersey, his hands immersed deeply in those pockets our fathers (and the heroes of Rabelais) used to wear behind a front flap, he would have attracted my notice even if he had not, unaware of my presence so close behind him, been humming to himself the chorus of a song that used to be very popular on gabbarts,[1] but is now gone out of date, like 'The Captain with the Whiskers took a Sly Glance at me'. You may have heard it thirty years ago, before the steam puffer[2] came in to sweep the sailing smack from all the seas that lie between Bowling and Stornoway. It runs —

> *"Young Munro he took a notion*
> *For to sail across the sea,*
> *And he left his true love weeping,*
> *All alone on Greenock Quay,"*

And by that sign, and by his red beard, and by a curious gesture he had, as if he were now and then going to scratch his ear and only determined not to do it when his hand was up, I knew he was one of the Macfarlanes. There were ten Macfarlanes, all men, except one, and he was a valet, but the family did their best to conceal the fact, and said he was away on the yachts, and making that much money he had not time to write a scrape home.

'I think I ought to know you,' I said to the vocalist with the hard hat. 'You are a Macfarlane: either the Beekan, or Kail, or the Nipper, or Keep Dark, or Para Handy —'

'As sure as daith,' said he, 'I'm chust Para Handy, and I ken your name fine, but I cannot chust mind your face.' He had turned round on the pawl[3] he sat on, without taking his hands from his pockets, and looked up

---

1. *A shallow draught sailing vessel used in the Scottish coastal trade.*

2. *A small steam lighter. Puffers were extensively used as general cargo carriers along the Western seaboard of Scotland. The puffer originated in the 1880's and were built in three types suited to canal, estuarine and off-shore work. The* Vital Spark *which, as Para Handy will shortly reveal, had made the crossing to Londonderry (without lights) was of the largest type. The name 'puffer' derives from the characteristic puffing sound made by the engine exhaust venting through the funnel.*

3. *A mooring post.*

at me where I stood beside him, watching a river steamer being warped into the pier.

'My goodness!' he said about ten minutes later,when he had wormed my whole history out of me; 'and you'll be writing things for the papers? Cot bless me! and do you tell me you can be makin' a living off that? I'm not asking you, mind, hoo mich you'll be makin', don't tell me; not a cheep! not a cheep! But I'll wudger it's more than Maclean the munister. But och! I'm not saying: it iss not my business. The munister has two hundred in the year and a coo's gress:[4] he iss aye the big man up yonder, but it iss me would like to show him he wass not so big a man as yourself. Eh? But not a cheep! not a cheep! A Macfarlane would never put his nose into another man's oar.'

'And where have you been this long while?' I asked, having let it sink into his mind that there was no chance today of his learning my exact income, expenditure, and how much I had in the bank.

'Me!' said he; 'I am going up and down like yon fellow in the Scruptures — what wass his name? Sampson — seeking what I may devour.[5] I am out of a chob. Chust that: out of a chob. You'll not be hearin' of anybody in your line that iss in want of a skipper?

Skippers, I said, were in rare demand in my line of business. We hadn't used a skipper for years.

'Chus that! chust that! I only mentioned it in case. You are making things for newspapers, my Cot! what will they not do now for the penny? Well, that is it; I am out of a chob; chust putting bye the time. I'm not vexed for myself, so mich as for poor Dougie. Dougie wass mate, and I wass skipper. I don't know if you kent the *Fital Spark?*'

The *Vital Spark,* I confessed, was well known to me as the most uncertain puffer that ever kept the Old New-Year[6] in Upper Lochfyne.

'That wass her!' said Macfarlane, almost weeping. 'There was never the bate of her, and I have sailed in her four years over twenty with my hert in my mooth for fear of her boiler. If you never saw the *Fital Spark,* she is aal hold, with the boiler behind, four men and a derrick, and a watter-butt

---

4. *The grazing for a cow—the parish Minister's glebe.*

5. *Para, though ready with a Scriptural quotation, frequently gets things a little confused. He is here quoting, not from the story of Samson, but from 1st Peter Ch.5 v.8 'Be sober, be vigilant; because your adversary the devil, as a roaring lion, walketh about, seeking whom he may devour:'*

6. *New Year's Day according to the old or Julian calendar—still celebrated in parts of the Highlands and Islands.*

and a pan loaf[7] in the fo'csle. Oh man! she wass the beauty! She was chust sublime! She should be carryin' nothing but gentry for passengers, or nice genteel luggage for the shooting-lodges, but there they would be spoilin' her and rubbin' all the pent off her with their coals, and sand, and whunstone, and oak bark, and timber, and trash like that.'

'I understood she had one weakness at least, that her boiler was apt to prime.'

'It's a — lie,' cried Macfarlane, quite furious; 'her boiler never primed more than wance a month, and that wass not with fair play. If Dougie wass here he would tell you.

'I wass ass prood of that boat ass the Duke of Argyll, ay, or Lord Breadalbane. If you would see me waalkin' aboot on her dake when we wass lyin' at the quay! There wasna the like of it in the West Hielan's. I wass chust sublime! She had a gold bead aboot her; it's no lie I am tellin' you, and I would be pentin' her oot of my own pocket every time we went to Arran for gravel. She drawed four feet forrit and nine aft, and she could go like the duvvle.'

'I have heard it put at five knots,' I said maliciously.

Macfarlane bounded from his seat. 'Five knots!' he cried. 'Show me the man that says five knots, and I will make him swallow the hatchet. Six knots, ass sure ass my name is Macfarlane; many a time between the Skate and Otter.[8] If Dougie wass here he would tell you. But I am not braggin' aboot her sailin'; it wass her looks. Man, she was smert, smert! Every time she wass new pented I would be puttin' on my Sunday clothes. There wass a time yonder they would be callin' me Two-flag Peter in Loch Fyne. It wass wance the Queen had a jubilee, and we had but the wan flag, but a Macfarlane never wass bate, and I put up the wan flag and a regatta shirt, and I'm telling you she looked chust sublime!

'I forget who it was once told me she was very wet,' I cooed blandly; 'that with a head wind the *Vital Spark* nearly went out altogether. Of course, people will say nasty things about these hookers. They say she was very ill to trim, too.'

Macfarlane jumped up again, grinding his teeth, and his face purple. He could hardly speak with indignation. 'Trum!' he shouted. 'Did you say "trum"? You could trum her with the wan hand behind your back and you lookin' the other way. To the duvvle with your trum! And they would be sayin' she wass wet! If Dougie wass here he would tell you. She would not

7. *A type of bread, popular in Scotland, with a smooth crust; baked in a tin or pan.*

8. *A stretch of Loch Fyne between Otter Point and Skate Island.*

take in wan cup of watter unless it wass for synin' [9] oot the dishes. She wass that dry she would not wet a postage stamp unless we slung it over the side in a pail. She wass sublime, chust sublime!

'I am telling you there iss not many men following the sea that could sail the *Fital Spark* the way I could. There iss not a rock, no, nor a chuckie stone inside the Cumbrie Heid that I do not have a name for. I would ken them fine in the dark by the smell, and that iss not easy, I'm telling you. And I am not wan of your dry-land sailors. I wass wance at Londonderry with her. We went at night and did Dougie no' go away and forget oil, so that we had no lamps, and chust had to sail in the dark with our ears wide open. If Dougie wass here he would tell you. Now and then Dougie would be striking a match for fear of a collusion.'

'Where did he show it?' I asked innocently. 'Forward or aft?'

'Aft,' said the mariner suspiciously. 'What for would it be aft? Do you mean to say there could be a collusion aft? I am telling you she could do her six knots before she cracked her shaft. It wass in the bow, of course; Dougie had the matches. She wass chust sublime. A gold bead oot of my own pocket, four men and a derrick, and a water butt and a pan loaf in the fo'c'sle. My bonnie wee *Fital Spark!*'

He began to show symptoms of tears, and I hate to see an ancient mariner's tears, so I hurriedly asked him how he had lost the command.

'I will tell you that,' said he. 'It was Dougie's fault. We had yonder a cargo of coals for Tarbert, and we got doon the length of Greenock, going fine, fine. It wass the day after the New Year, and I wass in fine trum, and Dougie said, "Wull we stand in here for orders?" and so we went into Greenock for some marmalade, and did we no' stay three days? Dougie and me wass going about Greenock looking for signboards with Hielan' names on them, and every signboard we could see with Campbell, or Macintyre, on it, or Morrison, Dougie would go in and ask if the man came from Kilmartin or anyway roond aboot there, and if the man said no, Dougie would say, "It's a great peety, for I have cousins of the same name, but maybe you'll have time to come oot for a dram?" [10] Dougie was chust sublime!

'Every day we would be getting sixpenny telegrams from the man the coals was for at Tarbert, but och! we did not think he wass in such an aawful hurry, and then he came himself to Greenock with the

9. *Rinsing*

10. *A small measure of liquid; hence a drink. Usually used of whisky, or as Para will be frequently found to refer to it 'Brutish spirits'.*

Grenadier, [11] and the only wans that wass not in the polis-office wass myself and the derrick. He bailed the laads out of the polis-office, and "Now," he said "you will chust sail her up as fast as you can, like smert laads, for my customers iss waiting for their coals, and I will go over and see my good-sister [12] at Helensburgh, and go back to Tarbert the day efter tomorrow." "Hoo can we be going and us with no money?" said Dougie — man, he wass sublime! So the man gave me a paper pound of money, and went away to Helensburgh, and Dougie wass coilin' up a hawser forrit ready to start from the quay. When he wass away, Dougie said we would maybe chust be as weel to wait another tide, and I said I didna know, but what did he think, and he said, "Ach, of course!" and we went aal back into Greenock. "Let me see that pound!" said Dougie, and did I not give it to him? and then he rang the bell of the public-hoose we were in, and asked for four tacks and a wee hammer. When he got the four tacks and the wee hammer he nailed the pound note on the door, and said to the man, "Chust come in with a dram every time we ring the bell till that's done!" If Dougie wass here he would tell you. Two days efter that the owner of the *Fital Spark* came doon from Gleska and five men with him, and they went away with her to Tarbert.'

'And so you lost the old command,' I said, preparing to go off. 'Well, I hope something will turn up soon.'

'There wass some talk about a dram,' said the mariner. 'I thought you said something aboot a dram, but och! there's no occasion!

A week later, I am glad to say, the Captain and his old crew were re-instated on the *Vital Spark.*

11. *Paddle steamer built in 1895 by J.&.G.Thomson at Clydebank for Messrs. David MacBrayne. Normally used on the winter service to and from Loch Fyne.*

12. *Sister-in-law*

2 THE PRIZE CANARY

CANARIES! said Para Handy contemptuously, 'I have a canary yonder at home that would give you a sore heid to hear him singing. He's chust sublime. Have I no', Dougie?'

It was the first time the mate had ever heard of the Captain as a bird-fancier, but he was a loyal friend, and at Para Handy's wink he said promptly, 'You have that, Peter. Wan of the finest ever stepped. Many a sore heid I had wi't.

'What kind of a canary is it?' asked the Brodick man jealously. 'Is it a Norwich?'

Para Handy put up his hand as usual to scratch his ear, and checked the act halfway. 'No, nor a Sandwich; it's chust a plain yellow wan,' he siad coolly. 'I'll wudger ye a pound it could sing the best you have blin'. It whustles even-on,[1] night and day, till I have to put it under a bowl o'watter if I'm wantin' my night's sleep.'

The competitive passions of the Brodick man were roused. He considered that among his dozen prize canaries he had at least one that could beat anything likely to be in the possession of the Captain of the *Vital Spark,* which was lying at Brodick when this conversation took place. He produced it — an emaciated, sickle-shaped, small-headed, bead-eyed, business-looking bird, which he called the Wee Free.[2] He was prepared to put up the pound for a singing contest anywhere in Arran, date hereafter to be arranged.

'That's all right,' said Para Handy, 'I'll take you on. We'll be doon this way for a cargo of grevel in a week, and if the money's wi' the man in the shippin'-box at the quay, my canary'll lift it.'

'But what aboot your pound?' asked the Brodick man. 'You must wudger a pound too.'

'Is that the way o't?' said the Captain. 'I wass never up to the gemblin',

---

1. *Continuously or persistently.*

2. *The popular nickname for the small part of the Free Church of Scotland which refused to enter into the Union with the United Presbyterian Church in 1900. The Free Kirk itself had been formed in the great Disruption of 1843 when a third of the members of the Church of Scotland left the Established Church over the issue of state control and the right of congregations to appoint the ministers of their choice. After the Union of 1900 there was a long legal battle, ending in the House of Lords, over the ownership of the property of the Free Church. In the end the Wee Frees were held to be the rightful possessors of the property of the Church, not the much larger portion which had entered the Union.*

but I'll risk the pound,' and so the contest was arranged.

'But you havena a canary at aal, have you?' said Dougie, later in the day, as the *Vital Spark* was puffing on her deliberate way to Glasgow.

'Me?' said Para Handy, 'I would as soon think of keepin' a hoolet.[3] But, och, there's plenty in Gleska if you have the money. From the needle to the anchor. Forbye, I ken a gentleman that breeds canaries; he's a riveter, and if I wass gettin' him in good trum he would maybe give a lend o' wan. If no', we'll take a dander[4] up to the Bird Market, and pick up a smert wan that'll put the hems[5] on Sandy Kerr's Wee Free. No man wi' any releegion aboot him would caal his canary a Wee Free.'

The Captain and the mate of the *Vital Spark* left their noble ship at the wharf that evening — it was a Saturday — and went in quest of the gentleman who bred canaries. He was discovered in the midst of an altercation with his wife which involved the total destruction of all the dishes on the kitchen dresser, and, with a shrewdness and consideration that were never absent in the Captain, he apologized for the untimely intrusion and prepared to go away. 'I see you're busy,' he said, looking in on a floor covered with the debris of the delf[6] which this ardent lover of bird life was smashing in order to impress his wife with the fact that he was really annoyed about something — 'I see you're busy. Fine, man, fine! A wife need never weary in this hoose — it's that cheery. Dougie and me was chust wantin' a wee lend of a canary for a day or two, but och, it doesna matter, seein' ye're so throng; we'll chust try the shops.'

It was indicative of the fine kindly humanity of the riveter who loved canaries that this one unhesitatingly stopped his labours, having disposed of the last plate, and said, 'I couldna dae't, chaps; I wadna trust a canary oot o' the hoose; there's nae sayin' the ill-usage it micht get. It would break my he'rt to ha'e onything gang wrang wi' ony o' my birds.'

'Chust that, Wull, chust that!' said Para Handy agreeably. 'Your feelings does you credit. I would be awful vexed if you broke your he'rt; it'll soon be the only hale thing left in the hoose. If I wass you, and had such a spite at the delf, I would use dunnymite,' and Dougie and he departed.

'That's the sort of thing that keeps me from gettin' merrit,' the Captain,

<hr>

3. *owl*

4. *Stroll.*

5. *Overcome.*

6. *Delftware, earthenware.*

with a sigh, confided to his mate, when they got down the stair. 'Look at the money it costs for dishes every Setturday night.'

'Them riveters iss awfu' chaps for sport,' said Dougie irrelevantly.

'There's nothing for't now but the Bird Market,' said the Captain, leading the way east along Argyle Street. They had no clear idea where that institution was, but at the corner of Jamaica Street[7] consulted several Celtic compatriots, who put them on the right track. Having reached the Bird market,[8] the Captain explained his wants to a party who had 'Guaranteed A1 Songsters' to sell at two shillings. This person was particularly enthusiastic about one bird which in the meantime was as silent as 'the harp that once through Tara's halls.' He gave them his solemn assurance it was a genuine prize roller canary; that when it started whistling, as it generally did at breakfast time, it sang till the gas was lit, with not even a pause for refreshment. For that reason it was an economical canary to keep; it practically cost nothing for seed for this canary. If it was a songster suitable for use on a ship that was wanted, he went on, with a rapid assumption that his customers were of a maritime profession, this bird was peculiarly adapted for the post. It was a genuine imported bird, and had already made a sea voyage. To sell a bird of such exquisite parts for two shillings was sheer commercial suicide; he admitted it, but he was anxious that it should have a good home.

'I wish I could hear it whustlin',' said the Captain, peering through the spars at the very dejected bird, which was a moulting hen.

'It never sings efter the gas is lighted,' said the vendor regretfully, 'that's the only thing that's wrang wi't. If that bird wad sing at nicht when the gas was lit, it wad solve the problem o' perpetual motion.'

Para Handy, considerably impressed by this high warrandice,[9] bought the canary, which was removed from the cage and placed in a brown paper sugar-bag, ventilated by holes which the bird-seller made in it with the stub of a lead pencil.

Will you no' need a cage?' asked Dougie.

7. *Para and Dougie have walked towards the centre of the City along Argyle Street, passing under the bridge formed by the railway lines leaving the Caledonian Railway Company's Central Station. This bridge covers the area between Hope Street and Jamaica Street and was commonly known as the 'Highlandman's Umbrella' from its popularity as a place of meeting and resort for the City's large Highland population. Hence Para's ready ability to consult 'several Celtic compatriots'.*

8. *Situated in Oswald Street near the Central Station.*

9. *A Scots legal term: a guarantee of indemnity.*

'Not at aal, not at aal!' the Captain protested; 'wance we get him doon to Brodick we'll get plenty o' cages,' and away they went with their pruchase, Para Handy elate at the imminent prospect of his prize canary winning an easy pound. Dougie carefully carried the bag containing the bird.

Some days after, the *Vital Spark* arrived at Brodick, but the Captain, who had not yet staked his pound with the man in the shipping-box as agreed on, curiously enough showed no disposition to bring off the challenge meeting between the birds. It was by accident he met the Brodick man one day on the quay.

'Talking about birds,' said Para Handy, with some diffidence, 'Dougie and me had a canary yonder —'

'That's aal off,' said the Brodick man hurriedly, getting very red in the face, showing so much embarrassment, indeed, that the Captain of the *Vital Spark* smelt a rat.

'What way off?' he asked. 'It sticks in my mind that there wass a kind of a wudger, and that there's a pound note in the shupping-box for the best canary.'

'Did you bring your canary?' asked the Brodick man anxiously.

'It's doon there in the vessel singin' like to take the rivets oot o' her,' said Para Handy. 'It's chust sublime to listen to.'

'Weel, the fact iss, I'm not goin' to challenge,' said the Brodick man. 'I have a wife yonder, and she's sore against bettin' and wudgerin' and gemblin', and she'll no let me take my champion bird Wee Free over the door.'

'Chust that!' said Para Handy. 'That's a peety. Weel, weel, the pund'll come in handy. I'll chust go away down to the shupping-box and lift it. Seeing I won, I'll stand you a drink.'

The Brodick man maintained with warmth that as Para Handy had not yet lodged his stake of a pound the match was off; an excited discussion followed, and the upshot was a compromise. The Brodick man, having failed to produce his bird, was to forfeit ten shillings, and treat the crew of the *Vital Spark*.

They were being treated, and the ten shillings were in Para Handy's possession, when the Brodick sportsman rose to make some disconcerting remark.

'You think you are very smert, Macfarlane,' he said, addressing the Captain. 'You are thinkin' you did a good stroke to get the ten shullin's, but if you wass smerter it iss not the ten shullin's you would have at aal, but the pound. I had you fine, Macfarlane. My wife never said a word aboot the wudger, but my bird is in the pook,[10] and couldna sing a note this week. That's the way I backed oot.'

Para Handy displayed neither resentment nor surprise. He took a deep draught of beer out of a quart pot, and smiled with mingled tolerance and pity on the Brodick man.

'Ay, ay!' he said, 'and you think you have done a smert thing. You have mich cause to be ashamed of yourself. You are nothing better than a common swundler. But och, it doesna matter, the fact iss, oor bird's deid.'

'Deid!' cried the Brodick man. 'What do you mean by deid?'

Chust that it's no livin',' said Para Handy cooly. 'Dougie and me bought wan in the Bird Market, and Dougie was carryin' it doon to the vessel in a sugar-poke when he met some fellows he kent in Chamaica Street, and went for a dram, or maybe two. Efter a while he didna mind what he had in the poke, and he put it in his troosers pockets, thinkin' it wass something extra for the Sunday's dinner. When he brought the poor wee bird oot of his pocket in the mornin', it was chust a' remains.'

10. *Moulting.*

Jamaica Street *Argyll & Bute District Libraries*

3 THE MALINGERER

THE crew of the *Vital Spark* were all willing workers, except The Tar, who was usually as tired when he rose in the morning as when he went to bed. He said himself it was his health, and that he had never got his strength right back since he had the whooping-cough twice when he was a boy. The Captain was generally sympathetic, and was inclined to believe The Tar was destined to have a short life unless he got married and had a wife to look after him. 'A wife's the very thing for you,' he would urge; 'it's no' canny,[1] a man as delicate as you to be having nobody to depend on.'

'I couldna afford a wife,' The Tar always maintained. 'They're all too grand for the like of me.'

'Och ay! but you might look aboot you and find a wee, no' aawfu' bonny wan,' said Para Handy.

'If she was blin', or the like of that, you would have a better chance of gettin' her,' chimed in Dougie, who always scoffed at The Tar's periodical illnesses, and cruelly ascribed his lack of energy to sheer laziness.

The unfortunate Tar's weakness always seemed to come on him when there was most to do. It generally took the form of sleepiness, so that sometimes when he was supposed to be preparing the dinner he would be found sound asleep on the head of a bucket, with a half-peeled potato in his hand. He once crept out of the fo'c'sle rubbing his eyes after a twelve hours' sleep, saying, 'Tell me this and tell me no more, am I going to my bed or comin' from it?'

But there was something unusual and alarming about the illness which overtook The Tar on their way up Loch Fyne to lift a cargo of timber. First he had shivers all down his back; then he got so stiff that he could not bend to lift a bucket, but had to kick it along the deck in front of him, which made Dougie admiringly say, 'Man! you are an aawful handy man with you feet, Colin'; his appetite, he declared, totally disappeared immediately after an unusually hearty breakfast composed of six herrings and two eggs; and finally he expressed his belief that there was nothing for it but his bed.

'I'll maybe no trouble you long, boys,' he moaned lugubriously. 'My heid's birling roond that fast that I canna even mind my own name two meenutes.'

'You should write in on a wee bit paper,' said Dougie unfeelingly, 'and keep it inside your bonnet, so that you could look it up at any time you were needin'.'

1. *It's unnatural or it's imprudent.*

11

Para Handy had kinder feelings, and told The Tar to go and lie down for an hour or two and take a wee drop of something.

'Maybe a drop of brandy would help me,' said The Tar, promptly preparing to avail himself of the Captain's advice.

'No, not brandy; a drop of good Brutish spurits will suit you better, Colin,' said the Captain, and went below to dispense the prescription himself.

The gusto with which The Tar swallowed the prescribed dram of British spirits and took a chew of tobacco after it to enhance the effect, made Para Handy somewhat suspicious, and he said to Dougie when he got on deck, leaving The Tar already in a gentle slumber.

'That rascal's chust scheming,' said Dougie emphatically. 'There iss nothing in world wrong with him but the laziness. If you'll notice, he aalways gets no weel when we're going to lift timber, because it iss harder on him at the winch.'

The Captain was indignant, and was for going down there and then with a rope's-end to rouse the patient, but Dougie confided to him a method of punishing the malingerer and at the same time getting some innocent amusement for themselves.

Dinner-time came round. The Tar instinctively wakened and lay wondering what they would take down to him to eat. The *Vital Spark* was puff-puffing her deliberate way up the loch, and there was an unusual stillness on deck. It seemed to The Tar that the Captain and Dougie were moving about on tiptoe and speaking in whispers. The uncomfortable feeling this created on his mind was increased when his two shipmates came down with slippers on instead of their ordinary sea-boots, creeping down the companion with great caution, carrying a bowl of gruel.

'What's that for?' asked The Tar sharply. 'Are you going to paste up any bills?'

'Wheest, Colin,' said Para Handy, in a sick-room whisper. 'You must not excite yourself, but take this gruel. It'll do you no herm. Poor fellow, you're looking aawful bad.' They hung over his bunk with an attitude of chastened grief, and Dougie made to help him to the gruel with a spoon as if he were unable to feed himself.

'Have you no beef?' asked The Tar, looking at the gruel with disgust. 'I'll need to keep up my strength with something more than gruel.'

'You daurna for your life take anything but gruel,' said the Captain sorrowfully. 'It would be the death of you at wance to take beef, though there's plenty in the pot. Chust take this, like a good laad, and don't speak. My Chove! you are looking far through.'

12

'Your nose is as sharp as a preen,'[2] said Dougie in an awed whisper, and with a piece of engine-room waste wiped the brow of The Tar, who was beginning to perspire with alarm.

'I don't think I'm so bad ass aal that,' said the patient. 'It wass chust a turn; a day in my bed'll put me aal right — or maybe two.'

They shook their heads sorrowfully, and the Captain turned away as if to hide a tear. Dougie blew his nose with much ostentation and stifled a sob.

'What's the metter wi' you?' asked The Tar, looking at them in amazement and fear.

'Nothing, nothing, Colin,' said the Captain. 'Don't say a word. Iss there anything we could get for you?'

'My heid's bad yet,' the patient replied. 'Perhaps a drop of spirits —'

'There's no' another drop in the ship,' said the Captain.

The patient moaned. 'And I don't suppose there's any beer either?' he said hopelessly.

He was told there was no beer, and instructed to cry if he was requiring any one to come to his assistance, after which the two nurses crept quietly on deck again, leaving him in a very uneasy frame of mind.

They got into the quay late in the afternoon and the Captain and mate came down again quietly, with their caps in their hands, to discover The Tar surreptitiously smoking in his bunk to dull the pangs of hunger that now beset him, for they had given him nothing since the gruel.

'It's not for you, it's not for you at aal, smokin'!' cried Para Handy in horror, taking the pipe out of his hand. 'With the trouble you have, smoking drives it in to the heart and kills you at wance.'

'What trouble do you think it iss?' asked the patient seriously.

'Dougie says it's — it's — what did you say it wass, Dougie?'

'It's convolvulus in the inside,' said Dougie solemnly; 'I had two aunties that died of it in their unfancy.'

'I'm going to get up at wance!' said The Tar, making to rise, but they thrust him back in his blankets, saying the convolvulus would burst at the first effort of the kind he made.

He began to weep. 'Fancy a trouble like that coming on me and me quite young!' he said, pitying himself seriously. 'There wass never wan in oor femily had it.'

'It's sleep brings it on,' said Dougie, with the air of a specialist who would ordinarily charge a fee of ten guineas — 'sleep and sitting doon.

2. *Pin.*

13

There iss nothing to keep off convolvulus but exercise and rising early in the morning. Poor fellow! But you'll maybe get better; when there's hope there's life. the Captain and me wass wondering if there wass anything we could buy ashore for you — some grapes, maybe, or a shullin' bottle of sherry wine.'

'Mercy on me! am I ass far through as that?' said The Tar.

'Or maybe you would like Macphail, the encheneer, to come doon and read the Scruptures a while to you' said Para Handy.

'Macphail!' cried the poor Tar; 'I wudna let a man like that read a songbook to me.'

They clapped him affectionately on the shoulders; Dougie made as if to shake his hand, and checked himself; then the Captain and mate went softly on deck again, and the patient was left with his fears. He felt utterly incapable of getting up.

Para Handy and his mate went up the town and had a dram with the local joiner, who was also undertaker. With this functionary in their company they were moving towards the quay when Dougie saw in a grocer's shop-door a pictorial card bearing the well-known monkey portrait[3] advertising a certain soap that won't wash clothes. He went chuckling into the shop made some small purchase, and came out the possessor of the picture. Half an hour later, when it was dark, and The Tar was lying in an agony of hunger which he took to be the pains of internal convolvulus, Para Handy, Dougie, and the joiner came quietly down to the fo'c'sle, where he lay. They had no lamp, but they struck matches and looked at him in his bunk with countenances full of pity.

'A nose as sherp as a preen,' said Dougie, 'it must be the galloping kind of convolvulus.'

'Here's Macintyre the joiner would like to see you, Colin,' said Para Handy, and in the light of a match the patient saw the joiner cast a rapid professional eye over his proportions.

'What's the joiner wantin' here?' said The Tar, with a frightful suspicion.

'Nothing, Colin, nothing — six by two — I wass chust passing — six by two — chust passing, and the Captain asked me in to see you. It's — six by two, six by two — it's no' very healthy weather we're havin'. Chust that!'

The fo'c'sle was in darkness and The Tar felt already as if he was dead and buried. 'Am I lookin' very bad?' he ventured to ask Dougie.

3. *Monkey Brand soap. This widely used household soap featured a monkey wearing a dress suit in its advertisements. The text of the advertisement normally incorporated the phrase 'Won't wash clothes'.*

'Bad's no' the name for it,' said Dougie. 'Chust look at yourself in the enchineer's looking-gless.' he produced from under his arm the engineer's mirror, on the face of which he had gummed the portrait of the monkey cut out from the soap advertisement, which fitted neatly into the frame. The Captain struck a match, and in its brief and insufficient light The Tar looked at himself, as he thought, reflected in the glass.

'Man, I'm no' that awful changed either; if I had a shave and my face washed. I don't believe it's convolvulus at aal,' said he, quite hopefully, and jumped from his bunk.

For the rest of the week he put in the work of two men.

Launch of a puffer at Kirkintilloch *Strathkelvin District Libraries*

4 THE MATE'S WIFE

THAT the Captain of the *Vital Spark* should so persistently remain a bachelor surprised many people. He was just the sort of man, in many respects, who would fall an easy prey to the first woman on the look-out for a good home. He had rather a gallant way with the sex, generally said 'mem' to them all, regardless of class; liked their society when he had his Sunday clothes on, and never contradicted them. If he had pursued any other calling than that of mariner I think he would have been captured long ago; his escape doubtless lay in the fact that sailing about from place to place, only briefly touching at West-Coast quays, and then being usually grimed with coal-dust, he had never properly roused their interest and natural sporting instincts. They never knew what a grand opportunity they were losing.

'I'm astonished you never got married, Captain,' I said to him recently.

'Ach, I couldn't be bothered,' he replied, like a man who had given the matter his consideration before now. 'I'm that busy wi' the ship I havena time. There's an aawful lot of bother aboot a wife. Forbye, my hert's in the *Fital Spark* — there's no' a smerter boat in the tred. Wait you till I get her pented!'

'But a ship's not a wife, Captain,' I protested.

'No,' said he, 'but it's a responsibility. You can get a wife any time that'll stick to you the same as if she wass riveted as long's you draw your pay, but it takes a man with aal his senses aboot him to get a ship and keep her. And chust think on the expense! Oh, I'm not sayin', mind you, that I'll not try wan some day, but there's no hurry, no, not a bit.'

'But perhaps you'll put it off too long,' I said, 'and when you're in the humour to have them they won't have you.'

He laughed at the very idea.

'Man!' he said, 'it's easy seen you have not studied them. I ken them like the Kyles of Bute. The captain of a steamer iss the most popular man in the wide world — popularer than the munisters themselves, and the munisters iss that popular the weemen put bird-lime in front of the Manses to catch them, the same ass if they were green-linties.[1] It's worse with sea-captains — they're that dashing, and they're not aalways hinging aboot the hoose wi' their sluppers on.'

'There's another thing,' he added, after a little pause, 'I couldna put up with a woman comin' aboot the vessel every pay-day. No, no, I'm for none o' that. Dougie's wife's plenty.'

1. *Green linnets or greenfinches.* (Chloris chloris)

'But surely she does not invade you weekly?' I said, surprised.

'If the *Fital Spark's* anywhere inside Ardlamont on a Setturday,' said Para Handy, 'she's doon wi' the first steamer from Gleska,[2] and her door-key in her hand, the same ass if it wass a pistol to put to his heid. If Dougie was here himsel' he would tell you. She's a low-country woman, wi' no' a word o' Gaalic, so that she canna understand Dougie at his best. When it comes to bein' angry in English, she can easy bate him. Oh, a cluvver woman: she made Dougie a Rechabite,[3] and he's aalways wan when he's at home, and at keepin' him trum and tidy in his clothes she's chust sublime. But she's no' canny aboot a ship. The first week efter she merried him we were lyin' at Innellan, and doon she came on the Setturday wi' her door-key at full cock. When Dougie saw her comin' doon the quay he got white, and turned to me, sayin', "Peter, here's the Mustress; I wish I hadna touched that dram, she'll can tell it on me, and I'm no' feared for her, but it would hurt her feelings."

'"Man!" I said, "you're an aawful tumid man for a sailor: but haste you doon the fo'c'sle and you'll get a poke of peppermint sweeties in my other pocket I had for the church tomorrow. Chust you go like the duvvle, and I'll keep her in conversation till you get your breath shifted."

'Dougie bolted doon below, and wass up in a shot. "I got the sweeties, Peter," he said, "but, oh! she's as cunning as a jyler, and she'll chalouse something if she smells the peppermints. What would you say to the whole of us takin' wan or two sweeties so that we would be aal the same, and she wouldna suspect me?" "Very weel," I said, "anything to obleege a mate," and when the good leddy reached the side of the vessel the enchineer and The Tar and me and Dougie wass standin' in a row eating peppermints till you would think it wass the front sate of the Tobermory Free Church.

'"It's a fine day and an aufu' smell o' losengers," was the first words she said when she put her two feet on the deck. And she looked very keen at her man.

'"It is that, mem," "It's the cargo."

2. *Glasgow.*

3. *A member of the total abstinence society* 'The Independent Order of Rechabites'. *The Rechabites were formed in 1835 and in addition to practising and advocating total abstinence they also operated as a major Friendly Society. By 1910 the total British membership exceeded 200,000. The name comes from Jeremiah Ch.35, vv 5 & 6:—'And I set before the sons of the house of the Rechabites pots full of wine, and cups, and I said unto them, Drink ye wine. But they said, we will drink no wine: for Jonadab the son of Rechab our Father commanded us, saying ye shall drink no wine, neither ye, nor your sons for ever.'*

17

"'What cargo?" said she, looking at Dougie harder than ever. "I'll cargo him!"

"'I mean the cargo of the boat, mem," I said quite smert. "It's a cheneral cargo, and there's six ton of peppermint sweeties for the Tarbert fishermen."

"'What in the wide world dae the Tarbert fishermen dae wi' sae mony sweeties?" said she.

"'Och, it's chust to keep them from frightening away the herrin' when they're oot at the fishin'," I said. Man! I'm tellin' you I had aal my wuts aboot me that day! It wass lucky for us the hatches wass doon, so that she couldna see the cargo we had in the hold. There wasna wan sweetie in it.

'I couldna but be nice to the woman, for she wasna my wife, so I turned a bucket upside doon and gave her a sate, and let on that Dougie was chust ass mich a man of consequence on the *Fital Spark* as myself. It does not do to let a wife see wi' her own eyes that her man iss under you in your chob, for when she'll get him at home she'll egg him on to work harder and get your place, and where are you then, eh! where are you then, I'm asking? She wass a cluvver woman, but she had no sense. "Weel," said she, "I don't think muckle o' yer boat. I thocht it was a great big boat, wi' a cabin in it. Instead o' that, it's jist a wee coal yin."

'Man! do you know that vexed me; I say she wassna the kind of woman Dougie should have married at aal, at aal. Dougie's a chentleman like mysel'; he would never hurt your feelings unless he wass tryin'.[4]

"'There's nothing wrong with the *Fital Spark*, mem," I said to her. "She's the most namely ship in the tred; they'll be writing things aboot her in the papers, and men often come to take photographs of her."

'She chust sniffed her nose at that, the way merrit women have, and said, "Jist fancy that!"

"'Yes; chust fancy it!" I said to her. "Six knots in a gale of wind if Macphail the enchineer is in good trum, and maybe seven if it's Setturday, and him in a hurry to get home. She has the finest lines of any steamboat of her size coming oot of Clyde; if her lum wass pented yellow and she had a bottom strake or two of green, you would take her for a yat. Perhaps you would be thinkin' we should have a German band[5] on board of her, with the heid fuddler goin' aboot gaitherin' pennies in a shell, and the others keekin' over the ends of their flutes and cornucopias for fear he'll pocket

4. cf *Oscar Wilde (1854-1900)*:— '*A gentleman is one who never hurts anyone's feelings unintentionally.*'

5. *In the years before the 1914-18 War the Clyde pleasure steamers often carried a small group of German instrumentalists.*

some. What? H'm! Chust that!"

'Efter a bit she said she would like to see what sort of place her man and rest of us slept in, so there was nothing for it but to take her doon to the fo'c'sle, though it wass mich against my will. When she saw the fo'c'sle she wass nestier than ever. She said, "Surely this iss not a place for Christian men"; and I said, "No, mem, but we're chust sailors."

"'There's nae richt furniture in't," she said.

"'Not at present, mem," I said. "Perhaps you were expectin' a piano," but, och! she wass chust wan of them Gleska women, she didna know life. She went away up the toon there and then, and came back wi' a bit of waxcloth, a tin of black soap, a grocer's calendar, and a wee lookin'-gless, hung her bonnet and the door-key on a cleat, and started scrubbin' oot the fo'c'sle. Man, it wass chust peetiful! There wass a damp smell in the fo'c'sle I could feel for months efter, and I had a cold in my heid for a fortnight. When she had the floor of the fo'c'sle scrubbed, she laid the bit of waxcloth, got two nails from The Tar, and looked for a place to hang up the calendar and the wee lookin'-gless, though there wass not mich room for ornaments of the kind. "That's a little mair tidy-like," she said when she was feenished, and she came up lookin' for something else to wash. The Tar saw the danger and went ashore in a hurry.

"'Are ye merrit? she asked me before she left the vessel wi' Dougie's pay.

"'No, mem," I said, "I'm not merrit yet."

"'I could easy see that," she said, sniffin' her nose again, the same ass if I wass not a captain at aal, but chust before the mast. "I could easy see that. It's time you were hurryin' up. I ken the very wife wad suit you; she's a kizzen⁶ o' my ain, a weedow wumman no' a bit the worse o' the wear."

"'Chust that!" said I, "but I'm engaged."

"'Wha to?" she asked quite sherp, no' very sure o' me.

"'To wan of the Maids of Bute, mem," I told her, meanin' yon two pented stones you see from the steamer in the Kyles of Bute; and her bein' a Gleska woman, and not traivelled mich, she thocht I wass in earnest.

"'I don't ken the family," she said, "but it's my opeenion you wad be better wi' a sensible weedow."

"'Not at aal, mem," I said, "a sailor couldna have a better wife nor wan of the Maids of Bute; he'll maybe no' get mich tocher⁷ with her, but she'll no' come huntin' the quays for him or his wages on Setturday."'

6. *Cousin.*

7. *Dowry.*

19

5 PARA HANDY — POACHER

THE *Vital Spark* was lying at Greenock with a cargo of scrap-iron, on the top of which was stowed loosely an extraordinary variety of domestic furniture, from bird cages to cottage pianos. Para Handy had just had the hatches off when I came to the quay-side, and he was contemplating the contents of his hold with no very pleasant aspect.

'Rather a mixed cargo!' I ventured to say.

'Muxed's no' the word for't,' he said bitterly. 'It puts me in mind of an explosion. It's a flittin'¹ from Dunoon. There would be no flittin's in the *Fital Spark* if she wass my boat. But I'm only the captain, och aye! I'm only the captain, thirty-five shullin's a-week and liberty to put on a pea-jecket. To be puttin' scrap-iron and flittin's in a fine smert boat like this iss carryin' coals aboot in a coach and twice. It would make any man use Abyssinian language.'

'Abyssinian language?' I repeated, wondering.

'Chust that, Abyssinian language — swearing, and the like of that, you ken fine, yoursel', withoot me tellin' you. Fancy puttin' a flittin' in the *Fital Spark!* You would think she was a coal-laary, and her with two new coats of pent out of my own pocket since the New Year.'

'Have you been fishing?' I asked, desirous to change the subject, which was, plainly, a sore one with the Captain. And I indicated a small fishing-net which was lying in the bows.

'Chust the least wee bit touch,' he said, with a very profound wink. 'I have a bit of a net there no' the size of a pocket-naipkin, that I use noo and then at the river-mooths. I chust put it down — me and Dougie — and whiles the salmon or sea-troot meets wi' an accident and gets into't. Chust a small bit of a net, no' worth speakin' aboot, no' mich bigger nor a pocket-naipkin. They'll be calling it a splash-net, you ken yoursel' withoot me tellin' you.' And he winked knowingly again.

'Ah Captain!' I said, 'that's bad! Poaching with a splash-net! I didn't think you would have done it.'

'It's no' me; it's Dougie,' he retorted promptly. 'A fair duvvle for high jeenks, you canna keep him from it. I told him many a time that it wasna right, becaause we might be found oot and get the jyle for't, but he says they do it on aal the smertest yats. Yes, that iss what he said to me — "They do it on aal the first-cless yats; you'll be bragging the *Fital Spark* iss chust ass good ass any yat, and what for would you grudge a splash-net?"'

1. *A household removal*

'Still it's theft, Captain,' I insisted. 'And it's very, very bad for the rivers.'

'Chust that!' he said complacently. 'You'll likely be wan of them fellows that goes to the hotels for the fushing in the rivers. There's more sport aboot a splash-net; if Dougie wass here he would tell you.'

'I don't see where the sport comes in,' I remarked, and he laughed contemptuously.

'Sport!' he exclaimed. 'The best going. There wass wan time yonder we were up Loch Fyne on a Fast Day,[2] and no' a shop open in the place to buy onything for the next mornin's breakfast. Dougie says to me, "What do you think yoursel' aboot takin' the punt and the small bit of net no' worth mentionin', and going doon to the river mooth when it's dark and seeing if we'll no' get a fush?"

'"It's a peety to be poaching on the Fast Day," I said to him.

'"But it's no' the Fast Day in oor parish," he said. "We'll chust give it a trial, and if there's no fush at the start we'll come away back again." Oh! a consuderate fellow, Dougie; he saw my poseetion at wance, and that I wasna awfu' keen to be fushin' wi' a splash-net on the Fast Day. The end and the short of it wass that when it wass dark we took the net and the punt and rowed doon to the river and began to splash. We had got a fine haul at wance of six great big salmon, and every salmon Dougie would be takin' oot of the net he would be feeling it all over in a droll way, till I said to him, "What are you feel-feelin' for, Dougie, the same ass if they had pockets on them? I'm sure they're all right."

'"Oh, yes," he says, "right enough, but I wass frightened they might be the laird's[3] salmon, and I wass lookin' for the luggage label on them. There's none. It's all right; they're chust wild salmon that nobody planted."[4]

'Weel, we had got chust ass many salmon ass we had any need for when

2. *A weekday preceding the celebration of Holy Communion kept as a local holiday. A service of preparation for Communion was held on the Fast Day. At the time of the Para Handy stories Communion services were, in the Highlands, held at very infrequent intervals—typically twice a year. The emphasis that the Presbyterian reformers had put on the importance of the Sacrament and the need for preparation had led, somewhat paradoxically, to a decline in the frequency of celebration.*

3. *Landowner.*

4. *Dougie clearly believed in the old Gaelic doctrine that argued 'Slat a coille, breac a linne, fiadh a frithinn—tri mearlaidh de nach do gabh na Gaidheil riamh nàire' or 'A branch from the wood, a trout from the pool, a deer from the deer forest—three thefts of which Highlanders are never ashamed'.*

somebody birled a whustle, [5] and the river watchers put off in a small boat from a point outside of us to catch us. There wass no gettin' oot of the river mooth, so we left the boat and the net and the fush and ran ashore, and by-and-by we got up to the quay and on board the *Fital Spark,* and paaused and consudered things.

"'They'll ken it's oor boat," said Dougie, and his clothes wass up to the eyes in salmon scales.

"'There's no doo't aboot that," I says, "If it wassna the Fast Day I wouldna be so vexed; it'll be an awful disgrace to be found oot workin' a splash-net on the Fast Day. And it's a peety aboot the boat, it wass a good boat, I wish we could get her back."

"'Ay, it's a peety we lost her," said Dougie; "I wonder in the wide world who could have stole her when we were doon the fo'c'sle at oor supper?" Oh, a smert fellow, Dougie! when he said that I saw at wance what he meant.

"'I'll go up this meenute and report it to the polis office," I said quite firm and Dougie said he would go with me too, but that we would need to change oor clothes, for they were covered with fush-scales. We changed oor clothes and went up to the sercheant of polis, and reported that somebody had stolen oor boat. He wass sittin' readin his Bible, it bein' the Fast Day, wi' specs on, and he keeked up at us, and said, "You are very spruce, boys, with your good clothes on at this time of the night."

"'We aalways put on oor good clothes on the *Fital Spark* on a Fast Day," I says to him; "it's as little as we can do, though we don't belong to the parish."

'Next day there wass a great commotion in the place aboot some blackguards doon at the river mooth poachin' with a splash-net. The Factor [6] wass busy, and the heid gamekeeper wass busy, and the polis wass busy. We could see them from the dake of the *Fital Spark* going' aboot buzzin' like bum-bees.

"'Stop you!" said Dougie to me aal of a sudden. "They'll be doon here in a chiffy, and findin' us with them scales on oor clothes — we'll have to put on the Sunday wans again."

"'But they'll smell something if they see us in oor Sunday clothes," I said. "It's no' the Fast Day the day."

"'Maybe no' here," said Dougie, "but what's to hinder it bein' the Fast Day in oor own parish?"

5. *Blew a whistle.*

6. *A land agent acting for the estate owner.*

'We put on oor Sunday clothes again, and looked the Almanac to see if there wass any word in it of a Fast Day any place that day, but there was nothing in the Almanac but tides, and the Battle of Waterloo, and the weather for next winter. That's the worst of Almanacs; there's nothing in them you want. We were fair bate for a Fast Day any place, when The Tar came up and asked me if he could get to the funeral of a cousin of his in the place at two o'clock.

'"A funeral!" said Dougie. "The very thing. The Captain and me'll go to the funeral too. That's the way we have on oor Sunday clothes." Oh, a smert, smert fellow, Dougie!

'We had chust made up oor mind it wass the funeral we were dressed for, and no' a Fast Day any place, when the polisman and the heid gamekeeper came doon very suspeecious, and said they had oor boat. "And what's more," said the gamekeeper, "there's a splash-net and five stone of salmon in it. It hass been used, your boat, for poaching."

'"Is that a fact?" I says. "I hope you'll find the blackguards," and the gamekeeper gave a grunt, and said somebody would suffer for it, and went away busier than ever. But the polis sercheant stopped behind. "You're still in your Sunday clothes, boys," said he, "what iss the occasion today?"

'"We're going to the funeral," I said.

'"Chust that! I did not know you were untimate with the diseased," said the sercheant.

'"Neither we were," I said, "but we are going oot of respect for Colin." And we went to the funeral, and nobody suspected nothin', but we never got back the boat, for the gamekeeper wass chust needin' wan for a brother o' his own. Och ay! there's wonderful sport in a splash-net.'

6 THE SEA COOK

THE TAR'S duties included cooking for the ship's company. He was not exactly a chef who would bring credit to a first-class club or restaurant, but for some time after he joined the *Vital Spark* there was no occasion to complain of him. Quite often he would wash the breakfast-cups to have them clean for tea in the evening, and it was only when in a great hurry he dried plates with the ship's towel. But as time passed, and he found his shipmates not very particular about what they ate, he grew a little careless. For instance, Para Handy was one day very much annoyed to see The Tar carry forward the potatoes for dinner in his cap.

'That's a droll way to carry potatoes, Colin,' he said midly.

'Och! they'll do no herm; it's only an old kep anyway,' said The Tar. 'Catch me usin' my other kep for potatoes!'

'It was not exactly your kep I wass put aboot for,' said the Captain. 'It wass chust runnin' in my mind that maybe some sort of a dish would be nater and genteeler.[1] I'm no' compleenin', mind you, I'm chust mentioning it.'

'Holy smoke!' said The Tar. 'You're getting to be aawful polite wi' your plates for potatoes, and them no peeled!'

But the want of variety in The Tar's cooking grew worse and worse each voyage, and finally created a feeling of great annoyance to the crew. It was always essence of coffee, and herring — fresh, salt, kippered, or red — for breakfast, sausages or stewed steak and potatoes for dinner, and a special treat in the shape of ham and eggs for Sundays. One unlucky day for the others of the crew, however, he discovered the convenience of tinned corned beef, and would feed them on that for dinner three or four days a week. Of course they commented on this prevalence of tinned food, which the engineer with some humour always called "malleable mule', but The Tar had any number of reasons ready for its presence on the midday board.

'Sorry, boys,' he would say affably, 'but this is the duvvle of a place; no' a bit of butcher meat to be got in't till Wednesday, when it comes wi' the boat from Gleska.' Or 'The fire went oot on me, chaps, chust when I wass making a fine thing. Wait you till Setturday, and we'll have something rare!'

'Ay, ay; live, old horse, and you'll get corn,' the Captain would say under these circumstances, as he artistically carved the wedge of American meat. 'It's a mercy to get anything; back in your plate, Dougie.'

---

1. *More refined or polite.*

It became at last unbearable, and while The Tar was ashore one day in Tarbert, buying bottled coffee and tinned meat in bulk, a conference between the captain, the engineer, and the mate took place.

'I'm no' going to put up wi't any longer,' said the engineer emphatically. It's all very well for them that has no thinking to do wi' their heids to eat tinned mule even on, but an engineer that's thinking aboot his engines all the time, and sweatin' doon in a temperature o' 120, needs to keep his strength up.'

'What sort o' heid-work are you talking aboot?' said the Captain. 'Iss it readin' your penny novelles? Hoo's Lady Fitzgerald's man gettin' on?' This last allusion was to Macphail's passion for penny fiction, and particularly to a novelette story over which the engineer had once been foolish enough some years before to show great emotion.

'I move,' said Dougie, breaking in on what promised to be an unprofitable altercation — 'I move that The Tar be concurred.'

'Concurred!' said the engineer, with a contemptuous snort. 'I suppose you mean censured?'

'It's the same thing, only spelled different,' said the mate.

'What's censured?' asked the Captain.

'It's giving a fellow a duvvle of a clourin',' [2] answered Dougie promptly.

'No, no, I wouldna care to do that to The Tar. Maybe he's doin' the best he can, poor chap. The Tar never saw mich high life before he came on my boat, and we'll have to make an allowance for that.'

'Herrin' for breakfast seven days a week! it's a fair scandal,' said the engineer. 'If you were maister in your own boat, Macfarlane, you would have a different kind of man makin' your meat for you.'

'There's not mich that iss wholesomer than a good herrin',' said Para Handy. 'It's a fush that's chust sublime. But I'll not deny it would be good to have a change noo and then, if it wass only a finnen haddie.' [3]

'I have a cookery book o' the wife's yonder at home I'll bring wi' me the next time we're in Gleska, and it'll maybe give him a tip or two,' said the engineer, and this was, in the meantime, considered the most expedient thing to do.

Next trip, on the way to Brodick on a Saturday with a cargo of bricks, The Tar was delicately approached by the Captain, who had the cookery

2. *A beating or assault (physical or, as here, verbal).*

3. *Finnan haddock: a cured haddock. The name is usually held to derive from the Kincardineshire village of Findon. The Concise Scots Dictionary also suggests that the form 'Findram Haddie' may derive from an confusion with the Morayshire village of Findhorn.*

book in his hand. 'That wass a nice tender bit of tinned beef we had the day, Colin,' he said graciously. 'Capital, aaltogether! I could live myself on tinned beef from wan end of the year to the other, but Dougie and the enchineer there's compleenin' that you're givin' it to them too often. You would think they were lords! But perhaps I shouldna blame them, for the doctor told the enchineer he should take something tasty every day, and Dougie's aye frightened for tinned meat since he heard that the enchineer wance killed a man in the Australian bush.[4] What do you say yoursel' to trying something fancy in the cookery line?'

'There's some people hard to please,' said The Tar; 'I'm sure I'm doin' the best I can to satisfy you aal. Look at them red herrin's I made this mornin'!'

'They were chust sublime!' said the Captain, clapping him on the back. 'But chust try a change to keep their mooths shut. It'll only need to be for a little, for they'll soon tire o' fancy things. I have a kind of cookery book here you might get some tips in. It's no' mine, mind you, it's Macphail's.'

The Tar took the cookery book and turned over some pages with contemptuous and horny fingers.

'A lot o' nonsense!' he said. 'Listen to this: "Take the remains of any cold chicken, mix with potatoes, put in a pie-dish, and brown with a salamander." Where are you to get the cold chucken? and where are you to take it? Fancy callin' it a remains; it would be enough to keep you from eatin' chucken. And what's a salamander? There's no' wan on this vessel, at any rate.'

'It's chust another name for cinnamon, but you could leave it oot,' said the Captain.

'Holy smoke! listen to this,' proceeded The Tar: '"How to make clear stock. Take six or seven pounds of knuckle of beef or veal, half a pound of ham or bacon, a quarter of a pound of butter, two onions, one carrot, one turnip, half a head of salary, and two gallons of water." You couldna sup that in a week."

'Smaal quantities, smaal quantities, Colin,' explained the Captain. 'I'm sorry to put you to bother, but there's no other way of pleasin' them other fellows.'

'There's no' a thing in this book I would eat except a fowl that's described here,' said The Tar, after a further glance through the volume.

'The very thing!' cried the Captain, delighted. 'Try a fowl for Sunday,'

4. *This somewhat obscure remark is presumably a reference to the notorious Australian bushranger Ned Kelly (1855-1880) who carried out his depredations wearing armour made from sheet metal.*

26

and The Tar said he would do his best.

'I soon showed him who wass skipper on this boat,' said the Captain going aft to Dougie and the engineer. 'It's to be fowls on Sunday.'

There was an old-fashioned cutter yacht at anchor in Brodick Bay with a leg of mutton and two plucked fowls hanging openly under the overhang of her stern, which is sometimes even yet the only pantry a yacht of that type has, though the result is not very decorative.

'Look at that!' said the engineer to The Tar as the *Vital Spark* puffed past the yacht. 'There's sensible meat for sailors; no malleable mule. I'll bate you them fellows has a cook wi' aal his wuts aboot him.'

'It's aal right, Macphail,' said The Tar; 'chust you wait till tomorrow and I'll give you fancy cookin'.'

And sure enough on Sunday he had two boiled fowls for dinner. It was such an excellent dinner that even the engineer was delighted.

'I'll bate you that you made them hens ready oot o' the wife's cookery book,' he said. 'There's no' a better cookery book on the South-side of Gleska; the genuine Aunt Kate's. People come far and near for the lend o' that when they're havin' anything extra.'

'Where did you buy the hens?' inquired the Captain, nibbling contentedly at the last bone left after the repast.

'I didna buy them at aal,' said The Tar. 'I couldna be expected to buy chuckens on the money you alloo me. Forbye, it doesna say anything about buying in Macphail's cookery book. It says, 'Take two chickens and boil slowly.'' So I chust had to take them.'

'What do you mean by that?' asked Para Handy, with great apprehension.

'I chust went oot in a wee boat late last night and took them from the stern o' yon wee yacht.' said The Tar coolly; and a great silence fell upon the crew of the *Vital Spark*.

'Tomorrow,' said the Captain emphatically at last — 'tomorrow you'll have tinned meat; do you know that, Colin? And you'll never have chucken on the boat again, not if Macphail was breakin' his he'rt for it.'

7 A LOST MAN

IT was a dirty evening, coming on to dusk, and the *Vital Spark* went walloping drunkenly down Loch Fyne with a cargo of oak bark,[1] badly trimmed. She staggered to every shock of the sea; the waves came combing over her quarter, and Dougie the mate began to wish they had never sailed that day from Kilcatrine.. They had struggled round the point of Pennymore, the prospect looking every moment blacker, and he turned a dozen projects over in his mind for inducing Para Handy to anchor somewhere till the morning. At last he remembered Para's partiality for anything in the way of long-shore gaiety, and the lights of the village of Furnace gave him an idea.

'Ach! man, Peter,' did we no' go away and forget this wass the night of the baal at Furnace? What do you say to going in and joining the spree?'

'You're feared, Dougie,' said the Captain; 'you're scared to daith for your life, in case you'll have to die and leave your money. You're thinkin' you'll be drooned, and that's the way you want to put her into Furnace. Man! but you're tumid, tumid! Chust look at me — no' the least put aboot. That's becaause I'm a Macfarlane, and a Macfarlane never was bate yet, never in this world! I'm no' goin' to stop the night for any baal — we must be in Clyde on Friday; besides, we havena the clothes wi' us for a baal. Forbye, who'll buy the tickets? Eh? Tell me that! Who'll buy the tickets?'

'Ach! you don't need tickets for a Furnace baal' said Dougie, flicking the spray from his ear, and looking longingly at the village they were nearing. 'You don't need tickets for a Furnace baal as long as you ken the man at the door and taalk the Gaalic at him. And your clothes'll do fine if you oil your boots and put on a kind of collar. What's the hurry for Clyde? It'll no' run dry. In weather like this, too! It's chust a temptin' of Providence. I had a dream yonder last night that wasna canny. Chust a temptin' of Providence.'

'I wudna say but it is,' agreed the Captain weakly, putting the vessel a little to starboard; 'it's many a day since I was at a spree in Furnace. Are you sure the baal's the night?'

'Of course I am,' said Dougie emphatically; 'it only started yesterday.'

'Weel, if you're that keen on't, we'll maybe be chust as weel to put her in till the mornin',' said Para Handy, steering hard for Furnace Bay; and in a little he knocked down to the engines with the usual, 'Stop her, Macphail, when you're ready.'

1. *Once extensively used as a source of pyroligneous acid for the textile industry.*

All the crew of the *Vital Spark* went to the ball, but they did not dance much, though it was the boast of Para Handy that he was 'a fine strong dancer'. The last to come down to the vessel in the morning when the ball stopped, because the paraffin-oil was done, was the Captain, walking on his heels, with his pea-jacket tightly buttoned on his chest, and his round, go-ashore pot hat, as he used to say himself, 'on three hairs'. It was a sign that he felt intensely satisfied with everything.

'I'm feeling chust sublime,' he said to Dougie, smacking his lips and thumping himself on the chest as he took his place at the wheel, and the *Vital Spark* resumed her voyage down the loch. 'I am chust like the eagle that knew the youth in the Scruptures.[2] It's a fine, fine thing a spree, though I wass not in the trum for dancing. I met sixteen cousins yonder, and them all in the committee. They were the proud men last night to be having a captain for a cousin, and them only quarry-men. It's the educaation, Dougie; educaation gives you the nerve, and if you have the nerve you can go round the world.'

'You werena very far roond the world, whatever o't,' unkindly interjected the engineer, who stuck up his head at the moment.

The Captain made a push at him angrily with his foot. 'Go down, Macphail,' he said, 'and do not be making a display of your ignorance on this ship. Stop you till I get you at Bowling! Not around the world! Man, I wass twice at Ullapool, and took the *Fital Spark* to Ireland wance, without a light on her. There is not a port I am not acquent with from the Tail of the Bank to Cairndow, where they keep the two New Years.[3] And Campbeltown, ay, or Barra, or Tobermory. I'm telling you when I am in them places it's Captain Peter Macfarlane iss the mich-respected man. If you were a rale enchineer and not chust a fireman, I would be asking you to my ludgings to let you see the things I brought from my voyages.'

The engineer drew in his head and resumed the perusal of a penny novelette.

'He thinks I'm frightened for him' said the Captain, winking darkly to his mate. 'It iss because I am too cuvil to him: if he angers me, I'll show

---

2. *Para is thinking of Psalm 103 v.5 'Who satisfieth thy mouth with good things; so that thy youth is renewed like the eagle's.'*
In the familiar Scottish metrical version this runs:
  'Who with abundance of good things
  doth satisfy thy mouth
  So that, ev'n as the eagle's age
  renewed is thy youth.'

3. *See 'Para Handy, Master Mariner' note 6.*

him. It is chust spoiling the boat having a man like that in cherge of her enchines, and her such a fine smert boat, with me, and a man like me, in command of her.'

'And there's mysel', too, the mate,' said Dougie; 'I'm no' bad mysel'.'

Below Minard rocks the weather grew worse again: the same old seas smashed over the *Vital Spark*. 'She's pitching aboot chust like a washin'-boyne,'⁴ said Dougie apprehensively. 'That's the worst of them oak-bark cargoes.'

'Like a washin'-boyne!' cried Para Handy indignantly; 'she's chust sublime. I wass in boats in my time where you would need to be bailing the watter out of your top-boots every here and there. The smertest boat in the tred; stop you till I have a pound of my own, and I will paint her till you'll take her for a yat if it wasna for the lum. You and your washin'-boyne! A washin'-boyne wudna do you any herm, my laad, and that's telling you.'

They were passing Lochgair; the Steamer *Cygnet*⁵ overtook and passed them as if they had been standing, somebody shouting to them from her deck.

Para Handy refrained from looking. It always annoyed him to be passed this way by other craft; and in summer time, when the turbine *King Edward*⁶ or the *Lord of the Isles*⁷ went past him like a streak of lightning, he always retired below to hide his feelings. He did not look at the *Cygnet*.

---

4. *Wash tub.*

5. *This steamer was built for Messrs. David MacBrayne's cargo service between Glasgow and Inveraray. Launched by A. & J. Inglis at their Pointhouse yard in 1904 she was also used by MacBrayne's as a relief steamer on the Outer Isles run in the winter season.*

6. *The world's first commercial turbine passenger steamer. Built by William Denny & Bros. at Dumbarton in 1901 for the Turbine Passenger Steamer Syndicate. This group comprised Parsons Marine Steam Turbine Coy. Ltd., the pioneers of marine turbine propulsion, who were to build the King Edward's engines; Denny Bros., and John Williamson, a well-established independent steamer operator on the lower reaches of the Clyde. King Edward, a screw steamer, sailed on a service between Greenock, Dunoon, Rothesay and Campbeltown.*

7. *The second Clyde steamer to bear this name. This magnificent paddle steamer was built in 1891 for the Glasgow and Inveraray Steamboat Coy. by D.& W. Henderson at their Meadowside, Partick, yard. Designed for the daily Glasgow to Inveraray service she was transferred in 1903 to the Lochgoil and Inveraray Steamboat Coy. Ltd., and in 1912 sold to Turbine Steamers Ltd. who employed her on the daily cruise from Glasgow round the Isle of Bute.*

'Ay, ay,' he said to Dougie, 'if I was telling Mr. Macbrayne[8] the umpudence of them fellows, he would put a stop to it in a meenute, but I will not lose them their chobs; poor sowls! maybe they have wifes and families. That'll be Chonny Mactavish takin' his fun of me; you would think he wass a wean. Chust like them brats of boys that come to the riverside when we'll be going up the Clyde at Yoker and cry, "*Columbia*,[9] ahoy!" at us — the duvvle's own!'

As the *Cygnet* disappeared in the distance, with a figure waving at her stern, a huge sea struck the *Vital Spark* and swept her from stem to stern, almost washing the mate, who was hanging on to a stay, overboard.

'Tar! Tar!' cried the Captain. 'Go and get a ha'ad o' that bucket or it'll be over the side.'

There was no response. The Tar was not visible, and a wild dread took possession of Para Handy.

'Let us pause and consider,' said he to himself; 'was The Tar on board when we left Furnace?'

They searched the vessel high and low for the missing member of the crew, who was sometimes given to fall asleep in the fo'c'sle at the time he was most needed. But there was no sign of him. 'I ken fine he wass on board when we started,' said the Captain, distracted, 'for I heard him sputtin'. Look again, Dougie, like a good laad.' Dougie looked again, for he, too, was sure The Tar had returned from the ball with him. 'I saw him

8. *What became the most famous name in the West Coast shipping world came into prominence in 1879 when David MacBrayne, a partner in the long established firm of Messrs D Hutcheson & Bros, took over complete control of the firm and went into business under his own name. MacBraynes became particularly well known due to their brilliantly marketed 'Royal Route'—the excursion from Glasgow to Oban via Ardrishaig and the Crinan Canal. The route gained its name from Queen Victoria's use of it in 1847 and there are several references to it in the Para Handy stories. Even after rationalisation and nationalisation today's West Highland ferries still sail under the name of Caledonian MacBrayne.*

'Along the western sea-board . . . generations of young Highlanders have grown up with the idea that their very existence was more or less dependent on MacBrayne. But for MacBrayne, most of them would never have seen bananas or the white loaf of the lowlands; might still be burning coalfish oil in cruisies. . . .' Neil Munro (The Brave Days p.59)

9. *Unlike the other vessels mentioned in this story the* Columbia *was not on Clyde passenger service though for all that she was a regular and familiar sight on the river. The* Columbia *was the 8497 ton flagship of the Anchor Line, launched in 1902 from D & W Henderson's yard at Meadowside, Glasgow. She was used on the company's service from Glasgow to New York and was a familiar sight to 'them brats of boys' as she made her way down river from Yorkhill Quay.*

with my own eyes,' he said, 'two of him, the same as if he was a twins; that iss the curse of drink in a place like Furnace.' But the search was in vain, even though the engineer said he had seen The Tar an hour ago.

'Weel, there's a good man gone!' said Para Handy. 'Och! poor Tar! It was yon last smasher of a sea. He's over the side. Poor laad! poor laad! Cot bless me, dyin' without a word of Gaalic in his mooth! It's a chudgement on us for the way we were carryin' on, chust a chudgement; not another drop of drink will I drink, except maybe beer. Or at a New Year time. I'm blaming you Dougie, for making us stop at Furnace for a baal I wudna give a snuff for. You are chust a disgrace to the vessel, with your smokin' and your drinkin', and your ignorance. It iss time you were livin' a better life for the sake of your wife and femily. If it wass not for you makin' me go into Furnace last night, The Tar would be to the fore yet, and I would not need to be sending a telegram to his folk from Ardrishaig. If I was not steering the boat, I would break my he'rt greetin' for the poor laad that never did anybody any herm. Get oot the flag from below my bunk, give it a syne in the pail, and put it at half-mast, and we'll go into Ardrishaig and send a telegram — it'll be a sixpence. It'll be a telegram with a sore he'rt, I'll assure you. I do not know what I will say in it, Dougie. It will not do to break it too much to them; maybe we will send the two telegrams — that'll be a shilling. We'll say in the first wan — "Your son, Colin, left the boat today": and in the next wan we will say — "He iss not coming back, he iss drooned." Och! och! poor Tar, amn't I sorry for him? I was chust going to put up his wages a shillin' on Setterday.'

The *Vital Spark* went in close to Ardrishaig pier just as the *Cygnet* was leaving after taking in a cargo of herring-boxes. Para Handy and Dougie went ashore in the punt, the Captain with his hands washed and his watch-chain on as a tribute of respect for the deceased. Before they could send off the telegram it was necessary that they should brace themselves for the melancholy occasion. 'No drinking, chust wan gless of beer,' said Para Handy, and they entered a discreet contiguous public-house for this purpose.

The Tar himself was standing at the counter having a refreshment, with one eye wrapped up in a handkerchief.

'Dalmighty!' cried the Captain, staggered at the sight, and turning pale. 'What are you doing here with your eye in a sling?'

'What's your business?' retorted The Tar coolly. 'I'm no' in your employ anyway.'

'What way that?' asked Para Handy sharply.

'Did you no' give me this black eye and the sack last night at the baal,

32

and tell me I was never to set foot on the *Vital Spark* again? It was gey mean o' you to go away withoot lettin' me get my dunnage oot, and that's the way I came here with the *Cygnet* to meet you. Did you no' hear me roarin' on you when we passed?'

'Weel done! weel done!' said Para Handy soothingly, with a wink at his mate. 'But ach! I wass only in fun, Colin; it wass chust a jeenk; it wass chust a baur aalthegither. Come away back to the boat like a smert laad. I have a shilling here I wass going to spend anyway. Colin, what'll you take? We thought you were over the side and drooned, and you are here, quite dry as usual.'

T.S.S. King Edward *Argyll & Bute District Libraries*

8 HURRICANE JACK

I VERY often hear my friend the Captain speak of Hurricane Jack in terms of admiration and devotion, which would suggest that Jack is a sort of demigod. The Captain always refers to Hurricane Jack as the most experienced seaman of modern times, as the most fearless soul that ever wore oilskins, the handsomest man in Britain, so free with his money he would fling it at the birds, so generally accomplished that it would be a treat to be left a month on a desert island alone with him.

'Why is he called Hurricane Jack?' I asked the Captain once.

'What the duvvle else would you caal him?' asked Para Handy. 'Nobody ever caals him anything else than Hurricane Jeck.'

'Quite so, but why?' I persisted.

Para Handy scratched the back of his neck, made the usual gesture as if he were going to scratch his ear, and then checked himself in the usual way to survey his hand as if it were a beautiful example of Greek sculpture. His hand, I may say, is almost as large as a Belfast ham.

'What way wass he called Hurricane Jack?' said he. 'Well, I'll soon tell you that. He wass not always known by that name; that wass a name he got for the time he stole the sheep.'

'Stole the sheep!' I said, a little bewildered, for I failed to see how an incident of that kind would give rise to such a name.

'Yes; what you might call stole,' said Para Handy hastily; 'but, och! it wass only wan smaal wee sheep he lifted on a man that never went to the church, and chust let him take it! Hurricane Jeck would not steal a fly — no, nor two flies, from a Chrustian; he's the perfect chentleman in that.'

'Tell me all about it,' I said.

'I'll soon do that,' said he, putting out his hand to admire it again, and in doing so upsetting his glass. 'Tut, tut!' he said. 'Look what I have done — knocked doon my gless; it wass a good thing there wass nothing in it.'

'Hurricane Jeck,' said the Captain, when I had taken the hint and put something in it, 'iss a man that can sail anything and go anywhere, and aalways be the perfect chentleman. A millionaire's yat or a washing-boyne — it's aal the same to Jeck; he would sail the wan chust as smert as the other, and land on the quay as spruce ass if he wass newly come from a baal. Oh, man! the cut of his jeckets! And never anything else but 'lastic-sided boots, even in the coorsest weather! If you would see him, you would see a man that's chust sublime, and that careful about his 'lastic-sided boots he would never stand at the wheel unless there wass a bass[1] below his feet. He'll aye be oiling at his hair, and buying hard hats for going ashore with: I never saw a man wi' a finer heid for the hat, and in some of the vessels he wass in he would have the full of a bunker of hats. Hurricane Jeck wass brought up in the China clupper tred, only he wassna called Hurricane Jeck then, for he hadna stole the sheep till efter that. He wass captain of the *Dora Young,* wan of them cluppers; he's a hand on a gaabert the now, but aalways the perfect chentleman.'

'It seems a sad downcome for a man to be a gabbart hand after having commanded a China clipper,' I ventured to remark. 'What was the reason of his change?'

'Bad luck,' said Para Handy. 'Chust bad luck. The fellow never got fair-play. He would aye be somewhere takin' a gless of something wi' somebody, for he's a fine big cheery chap. I mind splendid when he wass captain on the clupper, he had a fine hoose of three rooms and a big decanter, wi' hot and cold watter, oot at Pollokshaws.[2] When you went oot to the hoose to see Hurricane Jeck in them days, time slupped bye. But he wassna known as Hurricane Jeck then, for it wass before he stole the sheep.'

'You were just going to tell me something about that,' I said.

'Jeck iss wan man in a hundred, and ass good ass two, if there wass anything in the way of trouble, for, man! he's strong, strong! He has a back on him like a shipping-box, and when he will come down Tarbert quay on a Friday night after a good fishing, and the trawlers are arguing, it's two yerds to the step with him and a bash in the side of his hat for fair defiance. But he never hit a man twice, for he's aye the perfect chentleman iss Hurricane Jeck till the time I'm going to tell you of, when he stole the sheep.

'I have not trevelled far mysel' yet, except Ullapool and the time I wass at Ireland; but Hurricane Jeck in his time has been at every place on the map, and some that's no'. Chust one of Britain's hardy sons — that's what he iss. As weel kent in Calcutta as if he wass in the Coocaddens,[3] and he could taalk a dozen of their foreign kinds of languages if he cared to take the bother. When he would be leaving a port, there wassna a leddy in the place but what would be doon on the quay wi' her Sunday clothes on and a bunch o' floo'ers for his cabin. And when he would be sayin' goodbye to

1. *Matting; especially that made of coconut fibre.*

2. *A highly respectable suburb of Glasgow lying on the south side of the city.*

3. *Cowcaddens. A district of central Glasgow lying to the north of Sauchiehall Street. Now largely given over to multi-storey car parks and motorway flyovers.*

them from the brudge, he would chust take off his hat and give it a shoogle,[4] and put it on again; his manners wass complete. The first thing he would do when he reached any place wass to go ashore and get his boots brushed and then sing "Rule Brittania" roond about the docks. It wass a sure way to get freend or foe aboot you, he said, and he wass aye as ready for the wan as for the other. Brutain's hardy son!

'He made the fastest passages in his time that wass ever made in the tea trade, and still and on he would meet you like a common working-man. There wass no pride or nonsense of that sort aboot Hurricane Jeck; but, mind you, though I'm callin' him Hurricane Jeck, he wasna Hurricane Jeck till the time he stole the sheep.'

'I don't like to press you, Captain, but I'm anxious to hear about that sheep,' I said patiently.

'I'm comin' to't,' said Para Handy. 'Jeck had the duvvle's own bad luck; he couldna take a gless by-ordinar' but the ship went wrong on him, and he lost wan job efter the other, but he wass never anything else but the perfect chentleman. When he had not a penny in his pocket he would borrow a shilling from you, and buy you a stick pipe for yourself chust for good nature —'

'A stick pipe?' I repeated interrogatively.

'Chust a stick pipe — or a wudden pipe, or whatever you like to call it. He had three medals and a clock that wouldna go for saving life at sea, but that wass before he wass Hurricane Jeck, mind you for at that time he hadna stole the sheep.'

'I'm dying to hear about that sheep,' I said.

'I'll soon tell you about the sheep' said Para Handy. 'It wass a thing that happened when him and me wass sailing on the *Elizabeth Ann,* a boat that belonged to Girvan, and a smert wan too, if she wass in any kind of trum at aal. We would be going here and there aboot the West Coast with wan thing and another, and not costing the owners mich for coals if coals wass our cargo. It wass wan Sunday we were passing Caticol in Arran, and in a place yonder where there wass not a hoose in sight we saw a herd of sheep eating grass near the shore. As luck would have it, there was not a bit of butcher-meat on board the *Elizabeth Ann* for the Sunday dinner, and Jeck cocked his eye at the sheep and says to me, "Yonder's some sheep lost, poor things; what do you say to taking the punt and going ashore to see if there's anybody's address on them?"

"Whatever you say yousel'," I said to Jeck, and we stopped the vessel

4. *Shake.*

and went ashore, the two of us, and looked the sheep high and low, but there wass no address on them. "They're lost, sure enough," said Jeck, pulling some heather and putting it in his pocket — he wassna Hurricane Jeck then — "they're lost, sure enough, Peter. Here's a nice wee wan nobody would ever miss, that chust the very thing for a coal vessel," and before you could say "knife" he had it killed and carried to the punt. Oh, he iss a smert, smert fellow with his hands; he could do anything.

'We rowed ass caalm ass we could oot to the vessel, and we had chust got the deid sheep on board when we heard a roarin' and whustling.

"'Taalk about Arran being releegious!' said Jeck. "Who's that whustling on the Lord's Day?'

'The man that wass whustling wass away up on the hill, and we could see him coming running doon the hill the same ass if he would break every leg he had on him.

"'I'll bate you he'll say it's his sheep," said Jeck. "Weel, we'll chust anchor the vessel here till we hear what he hass to say, for if we go away and never mind the cratur he'll find oot somewhere else it's the *Elizabeth Ann*."

'When the fermer and two shepherds came oot to the *Elizabeth Ann* in a boat, she wass lying at anchor, and we were all on deck, every man wi' a piece o' heather in his jecket.

"'I saw you stealing my sheep," said the fermer, coming on deck, furious. "I'll have every man of you jiled for this."

"'Iss the man oot of his wuts?" said Jeck. "Drink — chust drink! Nothing else but drink! If you were a sober Christian man, you would be in the church at this 'oor in Arran, and not oot on the hill recovering from last night's carry-on in Loch Ranza, and imagining you are seeing things that's not there at aal, at aal."

"'I saw you with my own eyes steal the sheep and take it on board," said the fermer, nearly choking with rage.

"'What you saw was my freend and me gathering a puckle heather for oor jeckets," said Jeck, "and if ye don't believe me you can search the ship from stem to stern."

"'I'll soon do that," said the fermer, and him and his shepherds went over every bit of the *Elizabeth Ann*. They never missed a corner you could hide a moose in, but there wass no sheep nor sign of sheep anywhere.

"'Look at that, Macalpine," said Jeck. "I have a good mind to have you up for inflammation of character. But what could you expect from a man that would be whustling on the hill like a peesweep[5] on a Sabbath when he

5. *Peewit, green plover or lapwing* (Vanellus vanellus).

should be in the church. It iss a good thing for you, Macalpine, it iss a Sabbath, and I can keep my temper."

"'I could swear I saw you lift the sheep," said the fermer quite vexed.

"'Saw your auntie! Drink; nothing but the cursed drink!" said Jeck, and the fermer and his shepherds went away with their tails behind their legs.

'We lay at anchor till it was getting dark, and then we lifted the anchor and took off the sheep that wass tied to it when we put it oot. "It's a good thing salt mutton," said Hurricane Jeck as we sailed away from Caticol, and efter that the name he always got wass Hurricane Jeck.'

'But why "Hurricane Jack"?' I asked, more bewildered than ever.

'Holy smoke! am I no' tellin' ye?' said Para Handy. "It wass because he stole the sheep.'

But I don't understand it yet.

Brodick and Goatfell *Argyll & Bute District Libraries*

9 QUEER CARGOES

'THE worst cargo ever I sailed wi',' said Macphail the engineer, 'was a wheen o' thae Mahommedan pilgrims: it wasna Eau de Colong they had on their hankies.'

'Mahommedans!' said Para Handy, with his usual suspicions of the engineer's foreign experience — 'Mahommedans! Where were they bound for? Was't Kirkintilloch?' [1]

'Kirkintilloch's no' in Mahommeda,' said Macphail nastily. 'I'm talkin' aboot rale sailin', no' wyding in dubs,[2] the way some folk does a' their days.'

'Chust that! chust that!' retorted the Captain sniffing. 'I thought it wass maybe on the the Port-Dundas Canal[3] ye had them.'

'There was ten or eleven o' them died every nicht,' proceeded Macphail, contemptuous of these interruptions. 'We just gied them the heave over the side, and then full speed aheid to make up for the seven meenutes.'

'Like enough you would ripe their pockets first,' chimed in Dougie. 'The worst cargo ever I sailed with wass leemonade bottles; you could hear them clinking aal night, and not wan drop of stumulents on board! It wass duvilish vexing.'

The worst cargo ever I set eyes on,' ventured The Tar timidly, in presence of these hardened mariners, 'wass sawdust for stuffing dolls.'

'Sawdust would suit you fine, Colin,' said the Captain. 'I'll warrant you got plenty of sleep that trup.

'You're there and you're talking about cargoes,' proceeded Para Handy, 'but there's not wan of you had the experience I had, and that wass with a cargo of shows for Tarbert Fair. They were to go with a luggage-steamer, but the luggage-steamer met with a kind of an accident, and wass late ot getting to the Broomielaw: she twisted wan of her port-holes or something like that, and we got the chob. It's me that wassna wantin' it, for it wass no credit to a smert boat like the *Fital Spark,* but you ken yoursel' what owners iss; they would carry coal tar made up in delf

---

1. *A Dumbartonshire town on the Forth and Clyde Canal with a small but vigorous shipbuilding industry, chiefly producing puffers like the* Vital Spark.

2. *Wading in a muddy pool.*

3. *Branch canal linking the Forth and Clyde Canal with Port Dundas in the north of Glasgow and connecting with the Monklands Canal.*

crates[4] if they get the freight for it.'

'I wouldna say but what you're right,' remarked Dougie agreeably.

'A stevedore would go wrong in the mind if he saw the hold of the vessel after them showmen got their stuff on board. You would think it wass a pawnshop struck wi' a sheet o' lightning. There wass everything ever you saw at a show except the coconuts and the comic polisman. We started at three o'clock in the mornin', and a lot of the show people made a bargain to come wi' us to look efter their stuff. There wass the Fattest Woman in the World, No-Boned Billy or the Boy Serpent, the Mesmerising Man, another man very namely among the Crowned Heads for walkin' on stilts, and the heid man o' the shows, a chap they called Mr. Archer. At the last meenute they put on a wee piebald pony that could pick oot any card you asked from a pack. If you don't believe me, Macphail, there's Dougie; you can ask him yoursel'.'

'You're quite right, Peter,' said Dougie emphatically. 'I'll never forget it. What are you goin' to tell them aboot the Fair?' he added suspiciously.

'It's a terrible life them show folk has!' resumed the Captain, without heeding the question. 'Only English people would put up with it; poor craturs, I wass sorry for them! Fancy them goin' aboot from place to place aal the year roond, wi' no homes! I would a hundred times sooner be a sailor the way I am. But they were nice enough to us, and we got on fine, and before you could say "knife" Dougie was flirtin' wi' the Fattest Woman in the World.'

'Don't believe him, boys,' said the mate, greatly embarrassed. 'I never even kent her Christian name.'

'When we got the shows discherged at Tarbert, Mr. Archer came and presented us aal with a free pass for everything except the stilts. "You'll no' need to put on your dress clothes," says he. He wass a cheery wee chap, though he wass chust an Englishman. Dougie and me went ashore and had a royal night of it. I don't know if ever you wass at a Tarbert Fair, Macphail — you were aye that busy learnin' the names of the foreign places you say you traivelled to, that you wouldn't have the time; but I'll warrant you it's worth while seein'. There's things to be seen there you wouldna see the like of in London. Dougie made for the tent of the mesmeriser and the Fattest Woman in the World whenever we got there: he thought she would maybe be dancin' or something of that sort, but aal she did was to sit on a chair and look fat. There was a crood roond her

4. *Crates made of delftware or earthenware. Para is being ironic and expressing his usual contempt for owners who fail to recognise the singular merits of the* Vital Spark.

nippin' her to make sure she wasna padded, and when we got in she cried, "Here's my intended man, Mr. Dugald; stand aside and let him to the front to see his bonny wee rosebud. Dugald, darling, you see I'm true to you and wearin' your ring yet," and she showed the crood a brass ring you could tie boats to.'

'She wass a caaution!' said Dougie. 'But what's the use of rakin' up them old stories?'

'Then we went to the place where No-Boned Billy or the Boy Serpent wass tying himself in knots and jumpin' through girrs. It was truly sublime! It bates me to know hoo they do it, but I suppose it's chust educaation.'

'It's nothing else,' said the mate. 'Educaation'll do anything for you if you take it when you're young, and have the money as weel.'

'Every noo and then we would be takin' a gless of yon red lemonade they sell at aal the Fairs, till Dougie got dizzy and had to go to a public-house for beer.'

'Don't say a word aboot yon,' interrupted the mate anxiously.

'It's aal right, Dougie we're among oorsel's. Weel, as I wass sayin', when he got the beer, Dougie, right or wrong, wass for goin' to see the fortune-teller. She wass an Italian-looking' body that did the spaein',[5] and for a sixpence she gave Dougie the finest fortune ever you heard of. He wass to be left a lot of money when he wass fifty-two, and mairry the dochter of a landed chentleman. But he wass to watch a man wi' curly hair that would cross his path, and he wass to mind and never go a voyage abroad in the month o' September. Dougie came out of the Italian spaewife's in fine trum wi' himsel', and nothing would do him but another vusit to the Fattest Woman in the World.'

'Noo, chust you be canny what you're at next!' again broke in the mate. 'You said you would never tell anybody.'

'Who's tellin' anybody?' asked Para Handy impatiently. 'I'm only mentionin' it to Macphail and Colin here. The mesmeriser wass readin' bumps when we got into the tent, and Dougie wass that full o' the fine fortune the Italian promised him that he must be up to have his bumps read. The mesmeriser felt aal the bumps on Dougie's heid, no' forgettin' the wan he got on the old New Year at Cairndow, and he said it wass wan of the sublimest heids he ever passed under his hands. "You are a sailor," he said to Dougie, "but accordin' to your bumps you should have been a munister. You had a fine, fine heid for waggin'. There's great strength of

5. *Fortune telling: cf Spaewife:—a woman who tells fortunes.*

41

will behind the ears, and the back of the foreheid's packed wi' animosity."

'When the readin' of the bumps was done, and Dougie wass nearly greetin' because his mother didna send him to the College in time, the mesmeriser said he would put him in a trance, and then he would see fine fun.'

'Stop it, Peter,' protested the mate. 'If you tell them, I'll never speak to you again.'

Para Handy paid no attention, but went on with his narrative. 'He got Dougie to stare him in the eye the time he wass working his hands like anything, and Dougie wass in a trance in five meenutes. Then the man made him think he wass a railway train, and Dougie went on his hands and knees up and doon the platform whustlin' for tunnels. Efter that he made him think he wass a singer — and a plank of wud — and a soger — and a hen. I wass black affronted to see the mate of the *Fital Spark* a hen. But the best of the baur wass when he took the Fattest Woman in the World up on the platform and mairried her to Dougie in front of the whole of Tarbert.'

'You gave me your word you would never mention it,' interrupted the mate, perspiring with annoyance.

'Then the mesmeriser made Dougie promise he would come back at twelve o'clock the next day and take his new wife on the honeymoon. When Dougie wass wakened oot of the trance, he didn't mind onything aboot it.'

'Neither I did,' said the mate.

'Next day, at ten meenutes to twelve, when we were makin' ready to start for the Clyde, my mate here took a kind of a tirrivee,[6] and wass for the shows again. I saw the dregs of the mesmerisin' wass on the poor laad, so I took him and gave him a gill of whisky with sulphur in it, and whipped him on board the boat and off to the Clyde before the trance came on at its worst. It never came back.'

'Iss that true?' asked The Tar.

'If Dougie wass here — Of course it iss true," said the Captain.

'All I can mind aboot it is the whisky and sulphur,' said Dougie. 'That's true enough.'

6. *A fit, tantrum or wild mood.*

THE BIRTH PLACE OF PARA HANDY

One of the major unsolved problems in Para Handy scholarship is the vexed question of our hero's birth place. As a larger than life character it is hardly surprising that he cannot easily be tied down to one place or time. In the next story he tells The Tar that he knows Loch Fyne well 'I ken every bit of it. . . . I wass born aal along this loch-side and brocht up wi an auntie.' In 'The Goat' (a tale not included in this collection) he reveals that he was at school in Tarbert, Loch Fyne and throughout the stories we read of his numerous relatives on Loch Fyne-side—not least of the sixteen cousins he met at the Furnace baal '. . . the proud men last night to be having a captain for a cousin and them only quarry-men. . . .'

However in 'Para Handy has an Eye to Business' we learn from Para's own lips of a totally different place of origin. Modestly he tells Sunny Jim (who has fanciful ideas about a puffer skipper's powers) '. . . its no' the way we're brought up on Loch Long; us Arrochar folk, when we're Captains believe in a bit o' compromise wi' the crews . . .' and later in the same tale says '. . . we're no' that daft, us folk from Arrochar. . . .'

Arrochar is, of course, at the very heart of the Clan Macfarlane lands and there is nothing inherently improbable in a Dumbartonshire, rather than an Argyllshire origin for Para.

We are however confronted with two contradictory and equally authoritative accounts of the birth of Para. It may be that no firm conclusion can be reached, although careful study of the registrations of birth for the counties of Argyll and Dumbarton in the 1860's might be instructive.   The statement that he 'wass born aal along this loch-side' is suspiciously vague and coupled with the statement that he was reared by an aunt may lead some to suspect some family tragedy or scandal.

10 IN SEARCH OF A WIFE

THE TAR had only got his first week's wages after they were raised a shilling, when the sense of boundless wealth took possession of him, and went to his head like glory. He wondered how on earth he could spend a pound a week. Nineteen shillings were only some loose coins in your pocket, that always fell through as if they were red-hot: a pound-note was different, the pleasure of not changing it till maybe tomorrow was like a wage in itself. He kept the pound-note untouched for three days, and then dreamed one night that he lost it through a hole in his pocket. There were really holes in his pockets, a fact that had never troubled him before; so the idea of getting a wife to mend them flashed on him. He was alarmed at the notion at first — it was so much out of his daily routine of getting up and putting on the fire, and cooking for the crew, and working the winch, and eating and sleeping — so he put it out of hs head; but it always came back when he thought of the responsibility of a pound a week, so at last he went up to Para Handy and said to him sheepishly, 'I wass thinking to mysel' yonder that maybe it wouldna be a bad plan for me to be takin' a kind of a wife.'

'Capital! First-rate! Good for you, Colin!' said the Captain. 'A wife's chust the very thing you're needing. Your guernsays iss no credit to the *Fital Spark* — indeed they'll be giving the boat a bad name; and I aalways like to see everything in nice trum aboot her. I would maybe try wan mysel' but I'm that busy on the boat with wan thing and another, me being Captain of her, I havena mich time for keeping a hoose. But och! there's no hurry for me; I am chust nine and two-twenties of years old, no' countin' the year I wass workin' in the sawmull. What wass the gyurl you were thinkin' on?'

'Och, I didna get that length,' said The Tar, getting very red in the face at having the business rushed like that.

'Weel, you would need to look slippy,' said Para Handy. 'There's fellows on shore with white collars on aal the time going aboot picking up the smert wans.'

'I wass chust thinkin' maybe you would hear of somebody aboot Loch Fyne that would be suitable: you ken the place better nor me.'

'I ken every bit of it,' said Para Handy, throwing out his chest. 'I wass born aal along this loch-side, and brocht up wi' an auntie. What kind of a wan would you be wantin'?'

'Och, I would chust leave that to yoursel',' said The Tar. 'Maybe if she had a puckle money it wouldna be any herm.

'Money!' cried the Captain. 'You canna be expectin' money wi' the first. But we'll consuder, Colin. We'll pause and consuder.'

Two days later the *Vital Spark* was going up to Inveraray for a cargo of timber, Para Handy steering, and singing softly to himself —

> *'As I gaed up yon Hieland hill,*
> *I met a bonny lassie;*
> *She looked at me and I at her,*
> *And oh, but she was saucy.*

> *With my rolling eye,*
> *Fal tee diddle dye,*
> *Rolling eye dum derry,*
> *With my rolling eye.'*

The Tar stood by him peeling potatoes, and the charming domestic sentiment of the song could not fail to suggest the subject of his recent thoughts. 'Did you have time to consuder yon?' he asked the Captain, looking up at him with comical coyness.

'Am I no' consudering it as hard as I'm able?' said Para Handy. 'Chust you swept aal them peelin's over the side and no' be spoiling the boat, my good laad.'

'I wass mindin, mysel', of a femily of gyurls called Macphail up in Easdale, or maybe it wass Luing,' said The Tar.

'Macphails!' cried Para Handy. 'I never hear the name of Macphail but I need to scratch mysel'. I wouldna alloo any man of the *Fital Spark* to mairry a Macphail, even if she wass the Prunce of Wales. Look at that man of oors that caals himsel' an enchineer; he's a Macphail, that's the way he canna help it.'

'Och, I wass chust in fun,' The Tar hastened to say soothingly. 'I don't think I would care for any of them Macphail gyurls whatever. Maybe you'll mind of something suitable before long.'

Para Handy slapped himself on the knee. 'By Chove!' said he, 'I have the very article that would fit you.'

'What's — what's her name?' asked The Tar, alarmed at the way destiny seemed to be rushing him into matrimony.

'Man, I don't know,' said the Captain, 'but she's the laandry-maid up here in the Shurriff's[1] — chust a regular beauty. I'll take you up and show her you tomorrow.'

1. *Sheriff. A locally based judge with wide-ranging civil and criminal jurisdiction.*

45

'Will we no' be awfu' busy tomorrow?' said The Tar hastily. 'Maybe it would be better to wait till we come back again. There's no' an awfu' hurry.'

'No hurry!' cried the Captain. 'It's the poor heid for business you have, Colin; a gyurl the same ass I'm thinkin' on for you will be snapped up whenever she gets her Mertinmas wages.'[2]

'I'm afraid she'll be too cluver for me, her being a laandry-maid,' said The Tar. 'They're awfu' high-steppers, laandry-maids, and awfu' stiff.'

'That's wi' working among starch,' explained Para Handy. 'It'll aal come oot in the washin'. Not another word, Colin; leave it to me. And maybe Dougie, och ay, Dougie and me'll see you right.'

So keenly did the Captain and Dougie enter into the matrimonial projects of The Tar that they did not even wait till the morrow, but set out to interview the young lady that evening. 'I'll no' put on my pea-jacket or my watch-chain in case she might take a fancy to mysel',' the Captain said to his mate. 'A man in a good poseetion like me canna be too caautious.' The Tar, at the critical moment, showed the utmost reluctance to join the expedition. He hummed and hawed, protested he 'didna like', and would prefer that they settled the business without him; but this was not according to Para Handy's ideas of business, and ultimately the three set out together with an arrangement that The Tar was to wait out in the Sheriff's garden while his ambassadors laid his suit in a preliminary form before a lady he had never set eyes on and who had never seen him.

There was a shower of rain, and the Captain and his mate had scarcely been ushered into the kitchen on a plea of 'important business' by the Captain, than The Tar took shelter in a large wooden larder at the back of the house.

Para Handy and Dougie took a seat in the kitchen at the invitation of its single occupant, a stout cook with a humorous eye.

'It was the laandry-maid we were wantin' to see, mem,' said the Captain, ducking his head forward several times and grinning widely to inspire confidence and create a genial atmosphere without any loss of time. 'We were chust passing the door, and we thought we would give her a roar in the by-going.'

'You mean Kate? asked the cook.

'Aye! chust that, chust that — Kate,' said the Captain, beaming warmly

2. *Martinmas—11th. November—was one of the traditional Scottish Quarter Days or term days on which rents were payable and agricultural and domestic servants' wages paid. By the time of this story the date of the Martinmas Term had been changed to 28th. November.*

till his whiskers curled. 'Hoo's the Shurriff keeping himsel'?' he added as an afterthought. 'Iss he in good trum them days?' And he winked expansively at the cook.

'Kate's not in,' said the domestic. 'She'll be back in a while if you wait.'

The Captain's face fell for a moment. 'Och perhaps you'll do fine yoursel',' said he cordially, at last. 'We have a fellow yonder on my boat that's come into some money, and what iss he determined on but to get married? He's awfu' backward, for he never saw much Life except the Tarbert Fair, and he asked us to come up here and put in a word for him.'

'Is that the way you do your courtin' on the coal-gabbarts?' said the cook, greatly amused.

'Coal-gaabert!' cried Para Handy, indignant. 'There iss no coal-gaabert in the business; I am the Captain of the *Fital Spark,* the smertest steamboat in the coastin' tred —'

'And I'm no' slack mysel'; I'm the mate,' said Dougie, wishing he had brought his trump.[3]

'He must be a soft creature not to speak for himself,' said the cook.

'Never mind that,' said the Captain; 'are you game to take him?'

The cook laughed. 'What about yoursel'?' she asked chaffingly, and the Captain blenched.

'Me!' he cried. 'I peety the wumman that would mairry me. If I wass not here, Dougie would tell you — would you no', Dougie? — I'm a fair duvvle for high jeenks. Forbye, I'm sometimes frightened for my health.'

'And what is he like, this awfu' blate[4] chap?' asked the cook.

'As smert a laad as ever stepped,' protested Para Handy. 'Us sailors iss sometimes pretty wild; it's wi' followin' the sea and fightin' hurricanes, here the day and away yesterday; but Colin iss ass dacent a laad ass ever came oot of Knapdale[5] if he wass chust letting himself go. Dougie himsel' will tell you.'

'There's nothing wrong wi' the fellow,' said Dougie. 'A fine riser in the mornin'.'

'And for cookin', there's no' his equal,' added the Captain.

'It seems to me it's my mistress you should have asked for,' said the cook; 'she's advertising for a scullery-maid.' But this sarcasm passed over the heads of the eager ambassadors.

'Stop you!' said the Captain, 'and I'll take him in himsel'; he's oot in the

3. *Jew's harp.*

4. *Shy.*

5. *A district of Argyllshire lying between Loch Fyne and Loch Sween.*

garden waiting for us.' And he and his mate went outside.

'Colin!' cried Para Handy, 'come away and be engaged, like a smert laad.' But there was no answer, and it was after considerable searching they discovered the ardent suitor sound asleep in the larder.

'It's no' the laandry-maid; but it's a far bigger wan,' exclaimed the Captain. 'She's chust sublime. Aal you have to do now is to come in and taalk nice to her.'

The Tar protested he couldn't talk to her unless he had some conversation lozenges.[6] Besides, it was the laundry-maid he had arranged for, not the cook.

'She'll do fine for a start; a fine gyurl,' the Captain assured him, and with some difficulty they induced The Tar to go with them to the back-door, only to find it emphatically shut in their faces.

'Let us paause and consuder, what day is this?' asked the Captain, when the emphasis of the rebuff had got time to sink into his understanding.

'Friday,' said Dougie.

'Tuts! wass I not sure of it? It's no' a lucky day for this kind of business. Never mind, Colin, we'll come tomorrow when the laandry-maid's in, and you'll bring a poke of conversation lozenges. You mustna be so stupid, man; you were awfu' tumid!'

'I wasna a bit tumid, but I wasna in trum,' said The Tar, who was walking down to the quay with a curious and unusual straddle.

'And what for would you not come at wance when I cried you in?' asked the Captain.

'Because,' said The Tar pathetically, 'I had a kind of accident yonder in the larder: I sat doon on a basket of country eggs.'

6. *A once popular type of sweetmeat printed with helpful messages such as 'I Love You', 'Be Mine', 'Until Tomorrow' and intended to aid bashful lovers like The Tar.*

11 THE SAILORS AND THE SALE

PARA HANDY'S great delight was to attend farm sales. 'A sale's a sublime thing,' he said, 'for if you don't like a thing you don't need to buy it. It's at the sales a good many of the other vessels in the tred get their sailors.' This passion for sales was so strong in him that if there was one anywhere within twelve miles of any port the *Vital Spark* was lying at, he would lose a tide or risk demurrage[1] rather than miss it. By working most part of a night he got a cargo of coals discharged at Lochgoilhead one day in time to permit of his attending a displenishing sale[2] ten miles away. He and the mate, Dougie, started in a brake that was conveying people to the sale; they were scarcely half-way there when the Captain sniffed.

'Hold on a meenute and listen, Dougie,' said he. 'Do you no' smell anything?'

Dougie sniffed too, and his face was lit up by a beautiful smile as of one who recognizes a friend. 'It's not lemon kali[3] at any rate,' he said knowingly, and chuckled in his beard.

'Boys!' said the Captain, turning round to address the other passengers in the brake, who were mainly cattle dealers and farmers — 'Boys! this iss going to be a majestic sale; we're five miles from the place and I can smell the whisky already.'

At that moment the driver of the brake bent to look under his seat, and look up again with great vexation written on his countenance. "Isn't it not chust duvvelish?' he said. 'Have I not gone away and put my left foot through a bottle of good spurits I wass bringing up wi' me in case anybody would take ill through the night.'

'Through the night!' exclaimed one of the farmers, who was plainly not long at the business. 'What night are you taalking aboot?'

'This night,' replied the driver promptly.

'But surely we'll be back at Lochgoilhead before night;' said the farmer, and all the others in the coach looked at him with mingled pity and surprise.

'It's a ferm sale we're going to, and not a rent collection,' said the

1. *The delay of a cargo due to the failure of a ship to sail or load; or the penalty imposed for the same.*

2. *A sale by auction of goods and livestock held when a farmer moved or went out of business.*

3. *Kali. 'A saline substance obtained by the calcination of saltwort.' (Oxford English Dictionary). Hence lemon kali=lemon soda. Kali derives from kalium. Kalium (K) is the chemical symbol for potassium.*

driver. 'And there's thirty-six gallons of ale ordered for it, no' to speak of refreshments.[4] If we're home in time for breakfast from this sale it's me that'll be the bonny surprised man, I'm telling you.'

At these farm sales old custom demands that food and drink should be supplied 'ad lib' by the outgoing tenant. It costs money, but it is a courtesy that pays in the long-run, for if the bidding hangs fire a brisk circulation of the refreshments stimulates competition among the buyers, and adds twenty per cent to the price of stots.[5] It would be an injustice to Para Handy and Dougie to say they attended sales from any consideration of this sort; they went because of the high jeenks. At the close of the day sometimes they found that they had purchased a variety of things not likely to be of much use on board a steam-lighter, as on the occasion when Dougie bought the rotary churn.

'Keep away from the hoosehold furniture aalthegither!' said the Captain, this day. 'We have too mich money in oor pockets between us, and it'll be safer no' to be in sight of the unctioneer till the beasts iss on, for we'll no' be tempted to buy beasts.'

'I would buy an elephant for the fun of the thing, let alone a coo or two,' said Dougie.

'That's put me in mind,' said the Captain, 'there's a cousin of my own yonder in Kilfinan wantin' a milk coo for the last twelvemonth; if I saw a bargain maybe I would take it. But we'll do nothing rash; maybe we're chust sailors, but we're no' daft aalthegither.'

By this time they were standing on the outside of a crowd of prospective purchasers interested in a collection of farm utensils and household sundries, the disposal of which preceeded the rouping[6] of the beasts. The forenoon was chilly; the chill appeared to affect the mood of the crowd, who looked coldly on the chain harrows, turnip-cutters, and other articles offered to them at prices which the auctioneer said it broke his heart ot mention, and it was to instil a little warmth into the proceedings that a handy man with red whiskers went round with refreshments on a tray.

'Streetch your hand and take a gless,' he said to the captain. 'It'll do you no herm.'

'Man, I'm not mich caring for it,' drawled the Captain. 'I had wan

---

4. *The driver clearly distinguishes between beer and spirits. 'A refreshment' is a popular Scottish euphemism for a glass of spirits; as in the phrase 'I don't really drink much, but I do take the occasional refreshment'.*

5. *Bullocks.*

6. *Sale by auction.*

yesterday. What do think, Dougie? Would it do any herm chust to take wan gless to show we're friendly to the sale of implements and things?'

'Whatever you say yoursel',' replied Dougie diffidently, but at the same time grasping the glass nearest him with no uncertain hand.

'Weel, here's good prices!' said the Captain, fixing to another glass, and after that the sun seemed to come out with a genial glow.

The lamentable fact must be recorded that before the beasts came up to the hammer the mate of the *Vital Spark* had become possessor of a pair of curling-stones — one of them badly chipped — a Dutch hoe, and a baking-board.

'What in the world are you going to do with that trash?' asked the Captain, returning from a visit to the outhouse where the ale was, to find his mate with the purchases at his feet.

'Och! it's aal right,' said Dougie, cocking his eye at him. 'I wassna giving a docken[7] for the things mysel', but I saw the unctioneer aye look-looking at me, and I didna like no' to take nothing. It's chust, as you might say, for the good of the hoose. Stop you and and you'll see some fun.'

'But it's a rideeculous thing buying curling-stones at this time of the year, and you no' a curler. What?'

Dougie scratched his neck and looked at his purchases. 'They didn't cost mich,' he said; 'and they're aye handy to have aboot you.'

When the cattle came under the hammer it was discovered that prices were going to be very low. All the likely buyers seemed to be concentrated round the beer-barrel in the barn, with the result that stots, queys,[8] cows, and calves were going at prices that brought the tears to the auctioneer's eyes. He hung so long on the sale of one particular cow for which he could only squeeze out offers up to five pounds that Para Handy took pity on him, and could not resist giving a nod that put ten shillings on to its price and secured the animal.

'Name, please?' said the auctioneer, cheering up wonderfully.

'Captain Macfarlane,' said Para Handy, and, very much distressed at his own impetuosity, took his mate aside. 'There you are, I bought your coo for you,' he said to Dougie.

'For me!' exclaimed his mate. 'What in the world would I be doing with a coo?'

---

7. *An object without value or significance: hence 'I didn't give a docken for the thing'='I cared nothing for the thing'.*

8. *Heifers.*

'You said yoursel' you would take a coo or two for the fun o' the thing,' said Para Handy.

'When I'm buying coos I'm buying them by my own word o' mooth; you can chust keep it for your cousin in Kilfinan. If I wass buyin a coo it wouldna be wan you could hang your hat on in fifty places. No, no, Peter, I'm Hielan', but I'm no' so Hielan' ass aal that.'

'My goodness!' said Para Handy, 'this iss the scrape! I will have to be taking her to Lochgoilhead, and hoisting her on the vessel, and milking her, and keeping her goodness knows what time till I'll have a cargo the length of Kilfinan. Forbye, my cousin and me's no' speakin' since Whitsunday last.'

'Go up to the unctioneer and tell him you didna buy it at all, that you were only noddin' because you had a tight collar,' suggested the mate, and the Captain acted on the suggestion; but the auctioneer was not to be takin in by any such story, and Para Handy and his mate were accordingly seen on the road to Lochgoil late that night with a cow, the possession of which took all the pleasure out of their days outing. Dougie's curling-stones, hoe, and baking board were to follow in a cart.

It was a long time after this before the *Vital Spark* had any occasion to go to Lochgoilhead. Macphail the engineer had only to mention the name of the place and allude casually to the price of beef or winter feeding, and the Captain would show the most extraordinary ill-temper. The fact was he had left his purchase at a farmer's at Lochgoilhead to keep for him till called for, and he never liked to think upon the day of reckoning. But the *Vital Spark* had to go to Lochgoilhead sooner or later, and the first time she did so the Captain went somewhat mournfully up to the farm where his cow was being kept for him.

'It's a fine day; hoo's the mustress?' he said to the farmer, who showed some irritation at never having heard from the owner of the cow for months.

'Fine, but what about your coo, Peter?'

'My Chove! iss she living yet?' said the Captain. 'I'll be due you a penny or two.'

'Five pounds, to be exact; and it'll be five pounds ten at the end of next month.'

'Chust the money I paid for her,' said Para Handy. 'Chust you keep her for me till the end of next month, and then pay yoursel' with her when my account iss up to the five pounds ten,' a bargain which was agreed on; and so ended Para Handy's most expensive high jeenk.

52

THE CAREER OF CAPTAIN PETER MACFARLANE

When we first meet Para Handy he had been sailing in the Vital Spark '. . . four years over twenty with my hert in my mooth for the fear of the boiler.' In these 24 years he had travelled widely—twice at Ullapool and '. . . wance at Londonderry . . .'. We may well believe that he is not one of 'your dry-land sailors', he has been '. . . twice wrecked in the North at places that's not on the maps.'

However his whole career was not spent on the *Vital Spark*, after all he confides to The Tar in 'In Search of a Wife' that he is '. . . chust nine and two twenties of years old, no' countin' the year I wass workin' in the sawmull.' We know from his tale of how he painted the Maids of Bute that he spent time as a deck hand on MacBrayne's *Inveraray Castle*. Above all he served with the redoubtable Hurricane Jack (who came from Kinlochaline '. . . and that iss ass good ass a Board of Tred certuficate . . .' on, amongst other ships, the gabbart *Margaret Ann*, the *Julia*, the *Aggie*, the *Mary Jane* as well as on the *Elizabeth Ann*. It was while serving on the latter ship that Hurricane Jack stole the sheep at Catacol and won his somewhat obscure nickname.

In addition to his long and varied service in the coasting trade which enabled him to boast 'There iss not a port I am not acquent with from the Tail of the Bank to Cairndow, where they keep the two New Years' he also served '. . . a season or two in the yats mysel'—the good old *Marjory . . .*'. However, despite the attractions of the yachts he concludes '. . . there's nothing bates the mercantile marine for makin' sailors. Brutain's hardy sons! We could do withoot yats, but where would we be withoot oor coalboats?'

12   A NIGHT ALARM

THE wheel of the *Vital Spark* was so close to the engines that the Captain could have given his orders in a whisper, but he was so proud of the boat that he liked to sail her with all the honours, so he always used the knocker. He would catch the brass knob and give one, two, or three knocks as the circumstances demanded, and put his mouth to the speaking-tube and cry coaxingly down to the engineer, 'Stop her Dan, when you're ready.' That would be when she was a few lengths off the quay. Dan, the engineer, never let on he heard the bell; he was very fond of reading penny novelettes, and it was only when he was spoken to soothingly down the tube that he would put aside *Lady Winifred's Legacy,* give a sigh, and stop his engine. Then he would stand upright — which brought his head over the level of the deck, and beside the Captain's top-boots — wiping his brow with a piece of waste the way real engineers do on the steamers that go to America. His great aim in taking a quay was to suggest to anybody hanging about it that it was frightfully hot in the engine-room — just like the Red Sea — while the fact was that most of the time there was a draught in the engine-room of the *Vital Spark* that would keep a cold store going without ice.

When he stuck up his head he always said to the Captain, 'You're aye wantin' something or other, fancy goin' awa' and spoilin' me in the middle o' a fine baur.'[1]

'I'm sorry, Dan,' Para Handy would say to him in an agony of remorse, for he was afraid of the engineer because that functionary had once been on a ship that made a voyage to Australia, and used to say he had killed a man in the Bush. When he was not sober it was two men, and he would weep. 'I'm sorry, Dan,' but I did not know you would be busy.' Then he would knock formally to reverse the engine, and cry down the tube, 'Back her, Dan, when you're ready; there's no hurry,' though the engineer was, as I have said, so close that he could have put his hand on his head.

Dan drew in his head, did a bit of juggling with the machinery, and resumed his novelette at the place where Lady Winifred lost her jewels at the ball. There was something breezy in the way he pulled in his head and moved in the engine-room that disturbed the Captain. 'Dan's no' in good trum the day,' he would say, in a hoarse whisper to the mate Dougie under these circumstances. 'You daurna say wan word to him but he flies in a tiravee.'

1. *An all purpose word which means, as the context indicates, a tale, joke, situation or exploit.*

54

'It's them cursed novelles,' was always Dougie's explanation; 'they would put any man wrong in the heid, let alone an enchineer. If it wass me wass skipper of this boat, I wadna be so soft with him, I'll assure you.'

'Ach, you couldna be hard on the chap and him a Macphail,' said the Captain. 'There wass never any holdin' o' them in. He's an aawful fellow for high jeenks; he killed a man in the Bush.'

One afternoon the *Vital Spark* came into Tarbert with a cargo of coals that could not be discharged till the morning, for Sandy Sinclair's horse and cart were engaged at a country funeral. The Captain hinted at repainting a strake[2] or two of the vessel, but his crew said they couldn't be bothered, forbye Dougie had three shillings; so they washed their faces after tea and went up the town. Peace brooded on the *Vital Spark,* though by some overlook Macphail had left her with almost a full head of steam. Sergeant Macleod, of the constabulary, came down when she lay deserted. 'By Cheorge!' said he to himself, 'them fellows iss coing to get into trouble this night, I'm tellin' you,' for he knew the *Vital Spark* of old. He drew his tippit[3] more firmly about him, breathed hard, and went up the town to survey the front of all the public-houses. Peace brooded on the *Vital Spark* — a benign and beautiful calm.

It was ten o'clock at night when her crew returned. They came down the quay in a condition which the most rigid moralist could only have described as jovial, and went to their bunks in the fo'c'sle. A drizzling rain was falling. That day the Captain had mounted a new cord on the steam whistle, so that he could blow it by a jerk from his position at the wheel. It was drawn back taut, and the free end of it was fastened to a stanchion. As the night passed and the rain continued falling, the cord contracted till at last it acted on the whistle, which opened with a loud and croupy[4] hoot that rang through the harbour and over the town. Otherwise peace still brooded on the *Vital Spark.* It took fifteen minutes to waken the Captain, and he started up in wild alarm. His crew were snoring in the light of a small globe lamp, and the engineer had a *Family Herald Supplement* on his chest.

'That's either some duvvlement of somebody's or a warnin',' said Para Handy, half irritated, half in superstitious alarm. 'Dougie, are you sleepin'?'

'What would I be here for if I wass not sleepin'?' said Dougie.

2. *A plank in a ship's hull.*

3. *A cape or cloak.*

4. *Wheezy, asthmatic.*

'Go up like a smert laad and see who's meddlin' my whustle.'

'I canna,' said Dougie; I havena but the wan o' my boots on. Send up The Tar.' The Tar was so plainly asleep from his snoring that it seemed no use to tackle him. The Captain looked at him. 'Man!' he said, 'he hass a nose that minds me o' a winter day, it's so short and dirty. He would be no use any way. It's the enchineer's chob, but I daurna waken him, he's such a man for high jeenks.' And still the whistle waked the echoes of Tarbert.

'If I wass skipper of this boat I would show him,' said Dougie, turning in his bunk, but showing no sign of any willingness to turn out. 'Give him a roar, Peter, or throw the heel of yon pan loaf at him.'

'I would do it in a meenute if he wasna a Macphail,' said the Captain, distracted. 'He wance killed a man in the Bush. But he's the enchineer; the whustle's in his depairtment. Maybe if I spoke nice to him he would see aboot it. Dan!' he cried softly across the fo'c'sle to the man with the *Family Herald Supplement* on his chest — 'Dan, show a leg, like a good laad, and go up and stop that cursed whistle.'

'Are you speakin' to me?' said the engineer, who was awake all the time.

'I was chust makin' a remark,' explained the Captain hurriedly. 'It's not of any great importance, but there's a whustle there, and it's wakin' the whole toon of Tarbert. If you werena awfu' throng⁵ sleepin', you might take a bit turn on dake and see what is't. Chust when you're ready, Dan, chust when you're ready.'

Dan ostentatiously turned on his side and loudly went to sleep again. And the whistle roared louder than ever.

The Captain began to lose his temper. 'Stop you till I get back to Bowling,' he said, 'and I'll give every man of you the whole jeeng-bang,⁶ and get rale men for the *Fital Spark*. Not a wan of you iss worth a spittle in the hour of dancher and trial. Look at Macphail there tryin' to snore like an enchineer with a certeeficate, and him only a fireman! I am not a bit frightened for him; I do not believe he ever killed a man in the bush at aal — he has not the game for it; I'll bate you he never wass near Australia — and what wass his mother but wan of the Macleans of Kenmore?⁷ Chust

5. *busy, occupied.*

6. *A tautology. The whole jeeng-bang (or jing bang)=all or everyone. Para intends to dismiss the entire crew on reaching Bowling.*

7. *Village by Loch Tay, Perthshire. The implication is that, coming from such inland stock, the engineer is in reality a land-lubber and not the terrifying deep-sea-going killer of his tales.*

that; wan of the Macleans of Kenmore! Him and his pride! If I had my Sunday clothes on I would give him my opeenion. And there you are Dougie! I thocht you were a man and not a mice. You are lying there in your ignorance, and never wass the length of Ullapool. Look at me — on the vessels three over twenty years, and twice wrecked in the North at places that's not on the maps.'

The two worthies thus addressed paid no attention and snored with suspicious steadiness, and the Captain turned his attention to The Tar.

'Colin!' he said more quietly, 'show a leg, like a cluvver fellow, and go up and put on the fire, for the breakfast.' But The Tar made no response, and in the depth of the fo'c'sle Para Handy's angry voice rose up again, as he got out of his bunk and prepared to pull on some clothes and go up on deck himself.

'Tar, by by-name and Tar by nature!' said he. 'You will stick to your bed that hard they could not take you off without a half-a-pound of saalt butter. My goodness! have I not a bonny crew? You are chust a wheen of crofters. When the owners of vessels wass wantin' men like you, they go to the Kilmichael cattle-market and drag you down with a rope to the seaside. You will not do the wan word I tell you. I'll wudger I'll not hammer down to you again, Dan, or use the speakin'-tube, the same ass if you were a rale encheneer, I'll chust touch you with the toe of my boot when I want you to back her, mind that! There iss not a finer nor a faster vessel than the *Fital Spark* in the tred; she iss chust sublime, and you go and make a fool of her with your drinking and your laziness and your ignorance.'

He got up on deck in a passion, to find a great many Tarbert people running down the quay to see what was wrong, and Sergeant Macleod at the head of them.

'Come! come! Peter, what iss this whustlin' for on a wet night like this at two o'clock in the mornin'?' asked the sergeant, with a foot on the bulwark. 'What are you blow-blow-blowin' at your whustle like that for?'

'Chust for fun,' said the Captain. 'I'm a terrible fellow for high jeenks. I have three fine stots from the Kilmichael market down below here, and they canna sleep unless they hear a whistle.'

'The man's in the horrors!'[8] said the sergeant in a whisper to some townsmen beside him on the quay. 'I must take him to the lock-up and make a case of him, and its no' a very nice chob, for he's ass strong ass a horse. Wass I not sure there would be trouble when I saw the *Fital Spark*

8. *Suffering from* delirium tremens

the day? It must be the lock-up for him, and maybe Lochgilphead, but it iss a case for deleeberation and caaution — great caaution.'

'Captain Macfarlane,' he said in a bland voice to the Captain, who stood defiant on the deck, making no attempt to stop the whistling. 'Mr. Campbell the banker wass wantin' to see you for a meenute up the toon. Chust a meenute! He asked me to come doon and tell you.'

'What will the banker be wantin' wi' me?' said the Captain looking down and suspecting nothing. 'It's a droll time o' night to be sendin' for onybody.'

'So it is, Captain Macfarlane,' admitted the constable mildly. 'I do not know exactly what he wants, but it iss in a great hurry. He said he would not keep you wan meenute. I think it will be to taalk about your cousin Cherlie's money.'

'I'll go wi' you whenever I get on my bonnet,' said the Captain, preparing to go below.

'Never mind your bonnet; it iss chust a step or two, and you'll be back in five meenutes,' said the sergeant; and, thus cajoled, the Captain of the *Vital Spark,* having cut the cord and stopped the whistle, went lamb-like to the police office.

Peace fell again upon the *Vital Spark.*

Tarbert Harbour *Argyll & Bute District Libraries*

13 A DESPERATE CHARACTER

THOUGH Para Handy went, like a lamb, with Sergeant Macleod, he had not to suffer the ignominy of the police office, for the sergeant found out on the way that the Captain belonged to the Wee Free, and that made a great deal of difference. Instead of putting the mariner into a cell, he took him into his own house, made a summary investigation into the cause of the whistling of the *Vital Spark,* found the whole thing was an accident, dismissed the accused without a stain on his character, gave him a dram, and promised to take him down a pair of white hares for a present before the vessel left Tarbert.

'I am glad to see you belong to the right Church, Peter,' he said. 'Did I not think you were chust wan of them unfuduls that carries the rud-edged hime-books[1] and sits at the prayer,[2] and here you are chust a dacent Christian like mysel'. My goodness! It shows you a man cannot be too caautious. Last year there wass but a small remnant of us Christians to the fore here — myself and Macdougall the merchant, and myself and the Campbells up in Clonary Farm, and myself and the steamboat aagent, and myself and my cousins at Dunmore; but it'll be changed days when we get a ha'ad o' the church. They'll be sayin' there's no hell; we'll show them, I'll assure you! We are few, but firm — firm; there's no bowin' of the knee[3] with us, and many a pair of white hares I'll be gettin' from the Campbells up in Clonary. I have chust got to say the word that wan of the rale old Frees iss in a vessel at the quay, and there will be a pair of white hares doon for you tomorrow.'

'I'm a staunch Free,' said Para Handy, upsetting his glass, which by this time had hardly a drop left in it. 'Tut! tut!' he exclaimed apologetically, 'it's a good thing I never broke the gless. Stop! stop! stop in a meenute; I'm sure I'm no needing any more. But it's a cold wet nicht, whatever. I'm a staunch Free. I never had a hime-book on board my boat; if Dougie wass here he would tell you.'

1. *Red-edged hymn books. The Free Church (v.s.) eschewed the use of hymns, confining its praise to the metrical versions of the Psalms of David and the Scottish Paraphrases.*

2. *The established Church of Scotland followed the custom of standing to sing and sitting to pray. The 'Wee Frees' observed the opposite convention.*

3. *cf Romans, Ch.11, v.4 'I have reserved to myself seven thousand men, who have not bowed the knee to the image of Baal.' Note that this Baal—a false god or idol—should be clearly distinguished from the type of baal held at Furnace (v.s. A Lost Man)*

'You'll no' get very often to the church, wi' you goin' about from place to place followin' the sea?' said the sergeant.

'That's the worst of it,' said Para Handy, heaving a tremendous sigh. 'There's no mich fun on a coal vessel; if it wasna the *Fital Spark* wass the smertest in the tred, and me the skipper of her, I would mairry a fine strong wife and start a business. There wass wan time yonder, when I wass younger, I wass very keen to be a polisman.'

'The last chob!' cried the sergeant. 'The very last chob on earth! You would be better to be trapping rabbits. It iss not an occupation for any man that has a kind he'rt, and I have a he'rt mysel' that's no slack in that direction, I'm tellin' you. Many a time I'll have to take a poor laad in and cherge him, and he'll be fined, and it's mysel' that's the first to get the money for his fine.'

'Do you tell me you pay the fine oot of your own pocket?' asked Para Handy, astonished.

'Not a bit of it; I have aal my faculties about me. I go round and raise a subscription,' explained the sergeant. 'I chust go roond and say the poor laad didna mean any herm, and his mother wass a weedow, and it iss aal right, och aye! it is aal right at wance wi' the folk in Tarbert. Kind, kind he'rts in Tarbert — if there's any fushing. But the polis iss no chob for a man like me. Still and on it's a good pay, and the uniform, and a fine pair of boots, and an honour, so I'm no' complaining. Not a bit!'

Para Handy put up his hand with his customary gesture to scratch his ear, but as usual thought better of it, and sheered off. 'Do you ken oor Dougie?' he asked.

'Iss it your mate?' replied the constable. 'They're telling me aboot him, but I never had him in my hands.'

'It's easy seen you're no long in Tarbert,' said the Captain. 'He wass wan time namely here for makin' trouble; but that wass before he wass a kind of a Rechabite. Did you hear aboot him up in Castlebay in Barra?'

'No,' said the sergeant.

'Dougie will be aye bouncin' he was wan time on the yats, and wearing a red night-kep aal the time, and whitening on his boots, the same ass if he wass a doorstep,[4] but man! he's tumid, tumid! If there's a touch of a gale he starts at his prayers, and says he'll throw his trump over the side. He can play the trump sublime — reels and things you never heard the like of; and if he wass here, and him in trum, it's himself would show you. But when the weathers' scoury,[5] and the *Fital Spark* not at the quay, he'll

4. *A reference to the once common practice of using pipeclay to whiten doorsteps.*

5. *Rough.*

make up his mind to live a better life, and the first thing that he's going to stop's the trump. "Hold you on, Dougie," I'll be sayin' to him; "don't do anything desperate till we see if the weather'll no lift on the other side of Minard." It's a long way from Oban out to Barra; many a man that hass gold braid on his kep in the Clyde never went so far, but it's nothing at aal to the *Fital Spark*. But Dougie does not like that trup at aal, at aal. Give him Bowling to Blairmore in the month of August, and there's no' a finer sailor ever put on oilskins.'

'Och, the poor fellow!' said the sergeant, with true sympathy.

'Stop you!' proceeded Para Handy. 'When we would be crossing the Munch, Dougie would be going to sacrifice his trump, and start releegion every noo and then; but when we had the vessel tied to the quay at Castlebay, the merchants had to shut their shops and make a holiday.'

'My Chove! do you tell me?' cried the sergeant.

'If Dougie was here himsel' he would tell you,' said the Captain. 'It needed but the wan or two drams, and Dougie would start walkin' on his heels to put an end to Castlebay. There iss not many shops in the place aaltogither, and the shopkeepers are aal MacNeils, and cousins to wan another, so when Dougie was waalkin' on his heels and in trum for high jeenks, they had a taalk together, and agreed it would be better chust to put on the shutters.'

'Isn't he the desperate character! said the constable. 'Could they no' have got the polis?'

'There's no a polisman in the island of Barra,' said Para Handy. 'If there wass any need for polismen they would have to send to Lochmaddy, and it would be two or three days before they could put Dougie on his trial. Forbye, they kent Dougie fine; they hadna any ill-wull to the laad, and maybe it wass a time there wasna very mich business doin' anyway. When Dougie would find the shops shut he would be as vexed as anything, and make for the school. He would go into the school and give the children a lecture on music and the curse of drink, with illustrations on the trump. At last they used to shut the school too, and give the weans a holiday, whenever the *Fital Spark* was seen off Castle Kismul.[6] He wass awfu' popular, Dougie, wi' the weans in Castlebay.'

'A man like that should not be at lerge.' said the constable emphatically.

'Och! he wass only in fun; there wass no more herm in Dougie than a fly. Chust fond of high jeenks and recreation; many a place in the

6. *The seat of the MacNeills of Barra. Situated on a rock in Castlebay harbour.*

Highlands would be gled to get the lend of him to keep them cheery in the winter-time. There's no herm in Dougie, not at aal, chust a love of sport and recreation. If he wass here himsel' he would tell you.'

'It iss a good thing for him he does not come to Tarbert for his recreation,' said the constable sternly; 'we're no' so Hielan' in Tarbert ass to shut the shops when a man iss makin' himsel' a nuisance. By Cheorge! if he starts any of his high jeenks in Tarbert he'll suffer the Laaw.'

'There iss no fear of Tarbert nowadays, 'said the Captain, 'for Dougie iss a changed man. He mairried a kind of a wife yonder at Greenock, and she made him a Good Templar,[7] or a Rechabite, or something of the sort where you get ten shillin's a week if your leg's broken fallin' doon the stair, and nobody saw you. Dougie's noo a staunch teetotaller except aboot the time of the old New Year, or when he'll maybe be takin' a dram for medicine. It iss a good thing for his wife, but it leaves an awfu' want in Barra and them other places where they kent him in his best trum.'

7. *Member of a temperance order.*

Tarbert Pier *Argyll & Bute District Libraries*

14 THE TAR'S WEDDING

IT was months after The Tar's consultation with Para Handy about a wife: The Tar seemed to have given up the idea of indulgence in any such extravagance, and Para Handy had ceased to recommend various 'smert, muddle-aged ones wi' a puckle[1] money' to the consideration of the young man, when the latter one day sheepishly approached him, spat awkwardly through the clefts of his teeth at a patch in the funnel of the *Vital Spark*, and remarked, 'I wass thinkin' to mysel' yonder, Captain, that if there wass nothing parteecular doing next Setturday, I would maybe get mairried.'

'Holy smoke!' said the Captain; 'you canna expect me to get a wife suitable for you in that time. It's no reasonable. Man, you're gettin' droll — chust droll!'

'Och, I needn't be puttin' you to any trouble,' said The Tar, rubbing the back of his neck with a hand as rough as a rasp. 'I wass lookin' aboot mysel', and there's wan yonder in Campbeltown'll have me. In fact, it's settled. I thocht that when we were in Campbeltown next Setturday, we could do the chob and be dune wi't. We were roared[2] last Sunday —'

'Roared!' said the Captain. 'Iss it cried, you mean?'

'Yes, chust cried,' said The Tar, 'but the gyurl's kind of dull in the hearing,' and it would likely need to be a roar. You'll maybe ken her — she's wan of the MacCallums.'

'A fine gyurl,' said the Captain, who had not the faintest idea of her identity, and had never set eyes on her, but could always be depended on for politeness. 'A fine gyurl!' Truly sublime! I'm not askin' if there's any money; eh? — not a word! It's none of my business, but, tuts! what's the money anyway, when there's love?'

'Shut up aboot that!' said the scandalized Tar, getting very red. 'If you're goin' to speak aboot love, be dacent and speak aboot it in the Gaalic. But we're no' taalkin' aboot love; we're taalkin' aboot my merrage. Is it aal right for Setturday?'

'You're a cunning man to keep it dark till this,' said the Captain, 'but I'll put nothing in the way, seein' it's your first caper of the kind. We'll have high jeenks at Campbeltown.'

The marriage took place in the bride's mother's house, up a stair that was greatly impeded by festoons of fishing-nets, old oars, and net-bows on the walls, and the presence of six stalwart Tarbert trawlers, cousins of

1. *An indeterminate small quantity.*

2. *The calling of the banns.*

The Tar's, who were asked to the wedding, but were so large and had so many guernseys on, they would of themselves have filled the room in which the ceremony took place; so they had agreed, while the minister was there at all events, to take turn about of going in to countenance the proceedings. What space there was within was monopolized by the relatives of the bride, by Para Handy and Dougie, The Tar in a new slop-shop[3] serge suit, apparently cut out by means of a hatchet, the bride — a good deal prettier than a Goth like The Tar deserved — and the minister. The wedding-supper was laid out in a neighbour's house on the same stair-landing.

A solemn hush marked the early part of the proceedings, marred only by the sound of something frying in the other house and the shouts of children crying for bowl-money[4] in the street. The minister was a teetotaller, an unfortunate circumstance which the Captain had discovered very early, and he was very pleased with the decorum of the company. The MacCallums were not church-goers in any satisfactory sense, but they and their company seemed to understand what was due to a Saturday night marriage and the presence of 'the cloth'. The clergyman had hardly finished the ceremony when the Captain began manoeuvring for his removal. He had possessed himself a bottle of ginger cordial and a plate of cake.

'You must drink the young couple's health, Mr. Grant,' he said. We ken it's you that's the busy man on the Setturday night, and indeed it's a night for the whole of us goin' home early. I have a ship yonder, the *Fital Spark*, that I left in cherge of an encheneer by the name of Macphail, no' to be trusted with such a responsibility.'

The minister drank the cheerful potion, nibbled the corner of a piece of cake, and squeezed his way downstairs between the Tarbert trawlers.

'We're chust goin' away oorsel's in ten meenutes,' said the Captain after him.

'Noo that's all right,' said Para Handy, who in virtue of his office had constituted himself master of ceremonies. 'He's a nice man, Mr. Grant, but he's not strong, and it would be a peety to be keeping him late out of his bed on a Setturday night. I like, mysel', yon old-fashioned munisters that had nothing wrong wi' them, and took a Chrustian dram. Pass oot

3. *A ship's store or sailor's outfitters.*

4. *It was the custom at Scottish weddings for coins to be thrown to on-looking children as a means of ensuring good luck and prosperity for the newly married couple. This distribution was variously known as 'bowl money', a 'pour out', a 'scatter' or a 'scramble'.*

that bottle of chinger cordial to the lads from Tarbert and you'll see fine fun.'

He was the life and soul of the evening after that. It was he who pulled the corks, who cut the cold ham, who kissed the bride first, who sang the first song, and danced with the new mother-in-law. 'You're an aawful man, Captain Macfarlane,' she said in fits of laughter at his fun.

'Not me!' said he, lumberingly dragging her round in a polka to the strains of Dougie's trump. 'I'm a quate fellow, but when I'm in trum I like a high jeenk noo and then. Excuse my feet. It's no' every day we're merryin' The Tar. A fine, smert, handy fellow, Mrs. MacCallum; you didn't make a bad bargain of it with your son-in-law. Excuse my feet. A sailor every inch of him, once you get him wakened. A pound a-week of wages an' no incumbrance. My feet again, excuse them!'

'It's little enough for two,' said Mrs. MacCallum; 'but a man's aye a man,' and she looked the Captain in the eye with disconcerting admiration.

'By Chove! she's a weedow wuman,' thought the Captain; 'I'll have to ca' canny, or I'll be in for an engagement.'

'I aye like sailors,' said Mrs. MacCallum; 'John — that's the depairted, I'm his relic[5] — was wan.'

'A poor life, though,' said the Captain, 'especially on the steamers, like us. But your man, maybe, was sailin' foreign, an' made money? It's always a consuderation for a weedow.'

'Not a penny,' said the indiscreet Mrs. MacCallum, as Para Handy wheeled her into a chair.

At eleven o'clock The Tar was missing. He had last been seen pulling off his new boots, which were too small for him, on the stair-head; and it was only after considerable searching the Captain and one of the Tarbert cousins found him sound asleep on the top of a chest in the neighbour's house.

'Colin,' said the Captain, shaking him awake, 'sit up and try and take something. See at the rest of us, as jovial as anything, and no' a man hit yet. Sit up and be smert for the credit of the *Fital Spark.*

'Are you angry wi' me, Captain?' said The Tar.

'Not a bit of it, Colin! But you have the corkscrew in your pocket. I'm no' caring myself, but the Tarbert gentlemen will take it amiss. Forbye, there's your wife; you'll maybe have mind of her — wan Lucy MacCallum? She's in yonder, fine and cheery, wi' two of your Tarbert

5. *Relict; ie. a widow.*

65

cousins holding her hand.'

'Stop you! I'll hand them!' cried the exasperated bride-groom, and bounded into the presence of the marriage-party in the house opposite, with a demonstration that finally led to the breaking-up of the party.

Next day took place The Tar's curious kirking.[6] The MacCallums, as has been said, were not very regular churchgoers; in fact, they had overlooked the ordinances since the departed John died, and forgot that the church bell rang for the Sabbath-school an hour before it rang for the ordinary forenoon service.

Campbeltown itself witnessed the bewildering spectacle of The Tar and his bride, followed by the mother and Para Handy, marching deliberately up the street and into the church among the children. Five minutes later they emerged, looking very red and ashamed of themselves.

'If I knew there wass so mich bother to mind things, I would never have got married at all,' said the bridegroom.

6. *A formal visit to a church after a significant event such as a wedding. Newly elected local councils used to visit the parish church in a body on a Sunday soon after the election in a ceremony known as the 'Kirking of the Council'.*

Campbeltown *Argyll & Bute District Libraries*

15 A STROKE OF LUCK

IT was a night of harmony on the good ship *Vital Spark*. She was fast in the
mud at Colintraive quay, and, in the den of her, Para Handy was giving his
song, 'The Dancing Master' —

'Set to Jeanie Mertin, tee-teedalum, tee-tadulum,
Up the back and doon the muddle, tee-tadalum, tee-tadulum.
Ye're wrong, Jeck, I'm certain; tee-tadalum, tee-tadalum.'

while the mate played an accompaniment on the trump — that is to say,
the Jew's harp, a favourite instrument on steam-lighters where the
melodeon has not intruded. The Captain knew only two verses, but he
sang them over several times. 'You're getting better and better at it every
time,' The Tar assured him, for The Tar had got the promise of a rise that
day of a shilling a week on his pay. 'If I had chust on my other boots,' said
the Captain, delighted at this appreciation. 'This ones iss too light for
singin' with —' and he stamped harder than ever as he went on with the
song, for it was his idea that the singing of a song was a very ineffective and
uninteresting performance unless you beat time with your foot on the
floor.

The reason for the harmony on the vessel was that Dougie the mate had
had a stroke of luck that evening. He had picked up at the quay-side a
large and very coarse fish called a stenlock, or coal-fish,[1] and had
succeeded, by sheer effrontery, in passing it off as a cod worth two
shillings on a guileless Glasgow woman who had come for the week to one
of the Colintraive cottages.

'I'm only vexed I didna say it wass a salmon,' said Dougie, when he
came back to the vessel with his ill-got florin. 'I could have got twice ass
much for't.'

'She would ken fine it wasna a salmon when it wasna in a tin,' said the
Captain.

'There's many a salmon that iss not in a canister,' said the mate.

'Och ay, but she's from Gleska; they're awfu' Hielan'[2] in Gleska aboot

---

1. *Saithe or coley.*

2. *Very Highland: i.e. very simple or unsophisticated. It is curious to note Captain
Macfarlane using this characteristically Lowland epithet and speaking scornfully
(by implication) of his fellow Highlanders. Indeed Para seems oddly perverse in
this story. He later goes so far as to compare Loch Fyne, unfavourably, with the
dock area of Glasgow: 'There iss more life in wan day in the Broomielaw of Gleska
than there is in a fortnight in Loch Fyne.' This may be true but it is scarcely typical of
Para Handy's normal attitudes and opinions.*

fush and things like that,' said the Captain. 'But it's maybe a peety you didn't say it wass a salmon, for two shullin's iss not mich among four of us.'

'Among four of us!' repeated Dougie emphatically. 'It's little enough among wan, let alone four; I'm going to keep her to mysel'.'

'If that iss your opeenion, Dougie, you are maakin' a great mistake, and it'll maybe be better for you to shift your mind,' the Captain said meaningly. 'It iss the jyle you could be getting for swundling a poor cratur from Gleska that thinks stenlock iss a cod. Forbye, it iss a temendous risk, for you might be found oot, and it would be a disgrace to the *Fital Spark*.'

Dougie was impressed by the possibility of trouble with the law as a result of his fish transaction, which, to do him justice, he had gone about more as a practical joke than anything else. 'I'm vexed I did it, Peter,' he said, turning the two shillings over in his hand. 'I have a good mind to go up and tell the woman it was chust a baur.'

'Not at aal! not at aal!' cried Para Handy. 'It wass a fine cod right enough; we'll chust send The Tar up to the Inns with the two shullin's and the jar, and we'll drink the Gleska woman's health that does not ken wan fish from another. It will be a lesson to her to be careful; chust that, to be careful.'

So The Tar had gone to the Inn for the ale, and thus it was that harmony prevailed in the fo'c'sle of the *Vital Spark*.

'Iss that a song of your own doing?' asked Dougie, when the Captain was done.

'No,' said Para Handy, 'it iss a low-country song I heard wance in the Broomielaw. Yon iss the place for seeing life. I'm telling you it iss Gleska for gaiety if you have the money. There iss more life in wan day in the Broomielaw of Gleska than there iss in a fortnight on Loch Fyne.'

'I daarsay there iss,' said Dougie; 'no' countin' the herring.'

'Och! life, life!' said the Captain, with a pensive air of ancient memory; 'Gleska's the place for it. And the fellows iss there that iss not frightened, I'm telling you.'

'I learned my tred there,' mentioned the engineer, who had no accomplishments, and had not contributed anything to the evening's entertainment, and felt that it was time he was shining somehow.

'Iss that a fact, Macphail? I thocht it wass a coal-ree[3] in the country,' said Para Handy. 'I wass chust sayin', when Macphail put in his oar, that yon's the place for life. If I had my way of it, the *Fital Spark* would be

---

3. *A coal dump, a coal merchant's store. Para is of course implying that Macphail is a mere stoker, 'chust a fireman' and not a 'rale enchineer'.*

going up every day to the Chamaica Brudge the same as the *Columba*,[4] and I would be stepping ashore quite spruce with my Sunday clothes on, and no' lyin' here in a place like Colintraive, where there's no' even a polisman, with people that swundle a Gleska woman oot of only two shullin's. It wass not hardly worth your while, Dougie.' The ale was now finished.

The mate contributed a reel and strathspey on the trump to the evening's programme, during which The Tar fell fast asleep, from which he awakened to suggest that he should give them a guess.

'Weel done, Colin!' said the Captain, who had never before seen such enterprise on the part of The Tar. 'Tell us the guess if you can mind it.'

'It begins something like this,' said The Tar nervously: '"Whether would you raither —" That's the start of it.'

'Fine, Colin, fine!' said the Captain encouragingly. 'Take your breath and start again.'

'"Whether would you raither,"' proceeded The Tar — '"whether would you raither or walk there?"'

'Say't again, slow,' said Dougie, and The Tar repeated his extraordinary conundrum.

'If I had a piece of keelivine (lead pencil) and a lump of paper I could soon answer that guess,' said the engineer, and the Captain laughed.

'Man, Colin,' he said, 'you're missing half of the guess oot. There's no sense at aal in "Whether would you raither or walk there?"'

'That's the way I heard it, anyway,' said The Tar, sorry he had volunteered. '"Whether would you raither or walk there?" I mind fine it wass that.'

'Weel, we give it up anyway; what's the answer?' said the Captain.

'Man, I don't mind whether there was an answer or no',' confessed The Tar, scratching his head; and the Captain irritably hit him with a cap on the ear, after which the entertainment terminated, and the crew of the *Vital Spark* went to bed.

Next forenoon a very irate-looking Glasgow woman was to be observed coming down the quay, and Dougie promptly retired into the hold of the *Vital Spark*, leaving the lady's reception to the Captain.

'Where's that man away to?' she asked Para Handy. 'I want to speak to him.'

'He's engaged, mem,' said the Captain.

4. *MacBrayne's magnificent flagship—used on the prestige summer sailings from the Broomielaw to Ardrishaig, 'The Royal Route'.*

'I don't care if he's married,' said the Glasgow woman; 'I'm no' wantin' him. I jist wanted to say yon wass a bonny-like cod he sell't me yesterday. I biled it three oors this mornin', and it was like leather when a' wass done.'

'That's droll,' said the Captain. 'It wass a fine fush, I'll assure you; if Dougie was here himsel' he would tell you. Maybe you didna boil it right. Cods iss currious that way. What did you use?'

'Watter!' snapped the Glasgow woman; 'did you think I would use sand?'

'Chust that! chust that! Watter? Weel, you couldna use anything better for boilin' with than chust watter. What kind of coals did you use?'

'Jist plain black yins,' said the woman. 'I bocht them frae Cameron along the road there,' referring to a coal agent who was a trade rival to the local charterer of the *Vital Spark*.

'Cameron!' cried Para Handy. 'Wass I not sure there wass something or other wrong? Cameron's coals wouldna boil a wulk, let alone a fine cod. If Dougie wass here he would tell you that himsel'.'

Steamers leaving Broomielaw *Authors' Collection*

PARA'S OPINIONS

A man of firm views Para has expressed himself on a wide variety of topics including:—

Bowmore . . . *iss namely for its mudges' [Mudges]*

Captains *The Captain of a steamer iss the most popular man in the wide world—popularer than the munisters themselves, and the munisters iss that popular the women pit bird-lime in front of the manses to catch them. . . . It's worse with sea-captains—they're that dashing, and they're not aalways hinging aboot the hoose wi' their sluppers on.' [The Mate's Wife]*

Crew of the *Vital Spark*
'*. . . four men and a derrick' [Para Handy, Master Mariner]*
Dougie' *. . . ass cheery a man ass ever you met across a dram' [An Ocean Tragedy]*
Hurricane Jack *'A night wi' Jeck iss ass good as a college education' [Hurricane Jack]*
Macphail *'The want o' the hair's an aawful depredaation' [Mudges]*
'I wouldna alloo any man on the Fital Spark to mairry a Macphail even if she wass the Prunce of Wales' [In Search of a Wife]
Sunny Jim *'He's chust sublime. . . . If he wass managed right there would be money in him' [Treasure Trove]*
The Tar *'A sailor every inch of him, once you get him wakened' [The Tar's Wedding]*

Dancing *'I'm kind of oot o' the dancin', except La Va and Petronella I don't mind one step' [The Disappointment of Erchie's Niece]*
but see also
'I can stot through the middle o' a dance like a tuppeny kahoochy ball' [The Leap-Year Ball]

Drink *'A drop of good Brutish spurits will suit you better' [The Malingerer]*
'I hate them tea-pairties—chust a way of wasting the New Year' [The Baker's Little Widow]

Education *It's the educaation, Dougie; educaation gives you the nerve and if you have the nerve you can go round the world' [A Lost Man]*

The English *'. . . poor craturs, I wass sorry for them' [Queer Cargoes]*

Glasgow *'. . . it is Gleska for gaiety if you have the money. There iss more life in wan day in the Broomielaw of Gleska than there iss in a fortnight on Loch Fyne' [A Stroke of Luck]*

Herring *'It's a fush that's chust sublime'* [The Sea Cook]

High Jeenks *'. . . they're aye stottin' back and hittin' you on the nose . . .'* [Para Handy's Apprentice (Not in collection)]

Loch Fyne *'. . . wass the place for Life in them days—high jeenks and big hauls . . .'* [Herring: A Gossip]

Love *'. . . what's the money anyway, when there's love'* [The Tar's Wedding]

Ministers *'I like, mysel', yon old-fashioned munisters that had nothing wrong wi' them, and took a Chrustian dram.'* [The Tar's Wedding]

Music *'If I had chust on my other boots. This ones iss too light for singin' with—'* [A Stroke of Luck]

Shipowners *'. . . they would carry coal tar made up in delf crates if they get the freight for it'* [Queer Cargoes]

Smoking *'With the trouble you have, smoking drives it in to the hert and kills you at wance'* [The Malingerer]

The Vital Spark *'. . . nothing bates the mercantile marine . . . Brutain's hardy sons! We could do withoot yats, but where would we be withoot oor coal-boats?'* [Among the Yachts]
'The smertest boat in the tred' [Sources Various!]
'She would not take in wan cup of watter unless it wass for synin' oot the dishes' [Para Handy Master Mariner]

Women *'I ken them like the Kyles of Bute'* [The Mate's Wife]
'A fine gyurl! Truly sublime!' [The Tar's Wedding]

16 DOUGIE'S FAMILY

THE size of Dougie the mate's family might be considered a matter which was of importance to himself alone, but it was astonishing how much interest his shipmates took in it. When there was nothing else funny to talk about on the *Vital Spark,* the would turn their attention to the father of ten, and cunningly extract information from him about the frightful cost of boys' boots and the small measure of milk to be got for sixpence at Dwight's dairy in Plantation.[1]

They would listen sympathetically, and later on roast him unmercifully with comments upon the domestic facts he had innocently revealed to them.

It might happen that the vessel would be lying at a West Highland quay, and the Captain sitting on deck reading a week-old newspaper, when he would wink at Macphail and The Tar, and say, 'Cot bless me! boys, here's the price of boots goin' up; peety the poor faithers of big families.' Or, 'I see there's to be a new school started in Partick,[2] Dougie; did you flit[3] again?

'You think you're smert, Peter,' the mate would retort lugubriously. 'Fun's fun, but I'll no' stand fun aboot my femily.'

'Och! no offence, Dougald, no offence,' Para Handy would say soothingly. 'Hoo's the mustress keepin'?' and then ask a fill of tobacco to show his feelings were quite friendly.

In an ill-advised moment the parental pride and joy of the mate brought on board one day a cabinet photograph[4] of himself and his wife and the ten children.

'What do you think of that?' he said to Para Handy, who took the extreme tip of one corner of the card between the finger and thumb of a hand black with coal-grime, glanced at the group, and said —

'Whatna Sunday School trup's this?'

'It's no a trup at aal,' said Dougie with annoyance.

'Beg pardon, beg pardon,' said the Captain, 'I see noo I wass wrong; it's

1. *A dockside district in Govan, Glasgow, on the south side of the River Clyde.*

2. *Now a district of west Glasgow on the north side of the Clyde. At the time of this story a separate burgh whose inhabitants, many of Highland origin, took pride in asserting their civic independence.*

3. *Move house.*

4. *A standard size of print approximately 6″×4″.*

Quarrier's Homes.[5] Who's the chap wi' the whuskers in the muddle, that's greetin'?'

'Where's your eyes?' said Dougie. 'It's no' a Homes at aal; that's me, and I'm no greetin'. What would I greet for?'

'Faith, I believe you're right,' said the Captain. 'It's yoursel' plain enough, when I shut wan eye to look at it; but the collar and a clean face make a terrible dufference. Well, well, allooin' than it's you, and you're no greetin', it's rideeculous for you to be goin' to a dancin'-school.'

'It's no' a dancin'-school, it's the femily,' said the mate, losing his temper. 'Fun's fun, but if you think I'll stand —'

'Keep caalm, keep caalm!' interrupted the Captain hurriedly, realizing that he had carried the joke far enough. 'I might have kent fine it wass the femily; they're aal ass like you both ass anything, and that'll be Susan the eldest.'

'That!' said Dougie, quite mollified — 'that's the mustress hersel'.'

'Well, I'm jeegered,' said the Captain, with well-acted amazement. 'She's younger-looking than ever; that's a woman that's chust sublime.'

The mate was so pleased he made him a present of the photograph.

But it always had been, and always would be, a distressing task to Dougie to have to intimate to the crew (as he had to do once a year) that there was a new addition to the family, for it was on these occasions that the chaff of his shipmates was most ingenious and galling. Only once, by a trick, had he got the better of them and evaded his annual roastings. On that occasion he came to the *Vital Spark* with a black muffler on, and a sad countenance.

'I've lost my best freend,' said he, rubbing his eyes to make them red.

'Holy smoke!' said Para Handy, 'is Macmillan the pawn-broker deid?'

'It's no' him,' said Dougie, manfully restraining a sob, and he went on to tell them that it was his favourite uncle, Jamie. He put so much pathos into his description of Uncle Jamie's last hours, that when he wound up by mentioning, in an off-hand way, that his worries were complicated by the arrival of another daughter that morning, the crew had, naturally, not the heart to say anything about it.

Some weeks afterwards they discovered by accident that he never had an Uncle Jamie.

'Man! he's cunning!' said Para Handy, when this black evidence of Dougie's astuteness came out. 'Stop you till the next time, and we'll make him pay for it.'

5. *A home for orphan children at Bridge of Weir, Renfrewshire, founded in the 1860's by William Quarrier.*

The suitable occasion for making the mate smart doubly for his deceit came in due course. Macphail the engineer lived in the next tenement to Dougie's family in Plantation, and he came down to the quay one morning before the mate, with the important intelligence for the Captain that the portait group was now incomplete.

'Poor Dugald!' said the Captain sympathetically. 'Iss it a child or a lassie?'

'I don't ken,' said the engineer. 'I just got a rumour frae the night polisman, and he said the wife was fine.'

'Stop you and you'll see some fun with Dougie,' said the Captain. 'I'm mich mistaken if he'll swundle us this twict.'

Para Handy had gone ashore for something, and was back before his mate appeared on board the *Vital Spark,* which was just starting for Campbeltown with a cargo of bricks. The mate took the wheel, smoked ceaselessly at a short cutty pipe,[6] and said nothing; and nobody said anything to him.

'He's plannin' some other way oot of the scrape,' whispered the Captain once to the engineer; 'but he'll not get off so easy this time. Hold you on!'

It was dinner-time, and the captain, mate, and engineer were round the pot on deck aft, with The Tar at the wheel, within comfortable hearing distance, when Para Handy slyly broached the topic.

'Man, Dougie,' he said, 'what wass I doin' yonder last night but dreamin' in the Gaalic aboot you? I wass dreamin' you took charter of the *Fital Spark* doon to Ardkinglas with a picnic, and there wass not a park[7] in the place would hold the company.'

Dougie simply grunted.

'It wass a droll dream,' continued the Captain, diving for another potato. 'I wass chust wonderin' hoo you found them aal at home. Hoo's the mustress keepin'?'

The mate got very red. 'I wass chust goin' to tell you aboot her,' he said with considerable embarrassment.

'A curious dream it wass,' said Para Handy, postponing his pleasure, like the shrewd man he is, that he might enjoy it all the more when it came. 'I saw you ass plain ass anything, and the *Fital Spark* crooded high and low with the picnic, and you in the muddle playing your trump. The mustress wass there, too, quite spruce, and — But you were goin' to say something

6. *Short clay pipe.*

7. *Field, pastureland.*

75

aboot the mustress, Dougie. I hope she's in her usual?'

'That's chust it,' said Dougie, more and more embarrassed as he saw his news had to be given now, if ever. 'You would be thinkin' to yourself I wass late this mornin', but the fact iss we were in an aawful habble[8] in oor hoose —'

'Bless me! I hope the lum[9] didn't take fire nor nothing like that?' said Para Handy anxiously; and The Tar, at the wheel behind, was almost in a fit with suppressed laughter.

'Not at aal! Worse nor that!' said Dougie in melancholy tones. 'There's — there's — dash it! there's more boots than ever needed yonder!'

'Man, you're gettin' quite droll,' said Para Handy. 'Do you no' mind you told me aboot that wan chust three or four months ago?'

'You're a liar!' said Dougie, exasperated; 'it's a twelve-month since I told you aboot the last.'

'Not at aal! not at aal! your mind's failin',' protested the Captain. 'Five months ago at the most; you told me aboot it at the time. Surely there's some mistake?'

'No mistake at aal aboot it,' said the mate, shaking his head so sadly that the Captain's heart was melted.

'Never mind, Dougald,' he said, taking a little parcel out of his pocket. 'I'm only in fun. I heard aboot it this mornin' from Macphail, and here's a wee bit peeny[10] and pair o' sluppers that I bought for't.'

'To the muschief! It's no' an "it",' said Dougie; 'it's — it's — it's a twuns!'

'Holy smoke!' exclaimed Para Handy. 'Iss that no chust desperate?' And the mate was so much moved that he left half his dinner and went forward towards the bow.

Para Handy went forward to him in a little and said, 'Cheer up, Dougie; hoo wass I to ken it wass a twuns? If I had kent, it wouldna be the wan peeny and the wan sluppers; but I have two or three shillin's here, and I'll buy something else in Campbeltown.'

'I can only — I can only say thankye the noo, Peter; it wass very good of you,' said the mate, deeply touched, and attempting to shake the Captain's hand.

'Away!, away!' said Para Handy, getting very red himself; 'none of your chat! I'll buy peenies and sluppers if I like.'

8. *Upset or confusion.*

9. *Chimney.*

10. *Pinafore.*

17 THE BAKER'S LITTLE WIDOW

ON the night after New Year's Day the Captain did a high-spirited thing he had done on the corresponding day for the previous six years; he had his hair cut and his beard trimmed by Dougie the mate, made a specially careful toilet — taking all the tar out of his hands by copious applications of salt butter — wound up his watch (which was never honoured in this way more than once a twelvemonth), and went up the quay to propose to Mrs. Crawford. It was one of the rare occasions upon which he wore a topcoat, and envied Macphail his Cairngorm scarfpin. There was little otherwise to suggest the ardent wooer, for ardent wooers do not look as solemn as Para Handy looked. The truth is, he was becoming afraid that his persistency might wear down a heart of granite, and that this time the lady might accept him.

The crew of the *Vital Spark*, whom he thought quite ignorant of his tender passion for the baker's widow, took a secret but intense interest in his annual enterprise. He was supposed to be going to take tea with a cousin (as if captains took the tar off their hands to visit their own cousins!), and in order to make the deception more complete and allay any suspicions on the part, especially, of Macphail, who, as a great student of penny novelettes, was up to all the intrigues of love, the Captain casually mentioned that if it wasn't that it would vex his cousin he would sooner stay on the vessel and play Catch the Ten[1] with them.

'I hate them tea pairties,' he said; 'chust a way of wasting the New Year. But stay you here, boys, and I'll come back ass soon ass ever I can.'

'Bring back some buns, or cookies, or buscuits wi' you,' cried Dougie, as the Captain stepped on to the quay.

'What do you mean?' said Para Handy sharply, afraid he was discovered.

'Nothing, Peter, nothing at aal,' the mate assured him, nudging The Tar in the dark. 'Only it's likely you'll have more of them that you can eat at your cousins' tea-pairty.'

Reassured thus that his secret was still safe, Para Handy went slowly up the quay. As he went he stopped a moment to exchange a genial word with everybody he met, as if time was of no importance, and he was only ashore for a daunder. This was because, dressed as he was, if he walked quickly and was not particularly civil to everybody, the whole of Campbeltown (which is a very observant place) would suspect he was up to something and watch him.

1. *Card game.*

The widow's shop was at a conveniently quiet corner. He tacked back and forward off it in the darkness several times till a customer, who was being served, as he could see through the glass door, had come out, and a number of boys playing at 'guesses' at the window had passed on, and then he cleared his throat, unbuttoned his topcoat and jacket to show his watch-chain, and slid as gently as he could in at the glass door.

'Dear me, fancy seeing you, Captain Macfarlane!' said the widow Crawford, coming from the room at the back of the shop. 'Is it really yourself?'

'A good New Year to you,' said the Captain, hurried and confused. 'I wass chust goin' up the toon, and I thought I would give you a roar in the by-going. Are you keeping tip-top, Mery?'

His heart beat wildly; he looked at her sideways with a timid eye, for, hang it! she was more irresistible than ever. She was little, plump, smiling, rosy-cheeked, neat in dress, and just the exact age to make the Captain think he was young again.

'Will you not come ben and warm yourself?' It's a nasty damp night,' said Mrs. Crawford, pushing the back door, so that he got the most tempting vision of an interior with firelight dancing in it, a genial lamp, and a tea-table set.

'I'll chust sit doon and draw my breath for a meenute or two. You'll be busy?' said the Captain, rolling into the back room with an elephantine attempt (which she skilfully evaded) at playfully putting his arm round the widow's waist as he did so.

'You're as daft as ever, I see, Captain,' said the lady. 'I was just making myself a cup of tea; will you take one?'

'Och, it's puttin' you to bother,' said the Captain.

'Not a bit of it,' said the widow, and she whipped out a cup which was suspiciously handy in a cupboard, and told the Captain to take off his coat and he would get the good of it when he went out.

People talk about young girls as entrancing. To men of experience like the Captain girls are insipid. The prime of life in the other sex is something under fifty; and the widow, briskly making tea, smiling on him, shaking her head at him, pushing him on the shoulder when he was impudent, chaffing him, surrounding him with an intoxicating atmosphere of homeliness, comfort, and cuddleability, seemed to Para Handy there and then the most angelic creature on earth. The rain could be heard falling heavily outside, no customers were coming in, and the back room of the baker's shop was, under the circumstances, as fine an earthly makeshift for Paradise as man could ask for.

Para Handy dived his hand into his coat pocket. 'That minds me,' said he; 'I have a kind of bottle of scent here a friend o' mine, by the name of Hurricane Jeck, took home for me from America last week. It's the rale Florida Water; no' the like o't to be got here, and if you put the least sensation on your hanky you'll feel the smell of it a mile away. It's chust sublime.'

'Oh! it's so kind of you!' said the widow, beaming on him with the merriest, brownest, deepest, meltingest of eyes, and letting her plump little fingers linger a moment on his as she took the pefume bottle. The Captain felt as if golden harps were singing in the air, and fairies were tickling him down the back with peacocks' feathers.

'Mercy,' he said in a little, 'this iss splendid tea. Capital, aalthegither!'

'Tuts! Captain,' said she, 'is it only my tea you come to pay compliments to once a year? Good tea's common enough if you're willing to pay for it. What do you think of myself?'

The Captain neatly edged his chair round the corner of the table to get it close beside hers, and she just as neatly edged her chair round the other corner, leaving their relative positions exactly as they had been.

'No, no, Captain,' said she, twinkling; 'hands off the widow. I'm a done old woman, and it's very good of you to come and have tea with me; but I always thought sailors, with a sweet-heart, as they say, in every port, could say nice things to cheer up a lonely female heart. What we women need, Captain — the real necessity of our lives — is someone to love us. Even if he's at the other end of the world, and unlikely ever to be any nearer, it makes the work of the day cheery. But what am I haverin'[2] about?' she added, with a delicious, cosy, melting, musical sigh that bewitchingly heaved her blouse. 'Nobody cares for me, I'm too old.'

'Too old!' exclaimed the Captain, amused at the very idea. 'You're not a day over fifty. You're chust sublime.'

'Forty-nine past, to be particular,' said the widow, 'and feel like twenty. Oh! Captain, Captain! you men!'

'Mery,' entreated Para Handy, putting his hand to one side, 'caal me Peter, and gie me a haad o' your hand.' This time he edged his chair round quicker than she did hers, and captured her fingers. Now that he had them he didn't know very well what to do with them, but he decided after a little that a cute thing to do was to pull them one by one and try to make them crack. He did so, and got slapped on the ear for his pains.

'What do you mean by that?' said she.

2. *Havering: talking nonsense.*

'Och, it was chust a baur, Mery,' said Para Handy, 'Man, you're strong, strong! You would make a sublime wife for any sober, decent, good-looking, capable man. You would make a fine wife for a sailor, and I'm naming no names, mind ye; but' — here he winked in a manner that seemed to obliterate one complete side of his face — 'they caal him Peter. eh? What?'

'Nobody would have me,' said the widow, quite cheerfully, enjoying herself immensely. 'I'm old — well, kind of old, and plain, and I have no money.'

'Money!' said Para Handy contemptuously; 'the man I'm thinking of does not give wan docken for money. And you're no more old than I am mysel', and as for bein' plain, chust look at the lovely polka you have on and the rudeness of your face. If Dougie was here he would tell — no, no, don't mention a cheep³ to Dougie — not a cheep; he would maybe jalouse⁴ something.'

'This is the sixth time of asking, Captain,' said the widow. 'You must have your mind dreadful firm made up. But it's only at the New Year I see you; I'm afraid you're like all sailors — when you're away you forget all about me. Stretch your hand and have another London bun.'

'London buns iss no cure for my case,' said the Captain, taking one, however. 'I hope you'll say yes this time.'

'I'll — I'll think about it,' said the widow still smiling; 'and if you're passing this way next New Year and call in, I'll let you know.'

The crew of the *Vital Spark* waited on deck for the return of the skipper. Long before he came in sight they heard him clamping down the quay singing cheerfully to himself —

> *'Rolling home to bonnie Scotland,*
> *Rolling home, dear land, to thee;*
> *Rolling home to bonnie Scotland,*
> *Rolling home across the sea.'*

'Iss your cousin's tea-pairty over already?' said Dougie innocently. 'Wass there many at it?'

'Seven or eight,' said Para Handy promptly. 'I chust came away. And I'm feeling chust sublime. Wan of Brutain's hardy sons.'

He went down below, and hung up his topcoat and his watch and took

3. *Say a word.*
4. *Suspect.*

off his collar, which uncomfortably rasped his neck. 'Mery's the right sort,' said he to himself; 'she's no' going ram-stam[5] into the business. She's caautious like mysel'. Maybe next New Year she'll make her mind up.'

And the widow, putting up her shutters that night, hummed cheerfully to herself, and looked quite happy. 'I wish I HAD called him Peter,' she thought; 'next year I'll not be so blate.'

5. *Precipitately.*

Campbeltown — Street Scene *Argyll & Bute District Libraries*

18   THREE DRY DAYS

ON the first day of February the Captain of the *Vital Spark* made an amazing resolution. Life in the leisure hours of himself and his crew had been rather strenuous during the whole of January, for Dougie had broken with the Rechabites. When Dougie was not a Rechabite, he always carried about with him an infectious atmosphere of gaiety and a half-crown, and the whole ship's company took its tone from him. This is a great moral lesson. It shows how powerful for good or evil is the influence and example of One Strong Man. If Dougie had been more at home that month, instead of trading up the West Coast, his wife would have easily dispelled his spirit of gaiety by making him nurse the twins, and she would have taken him herself to be reinstalled in the Rechabites, for she was 'a fine, smert, managin' woman', as he admitted himself; but when sailors are so often and so far away from the benign influences of home, with nobody to search their pockets, it is little wonder they should sometimes be foolish.

So the Captain rose on the first day of the month with a frightful headache, and emphatically refused to adopt the customary method of curing it. 'No,' he said to his astonished mates, 'I'm no' goin up the Ferry Hoose nor anywhere else; I'm teetotal.'

'Teetotal!' exclaimed Dougie, much shocked. 'You shouldna make a joke aboot things like that, and you no' feelin' very weel; come on up and take your mornin'.'

'Not a drop!' said Para Handy firmly.

'Tut, tut,' chust wan beer,' pesisted the mate patiently.

'Not even if it wass jampaigne,' said the Captain, drying his head, which he had been treating to a cold douche. 'My mind's made up. Drink's a curse, and I'm done wi' t, for I canna stand it.'

'There's nobody askin' you to stand it,' explained the mate. 'I have a half-croon o' my own here.'

'It's no odds,' said the Captain, 'I'm on the teetotal tack. Not another drop will I taste —'

'Stop, stop!' interrupted Dougie, more shocked than ever. 'Don't do anything rash. You might be struck doon deid, and then you would be sorry for what you said. Do you mean to tell us that you're goin' to be teetotal aalthegither?'

'No,' said the Captain, 'I'm no' that desperate. I wouldna care chust to go aal that length, but I'm goin' to be teetotal for the month o' February.'

'Man, I think you're daft, Peter,' said the mate. 'February of aal months! In February the New Year's no right bye, and the Gleska Fair's chust comin' on; could you no' put it off for a more sensible time?'

'No,' said the Captain firmly, 'February's the month for me; there's two or three days less in't than any other month in the year.'

So the crew filed ashore almost speechless with astonishment — annoyed and depressed to some extent by this inflexible virtue on the part of Para Handy.

'He's gettin' quite droll in his old age,' was Dougie's explanation.

Fancy him goin' away and spoilin' the fun like that!' said The Tar incredulously.

'I aye said he hadna the game in him,' was the comment of Macphail the engineer.

Para Handy watched them going up the Ferry House, and wished it was the month of March.

The first day of his abstinence would have passed without much more inclination on his part to repent his new resolution were it not for the fact that half a score of circumstances conspired to make it a day of unusual trial. He met friends that day he had not met for months, all with plenty of time on their hands; Hurricane Jack, the irresistible, came alongside in another vessel, and was immediately for celebrating this coincidence by having half a day off, a proposal the Captain evaded for a while only by pretending to be seriously ill and under medical treatment; the coal merchant, whose cargo they had just discharged, presented the crew with a bottle of whisky; there was a ball at the George Hotel; there was a travelling piper on the streets with most inspiring melodies; the headache was away by noon — only a giant will-power could resist so many circumstances conducive to gaiety. But Para Handy never swerved in his resolution. He compromised with the friends who had plenty of time and the inclinations for merriment by taking fills of tobacco from them; confiscated the bottle of whisky as Captain, and locked it past with the assurance to his crew that it would be very much the more matured if kept till March; and the second time Hurricade Jack came along the quay to see if the Captain of the *Vital Spark* was not better yet, he accompanied him to the Ferry House, and startled him by saying he would have 'Wan small half of lime-juice on draught.'

'What's that, Peter?' said Hurricane Jack. 'Did I hear you say something aboot lime-juice, or does my ears deceive me?'

'It's chust for a bate,[1] Jeck — no offence,' explained the Captain

1. *Bet, wager.*

hurriedly. 'I have a bate on wi a chap that I'll no' drink anything stronger this month; but och! next month, if we're spared, wait you and you'll see some fine fun.'

Hurricane Jack looked at him with great disapproval. 'Macfarlane,' he said solemnly, 'you're goin' far wrong, and mind you I'm watchin' you. A gembler iss an abomination, and gemblin' at the expense of your inside iss worse than gemblin' on horses. Us workin' men have nothing but oor strength to go on, and if we do not keep up oor strength noo and then, where are we? You will chust have a smaal gill, and the man that made the bate wi' you'll never be any the wiser.'

'No, Jeck, thank you aal the same,' said the Captain, 'but I'll chust take the lime-juice. Where'll you be on the first o' Merch?'

Hurricane Jack grudgingly ordered the lime-juice, and asked the landlady to give the Captain a sweetie with it to put away the taste, then looked on with as aspect of mingled incredulity and disgust as Para Handy hurriedly gulped the unaccustomed beverage and chased it down with a drink of water.

'It's a fine thing a drap watter,' said Para Handy, gasping.

'No' a worse thing you could drink,' said Hurricane Jack. 'It rots your boots; what'll it no' do on your inside? Watter's fine for sailon' on — there's nothing better — but it's no' drink for sailors.'

On the second day of the great reform Para Handy spent his leisure hours fishing for saithe from the side of the vessel, and was, to all appearance, firmer than ever. He was threatened for a while by a good deal of interference from his crew, who resented the confiscation of the presentation bottle, but he turned the tables on them by coming out in the *rôle* of temperance lecturer. When they approached him, he sniffed suspiciously, and stared at their faces in a way that was simply galling — to Dougie particularly, who was naturally of a rubicund countenance. Then he sighed deeply, shook his head solemnly, and put on a fresh bait.

'Are you no' better yet?' Dougie asked. 'You're looking ass dull ass if the shup wass tied up to a heid-stone in the Necropolis o' Gleska.[2] None o' your didoes,[3] Peter; give us oot the spurits we got the present o'. It's Candlemas.'[4]

---

2. *The Glasgow Necropolis was one of the City's main burying places and from its establishment in 1833 was extensively used by the city's industrial and commercial elite.*

3. *Tricks.*

4. *February 2nd. One of the Scottish Quarter Days. The others being Whitsunday (15th May), Lammas (1st August) and Martinmas (11th November).*

Para Handy stared at his fishing-line, and said gently, as if he were speaking to himself, 'Poor sowls! poor sowls! Nothing in their heids but drink. It wass a happy day for me the day I gave it up, or I might be like the rest o' them. There's poor Dougald lettin' it get a terrible grup o' him; and The Tar chust driftin', driftin' to the poor's-hoose, and Macphail iss sure to be in the horrors before Setturday, for he hasna the heid for drink, him no' bein' right Hielan'.'

'Don't be rash; don't do anything you would be vexed for, but come on away up the toon and have a pant,'[5] said Dougie coaxingly. 'Man, you have only to make up your mind and shake it off, and you'll be ass cheery ass ever you were.'

'He's chust takin' a rise oot o' us; are you no' Captain?' said The Tar, anxious to leave his commander an honourable way of retreat from his preposterous position.

Para Handy went on fishing as if they were not present.

'Married men, too, with wifes and femilies,' he said musingly. 'If they chust knew what it wass, like me, to be risin' in the mornin' wi' a clear heid, and a good conscience, they would never touch it again. I never knew what happines wass till I joined the teetotal, and it'll be money in my pocket forbye.'

'You'll go on, and you'll go on with them expuriments too far till you'll be a vegetarian next,' said Dougie, turning away. 'Chust a vegetarian, tryin' to live on turnips and gress, the same ass a coo. If I was a Macfarlane I wouldna care to be a coo.'

Then they left him with an aspect more of sorrow than of anger, and he went on fishing.

The third day of the month was Saturday; there was nothing to do on the *Vital Spark,* which was waiting on a cargo of timber, so all the crew except the Captain spent the time ashore. Him they left severely alone, and the joys of fishing saithe and reading a week-old newspaper palled.

'The worst of bein' good iss that it leaves you duvelish lonely,' said the Captain to himself.

An hour later, he discovered that he had a touch of toothache, and, strongly inclined for a temporary suspension of the new rules for February, he went to the locker for the presentation bottle.

It was gone!

5. *A spree, a piece of fun.*

85

19 THE VALENTINE THAT MISSED FIRE

[This story was first published on 19th February 1906—as close to St Valentine's Day as could be arranged.]

A FORTNIGHT of strict teetotalism on the part of the Captain was too much of a joke for his crew. 'It's just bounce,' said the mate; 'he's showin' off. I'm a Rechabite for six years, every time I'm in Gleska; but I never let it put between me and a gless of good Brutish spurits wi' a shipmate in any port, Loch Fyne or foreign.'

'It's most annoyin'.' said The Tar. 'He asked me yesterday if my health wassna breakin' doon wi' drink, the same ass it would break doon wi' aal I take.'

'Chust what I told you; nothing but bounce!' said Dougie gloomily. 'Stop you! Next time he's in trum, I'll no' be so handy at pullin' corks for him. If I wass losin' my temper wi' him, I would give him a bit o' my mind.'

The engineer, wiping his brow with a wad of oily waste, put down the penny novelette he was reading and gave a contemptuous snort. 'I wonder to hear the two o' ye talkin',' said he. 'Ye're baith feared for him. I could soon fix him.'

'Could you, Macphail?' said Dougie. 'Your aawful game; what would you do?'

'I would send him a valentine that would vex him,' replied the engineer promptly; 'a fizzer o' a valentine that would mak' his hair curl for him.'

The mate impulsively smacked his thigh. 'My Chove! Macphail,' said he, 'it's the very ticket! What do you say to a valentine for the Captain, Colin?'

'Whatever you think yersel',' said The Tar.

That night Dougie and The Tar went ashore at Tarbert for a valentine. There was one shop-window up the town with a gorgeous display of penny 'mocks', designed and composed to give the recipient in every instance a dull, sickening thud on the bump of his self-esteem. The two mariners saw no valentine, however, that quite met the Captain's case.

'There'll be plenty o' other wans inside on the coonter,' said Dougie diplomatically. 'Away you in, Colin, and pick wan suitable and I'll stand here and watch.'

'Watch what?' inquired The Tar suspiciously. 'It would be more like the thing if you went in and bought it yoursel'; I'll maybe no' get wan that'll please you.'

'Aal you need to ask for iss a mock valentine, lerge size, and pretty broad, for a skipper wi' big feet. I would go in mysel' in a meenute if it wassna that — if it wassna that it would look droll, and me a muddle-aged man wi' whuskers.'

The Tar went into the shop reluctantly, and was horrified to find a rather pretty girl behind the counter. He couldn't for his life suggest mock valentines to her, and he could not with decency back out without explanation.

Have you any — have you any nice unvelopes?' he inquired bashfully, as she stood waiting his order.

'What size?' she asked.

'Lerge size, and pretty broad, for a skipper wi' big feet,' said The Tar in his confusion. Then he corrected himself, adding. 'Any size, muss, suitable for holdin' letters.'

'There's a great run on that kind of envelope this winter' the lady remarked, being a humorist. 'How many'

'A ha-pennyworth,' said The Tar. 'I'll chust take them wi' me.'

When The Tar came out of the shop the mate was invisible, and it was only after some search he found him in a neighbouring public-house.

'I chust came in here to put by the time,' said Dougie; 'but seein' you're here, what am I for?'

The Tar, realizing that there must be an unpleasant revelation immediately, produced the essential threepence and paid for beer.

'I hope you got yon?' said the mate anxiously.

'Ass sure ass daith, Dougie, I didna like to ask for it,' explained the young man pathetically. 'There's a gasalier[1] and two paraffin lamps bleezin' in the shop, and it would gie me a rud face to ask for a mock valentine in such an illumination. Iss there no other wee dark shop in the toon we could get what we want in?'

The mate surveyed him with a disgusted countenance. 'Man, you're a coward, Colin,' he said. 'The best in the land goes in and buys mock valentines, and it's no disgrace to nobody so long ass he has the money in his hand. If I had another gless o' beer I would go in mysel'.'

'You'll get that!' said The Tar gladly, and produced another threepence, after which they returned to the shop-window, where Dougie's courage apparently failed him, in spite of the extra glass of beer. It's no' that I give a docken for anybody,' he explained, 'but you see I'm that weel kent in Tarbert. What sort o' body keeps the shop?'

'Och, it's chust an old done man wi' a sore hand and wan eye no' neebours,' replied The Tar strategically. 'Ye needna be frightened for

1. *Gas light fitting.*

him; he'll no say a cheep. To bleezes wi' him!'

Dougie was greatly relieved at this intelligence. 'Toots!' he said. 'Iss that aal? Watch me!' and he went banging in at the door in three strides.

The lady of the shop was in a room behind. To call her attention Dougie cried, 'Shop!' and kicked the front of the counter, with his eyes already on a pile of valentines ready for a rush of business in that elegant form of billet-doux. When the pretty girl came skipping out of the back room, he was even more astounded and alarmed than The Tar had been.

'A fine night,' he remarked affably: 'iss your faither at the back?'

'I think you must have made a mistake in the shop,' said the lady. 'Who do you want?'

'Him with the sore hand and the wan eye no right neebours,' said the mate, not for a moment suspecting that The Tar had misled him. 'It's parteecular business; I'll no' keep him wan meenute.'

'There's nobody here but myself,' the girl informed him, and then he saw he had been deceived by his shipmate.

'Stop you till I get that Tar!' he exclaimed with natural exasperation, and was on the point of leaving when the pile of valentines met his eye again, and he decided to brazen it out.

'Maybe you'll do yoursel',' said he, with an insinuating leer at the shopkeeper. 'There iss a shipmate o' mine standin' oot there took a kind o' notion o' a mock valentine and doesna like to ask for't. He wass in a meenute or two ago — you would know him by the warts on his hand — but he hadna the nerve to ask for it.'

'There you are, all kinds,' said the lady, indicating the pile on the counter, with a smile of comprehension. 'A penny each.'

Dougie wet his thumb and clumsily turned over the valentines, seeking for one appropriate to a sea captain silly enough to be teetotal. 'It's chust for a baur, mind you,' he explained to the lady. 'No herm at all, at aal; chust a bit of high jeenk. Forbye it's no' for me: it's for the other fellow, and his name's Colin Turner, but he's blate, blate.' He raised his voice so that The Tar, standing outside the window, could hear him quite plainly; with the result that The Tar was so ashamed, he pulled down his cap on his face and hurriedly walked off to the quay.

'There's an awful lot o' them valentines for governesses and tylers² and polismen,' said Dougie; 'the merchant service doesna get mich of a chance. Have you nothing smert and nippy that'll fit a sea captain, and him teetotal?'

2. *Tailors. A tyler was also a minor official of a Masonic Lodge. For more on this confusion see Chapter 34 'Initiation'.*

The shopkeeper hurriedly went over her stock, and discovered that teetotalism was the one eccentricity valentines never dealt with; on the contrary, they were all for people with red noses and bibulous propensities.

'There's none for teetotal captains,' said she, 'but here's one for a captain that's not teetotal,' and she shoved a valentine with a most unpleasant-looking seaman, in a state of intoxication, walking arm-in-arm with a respectable-looking young woman.

'Man, that's the very tup!' said Dougie, delighted. 'It's ass clever a thing ass ever I seen. I wonder the way they can put them valentines thegather. Read what it says below, I havena my specs.'

The shopkeeper read the verse on the valentine:

> *'The girl that would marry a man like you*
> *Would have all the rest of her life to rue;*
> *A sailor soaked in salt water and rum*
> *Could never provide a happy home.'*

'Capital!' exclaimed the mate, highly delighted. 'Ass smert ass anything in the works of Burns. That wan'll do splendid.'

'I thought it was for a teetotal captain you wanted one,' said the lady, as she folded up the valentine.

'He's only teetotal to spite us,' said Dougie. 'And that valentine fits him fine, for he's coortin' a baker's weedow, and he thinks we don't know. Mind you, it's no' me that's goin' to send the valentine, it's Colin Turner; but there's no herm, chust a bit of a baur. You ken yoursel'.'

Then an embarrassing idea occurred to him — Who was to address the envelope?

'Do you keep mournin' unvelopes?' he asked.

'Black-edged envelopes — yes,' said the shopkeeper.

'Wan,' said Dougie; and when he got it he put the valentine inside and ventured to propose to the lady that, seeing she had pen and ink handy, she might address the envelope for him, otherwise the recipient would recognize Colin Turner's hand-of-write.

The lady obliged, and addressed the document to
CAPTAIN PETER MACFARLANE,
SS. VITAL SPARK,
TARBERT.

Dougie thanked her effusively on behalf of The Tar, paid for his purchase and a penny stamp, and went out. As he found his shipmate gone, he sealed the envelope and posted it.

When the letter-carrier came down Tarbert quay next morning, all the crew of the *Vital Spark* were on deck — the Captain in blissful unconsciousness of what was in store for him, the others anxious not to lose the expression of his countenance when he should open his valentine.

It was a busy day on the *Vital Spark;* all hands had to help get in a cargo of wood.

'A mournin' letter for you, Captain,' said the letter-carrier, handing down the missive.'

Para Handy looked startled, and walked aft to open it. He took one short but sufficient glimpse at the valentine, with a suspicious glance at the crew, who were apparently engrossed in admiration of the scenery round Tarbert. Then he went down the fo'c'sle, to come up a quarter of an hour later with his good clothes on, his hat, and a black tie.

'What the duvvle game iss he up to noo?' said Dougie, greatly astonished.

'I hope it didna turn his brain,' said The Tar. 'A fright sometimes does it. Wass it a very wild valentine, Dougie?'

Para Handy moved aft with a sad, resigned aspect, the mourning envelope in his hand. 'I'm sorry I'll have to go away till the efternoon, boys,' he said softly. 'See and get in that wud nice and smert before I come back.'

'What's wrong?' asked Dougie, mystified.

The Captain ostentatiously blew his nose, and explained that they might have noticed he had just got a mourning letter.

'Was't a mournin' wan? I never noticed,' said Dougie.

'Neither did I,' added The Tar hurriedly.

'Yes,' said the Captain sadly, showing them the envelope; 'my poor cousin Cherlie over in Dunmore iss no more; he just slipped away yesterday, and I'm goin' to take the day off and make arrangements.'

'Well I'm jiggered!' exclaimed Dougie, as they watched Para Handy walking off on what they realized was to be a nice holiday at their expense, for they would now have his share of the day's work to do as well as their own.

'Did ye ever see such a nate liar?' said The Tar, lost in admiration at the cunning of the Captain.

And then they fell upon the engineer, and abused him for suggesting the valentine.

20 THE DISAPPOINTMENT OF ERCHIE'S NIECE

PARA HANDY never had been at a Glasgow ball till he went to the Knapdale Natives', and he went there simply to please Hurricane Jack. That gallant and dashing mariner came to him one day at Bowling, treated him to three substantial refreshments in an incredibly short space of time, and then delivered a brilliant lecture on the duty of being patriotic to one's native place, 'backing up the boys', and buying a ticket for the assembly in question.

'But I'm not a native of Knapdale,' said the Captain. 'Forbye, I'm kind of oot o' the dancin'; except La Va and Petronella I don't mind wan step.'

'That's all right, Peter,' said Hurricane Jack encouragingly; 'there's nobody'll make you dance at a Knapdale ball if you're no' in trum for dancin'. I can get you on the committee, and aal you'll have to do will be to stand at the door of the committee room and keep the crood back from the beer-bottles. I'm no' there mysel' for amusement: do you ken Jean Mactaggart?'

'Not me,' said Para Handy. 'What Mactaggarts iss she off,[1] Jeck?'

'Carradale,' said Hurricane Jack modestly. 'A perfect beauty! We're engaged.'

The Captain shook hands mournfully with his friend and cheerlessly congratulated him. 'It's a responsibulity, Jeck,' he said, 'there's no doot it's a responsibulity, but you ken yoursel' best.'

'She's a nice enough gyurl so far ass I know,' said Hurricane Jack. 'Her brother's in the Western Ocean tred. What I'm wantin' you on the committee for iss to keep me back from the committee room, so that I'l not take a drop too much and affront the lassie. If you see me desperate keen on takin' more than would be dacent, take a dozen strong smert fellows in wi' you at my expense and barricade the door. I'll maybe taalk aboot tearin' the hoose doon, but och, that'll only be my nonsense.'

The Captain accepted the office, not without reluctance, and went to the hall, but Hurricane Jack failed to put in any appearance all night, and Para Handy considered himself the victim of a very stupid practical joke on the part of his friend.

Early next forenoon Hurricane Jack presented himself on board the *Vital Spark* and made an explanation. 'I'm black affronted,[2] Peter,' he said, 'but I couldna help it. I had a bit of an accident. You see it wass this

1. *To which family of Mactaggarts is she related?*

2. *Deeply embarrassed.*

91

way, Peter. Miss Mactaggart wass comin' special up from Carradale and stayin' with her uncle, old Macpherson. She was to put her clothes on there, and I wass to caal for her in wan of them cabs at seven o'clock. I wass ready at five, all spruce from clew to earing,[3] and hy heid wass that sore wi' wearin' a hat for baals that I got hold of a couple of men I knew in the China tred and went for chust one small wee gless. What happened efter that for an oor or two's a mystery, but I think I wass drugged. When I got to my senses I wass in a cab, and the driver roarin' doon the hatch to me askin' the address.

'"What street iss it you're for?" said he.

'"What streets have you?" I asked.

'"Aal you told me wass Macfarlane's shup," he said; "do you think we're anyway near it?"

'When he said that I put my heid oot by the gless and took an observation.

'"Iss this Carrick Street or Monday mornin'?" says I to him, and then he put me oot of his cab. The poor sowl had no fear in him; he must have been Irish. It wass not much of a cab; here's the door handles, a piece of wud, and the man's brass number; I chust took them with me for identification, and went home to my bed. When I wakened this mornin' and thought of Jean sittin' up aal night waitin' on me, I wass clean demented.'

'It's a kind of a peety, too, the way it happened,' said Para Handy sympathetically. 'It would put herself a bit aboot sittin' aal night wi' her sluppers on.'

'And a full set o' new sails,' said Hurricane Jack pathetically. 'She was sparin' no expense. This'll be a lesson to me. It'll do me good; I wish it hadna happened. What I called for wass to see if you'll be kind enough, seein' you were on the committee, to go up to 191 Barr Street, where she's stayin' wi' Macpherson, and put the thing ass nicely for me ass you can.'

Para Handy was naturally shy of the proposal. 'I never saw the lassie,' said he. 'Would it no' look droll for me to go instead of yoursel'?'

'It would look droll if you didna,' said Hurricane Jack emphatically. 'What are you on the committee for, and in charge of aal the beer, unless you're to explain things? I'll show you the close, and you'll go up and ask for two meenutes' private conversation with Miss Mactaggart, and you'll tell her that I'm far from weel. Say I wass on my way up last night in fine time and the cab collided with a tramway car. Break it nice, and no'

3. *From top to toe. The earing was the top corner of a square sail while the clew was the bottom corner.*

92

frighten the poor gyurl oot of her senses. Say I was oot of my conscience for seven 'oors, but that I'm gettin' the turn, and I'm no' a bit disfigured.'

Para Handy was still irresolute. 'She'll maybe want to nurse you, the way they do in Macphail's novelles,' said he, 'and what'll I tell her then?'

This was a staggerer for Hurricane Jack. He recognized the danger of arousing the womanly sympathies of Miss Mactaggart. But he was equal to all difficulties of this kind. 'Tell her,' said he, 'there's nobody to get speakin' to me for forty-eight 'oors, but that I'll likely be oot on Monday.'

The Captain agreed to undertake this delicate mission, but only on condition that Dougie the mate should accompany him to back him up in case his own resourcefulness as a liar should fail him at the critical moment.

'Very well,' said Hurricane Jack, 'take Dougie wi' you, but watch her uncle; 'I'm told he's cunning, cunning, though I never met him — a man Macpherson, by the name of Erchie. Whatever you tell her, if he's there at the time, tell it to her in the Gaalic.'

Para Handy and his mate that evening left Hurricane Jack at a discreet public bar called the 'Hot Blast', and went up to the house of Erchie Macpherson.[4] It was himself who came to answer their knock at his door, for he was alone in the house.

'We're no' for ony strings o' onions, or parrots, or onything o' that sort,' he said keeping one foot against the door and peering at them in the dim light of the rat-tail burner[5] on the stair-landing. 'And if it's the stair windows ye want to clean, they were done yesterday'.

'You should buy specs,' said the Captain promptly — 'they're no' that dear. Iss Miss Mactaggart in?'

Erchie opened the door widely, and gave his visitors admission to the kitchen.

'She's no' in the noo,' said he. 'Which o' ye happens to be the sailor chap that was to tak' her to the ball last nicht?'

'It wasna any o' us,' said Para Handy. 'It was another gentleman aalthegither.'

'I micht hae kent that,' said Erchie. 'Whit lock-up is he in? If it's his bail ye're here for, ye needna bother. I aye tell't my guid-sister's dochter she wasna ill to please when she took up wi' a sailor. I had a son that was yince

---

4. *Erchie MacPherson has been borrowed from another series of Neil Munro's tales: 'Erchie; my droll friend'. In addition to his Para Handy stories and the Erchie Macpherson tales, Munro also produced a set of stories about a commercial traveller 'Jimmy Swan; the joy traveller'.*

5. *Gas light.*

a sailor himself, but thank the Lord he's better, and he's in the Corporation noo.[6] Were ye wantin' to see Jean?'

'Chust for a meenute,' said Para Handy, quietly taking a seat on the jawbox.[7] 'Will she be long?'

'Five feet three,' said Erchie, 'and broad in proportion. She hasna come doon sae much as ye wad think at her disappointment.'

'That's nice,' said Para Handy. 'A thing o' the kind would tell terribly on some weemen. You're no' in the Shuppin' tred yoursel', I suppose? I ken a lot o' Macphersons in the coast line. But I'm no' askin', mind ye; it's chust for conversation. There wass a femily of Macphersons came from the same place ass mysel' on Lochfyne-side;[8] fine smert fellows they were, but I daresay no relation. Most respectable. Perhaps you ken the Gaalic?'

'Not me!' said Erchie frankly — 'jist plain Gleska. If I'm Hielan' I canna help it; my faither took the boat to the Broomielaw as soon as he got his senses.'

The conversation would have languished here if Dougie had not come to the rescue. 'What's your tred?' he asked bluntly.

'Whiles I beadle[9] and whiles I wait,' replied Erchie, who was not the man to be ashamed of his calling. 'At ither times I jist mind my ain affairs; ye should gie 't a trial — it'll no hurt ye.'

The seamen laughed at this sally: it was always a virtue of both of them that they could appreciate a joke at their own expense.

'No offence, no offence, Mr. Macpherson,' said Para Handy. 'I wish your niece would look slippy. You'll be sorry to hear aboot what happened to poor Jeck.'

Erchie turned quite serious. 'What's the maitter wi' him?' he said.

'The cab broke doon last night,' said the Captain solemnly 'and he got a duvvle of a smash.'

'Puir sowl!' said Erchie, honestly distressed. 'This'll be a sair blow for Jeanie.'

'He lost his conscience[10] for 'oors, but there's no disfeegurement, and he'll be speechless till Monday mornin'. It's a great peety. Such a splendid

---

6. *Erchie means that his son is now employed by the local authority.*

7. *Kitchen sink*

8. *Further important evidence on the vexed question of Para's place of birth.*

9. *Church officer, sexton. Erchie is here using the word as a verb; to beadle: to perform the duties of a beadle.*

10. *Consciousness.*

voice ass he had, too; it wass truly sublime. He's lyin' yonder wi' his heid in a sling and not wan word in him. He tell't me I was to say to —'

Here Dougie, seeing an inconsistency in the report, slyly nudged his captain, who stopped short and made a very good effort at a sigh of deep regret.

'I thocht ye said he couldna speak,' said Erchie suspiciously.

'My mistake, my mistake,' said the Captain. 'What I meant wass that he could only speak in Gaalic; the man's fair off his usual. Dougie'll tell you himsel'.'

Dougie shook his head lugubriously. 'Ay,' said he, 'he's yonder wi' fifteen doctors roond him waitin' for the turn.'

'What time did it happen?' inquired Erchie. 'Was it efter he was here?'

'He wass on his way here,' said Para Handy. 'It was exactly half-past seven, for his watch stopped in the smash.'

At this Erchie sat back in his chair and gave a disconcerting laugh. 'Man,' he said, 'ye're no bad at a baur, but ye've baith put yer feet in't this time. Will ye tak' a refreshment? There's a drop speerits in the hoose and a bottle or two o' porter.'

'I'm teetotal mysel' at present,' said Para Handy, 'but I have a nesty cold. I'll chust take the spurits while you're pullin' the porter. We'll drink a quick recovery to Jeck.'

'Wi' a' my he'rt,' said Erchie agreeably. 'I hope he'll be oot again afore Monday. Do ye no' ken he came here last nicht wi' the cab a' richt, but was that dazed Jeanie wadna gang wi' him. But she got to the ball a' the same, for she went wi' Mackay the polisman.'

'My Chove!' said the Captain, quite dumbfoundered. 'He doesna mind, himsel', a thing aboot it.'

'I daresay no',' said Erchie, 'that's the worst o' trevellin' in cabs; he should hae come in a motor-caur.'

When the Captain and Dougie came down Macpherson's stair, they considered the situation in the close.

'I think mysel',' said the Captain, 'it wouldna be salubrious for neither o' the two of us to go to the "Hot Blast" and break the news to Jeck the night.'

'Whatever ye think yersel',' said Dougie, and they headed straight for home.

21   PARA HANDY'S WEDDING

IT is possible that Para Handy might still have been a bachelor if Calum Cameron had not been jilted. Three days before Calum was to have been married, the girl exercised a girl's privilege and changed her mind. She explained her sad inconstancy by saying she had never cared for him, and only said 'yes' to get him off her face. It was an awkward business, because it left the baker's widow, Mrs. Crawford, with a large bride's-cake[1] on her hands. It is true the bride's-cake had been paid for, but in the painful circumstances neither of the parties to the broken contract would have anything to do with it, and it continued to lie in the baker's window, a pathetic evidence of woman's perfidy. All Campbeltown talked about it; people came five and six miles in from the country to look at it. When they saw what a handsome example of the confectioner's art it was, they shook their heads and said the lassie could have no heart, let alone good taste.

Mrs. Crawford, being a smart business woman, put a bill in the window with the legend —

EXCELLENT BRIDE'S-CAKE

SECOND HAND

17 / 6

But there were no offers, and she was on the point of disposing of it on the Art Union principle,[2] when, by one of those providential accidents that are very hard on the sufferer but lead by a myriad consequent circumstances to the most beneficient ends, a man in Carrick Street, Glasgow, broke his leg. The man never heard of Para Handy in all his life, nor of the *Vital Spark;* he had never been in Campbeltown, and if he had not kept a pet tortoise he would never have figured in this book, and Para Handy might not have been married, even though Calum Cameron's girl had been a jilt.

The Carrick Street man's tortoise had wandered out into the close in the evening; the owner, rushing out hurriedly at three minutes to ten to do some shopping, tripped over it, and was not prevented by the agony of his injured limb from seizing the offending animal and throwing it into the

1. *Wedding cake.*

2. *A once popular method of selling works of art. Subscribers took part in what was in effect a raffle.*

street, where it fell at the feet of Para Handy, who was passing at the time.

'A tortoise!' said the Captain, picking it up. 'The first time ever I kent they flew. I'll take it to Macphail — he's keen on birds anyway,' and down he took it to the engineer of the *Vital Spark*.

But Macphail refused to interest himself in a pet which commended itself neither by beauty of plumage nor sweetness of song, and for several days the unhappy tortoise took a deck passage on the *Vital Spark*, its constitution apparently little impaired by the fact that at times The Tar used it as a coal-hammer.

'I'll no' see the poor tortoise abused this way,' said Para Handy, when they got to Campbeltown one day; 'I'll take it up and give it to a friend o' mine,' and putting it into his pocket in the evening, he went up to the baker's shop.

The widow was at the moment fixing a card on the bride's-cake intimating that tickets for the raffle of it would cost sixpence each, and that the drawing would take place on the following Saturday. Her plump form was revealed in the small shop-window; the flush of exertion charmingly irradiated her countenance as she bent among her penny buns and bottles of fancy biscuits; Para Handy, gazing at her from the outside, thought he had never seen her look more attractive. She blushed more deeply when she saw him looking at her, and retired from the window with some embarrassment as he entered the shop.

'Fine night, Mery,' said the Captain. 'You're pushin' business desperate, surely when you're raffling bride's-cakes.'

'Will you not buy a ticket?' said the lady, smiling. 'You might be the lucky man to get the prize.'

'And what in the world would I do wi' a bride's-cake?' asked the Captain, his manly sailor's heart in a gentle palpitation. 'Where would I get a bride to — to — to fit it?'

'I'm sure and I don't know,' said the widow hurriedly, and she went on to explain the circumstances that had left it on her hands. The Captain listened attentively, eyed the elegant proportions of the cake in the window, and was seized by a desperate resolve.

'I never saw a finer bride's-cake,' he said; 'it's chust sublime! Do you think it would keep till the Gleska Fair?'

'It would keep a year for that part o't,' said the widow. 'What are you askin' that for?'

'If it'll keep to the Fair, and the Fair suits yoursel',' said Para Handy boldly, 'we'll have it between us. What do you say to that, Mery?' and he leaned amorously over the counter.

97

'Mercy on me! this is no' the New Year time,' exclaimed the widow; 'I thought you never had any mind of me except at the New Year. Is this a proposal, Captain?'

'Don't caal me Captain, caal me Peter, and gie me a haad o' your hand,' entreated Para Handy languishingly.

'Well then — Peter,' murmured the widow, and the Captain went back to the *Vital Spark* that night an engaged man: the bride's-cake was withdrawn from the window, and the tortoise took up its quarters in the back shop.

. . . . .

Of all the ordeals Para Handy had to pass through before his marriage, there was none that troubled him more than his introduction to her relatives, and the worst of them was Uncle Alick, who was very old, very deaf, and very averse to his niece marrying again. The Captain and his 'fiancée' visited him as in duty bound, and found him in a decidedly unfavourable temper.

'This is Peter,' said the widow by way of introduction; and the Captain stood awkwardly by her side, with his pea-jacket tightly buttoned to give him an appearance of slim, sprightly and dashing youthfulness.

'What Peter?' asked the uncle, not taking his pipe out of his mouth, and looking with a cold, indifferent eye upon his prospective relative.

'You know fine,' said the lady, flushing. 'It's my lad.'

'What did you say?' inquired Uncle Alick, with a hand behind his ear.

'My lad,' she cried. 'Peter Macfarlane — him that's the captain on the *Vital Spark*.'

'Catched him in a park,' said Uncle Alick. 'I'll wudger you didna need to run fast to catch him. Whatna park was it?'

'The *Vital Spark*,' roared the Captain, coming to Mary's assistance. 'I'm captain on her.'

'Are you, are you?' said Uncle Alick querulously. 'Weel, you needna roar at me like that; I'm no' that deaf. You'll be wan o' the Macfarlanes from Achnatra; they were aal kind of droll in the mind, but hermless.'

The Captain explained that he was a member of a different family altogether, but Uncle Alick displayed no interest in the explanation. 'It's none of my business,' said he.

'Mery thinks it is,' rejoined the Captain. 'That's the reason we're here.'

'Beer!' said Uncle Alick. 'No, no, I have no beer for you. I never keep drink of any sort in the hoose.'

'I never said beer,' exclaimed Para Handy.

'I'll be telling a lie then,' said Uncle Alick. 'The same as if I didna hear you with my own ears. You'll be the man that Mery's going to merry. I canna understand her; I'm sure she had plenty of trouble wi' Donald Crawford before he went and died on her. But it's none o' my business: I'm only an old done man, no' long for this world, and I'm no' goin' to interfere wi' her if she wass to merry a bleck. She never consulted me, though I'm the only uncle she has. You shouldna put yoursel's to bother tellin' me anything aboot it; I'm sure I would have heard aboot it from some o' the neebours. The neebours iss very good to me. They're sayin' it's a droll-like thing Mery merryin' again, and her wi' a nice wee shop o' her own. What I says to them iss, "It's her own business: perhaps she sees something takin' in the man that nobody else does. Maybe," I says to them, "he'll give up his vessel and help her in the shop."'

'Och, you're chust an old haiver!'[3] remarked the Captain *sotto voce*, and of course the deaf man heard him.

'A haiver!' said he. 'A nice-like thing to say aboot the only uncle Mery has, and him over eighty-six. But you're no' young yoursel'. Maybe it wass time for you to be givin' up the boats.'

'I'm no' thinkin' o' givin' them up, Uncle,' said Para Handy cheerfully. 'The *Fital Spark's* the smertest boat in the tred. A bonny-like hand I would be in a shop. No, no, herself here — Mery, can keep the shop or leave it chust ass it pleases hersel', it's aal wan to me; I'm quite joco. I hope you'll turn up at the weddin' on the fufteenth, for aal langsyne.'

'What's your wull?' inquired Uncle Alick.

'I hope you'll turn up at the weddin' and give us support,' bellowed the Captain.

'Give you sport,' said the old man indignantly. 'You'll surely get plenty of sport withoot takin' it off a poor old man like me.'

'Och! to the muschief!' exclaimed the Captain somewhat impatiently. 'Here's a half pound o' tobacco me and Mery brought you, and surely that'll put you in better trum.

'What wey did you no' say that at first?' said Uncle Alick. 'Hoo wass I to know you werena wantin' the lend o' money for the weddin'? Stop you and I'll see if there's any spurits handy.'

．　　．　　．　　．　　．

I was not at the wedding, but the Captain told me all about it some days afterwards. 'It would be worth a bit in the papers,' he said with

3. *to haiver=to talk nonsense, thus a haiver is one who talks in a foolish manner*

considerable elation. 'I'll wudger there wasna another weddin' like it in Kintyre for chenerations. The herrin' trawlers iss not back at their work yet, and herrin's up ten shullin's a box in Gleska. Dougie and The Tar and their wifes wass there, quite nate and tidy and every noo and then Macphail would be comin' doon to the boat and blowin' her whustle. Och, he's not a bad chap Macphail, either, but chust stupid with readin' them novelles.

'I never saw Mery lookin' more majestic; she wass chust sublime! Some of them said I wassna lookin' slack mysel', and I daarsay no', for I wass in splendid trum. When the knot was tied, and we sat doon to a bite, I found it wass a different bride's-cake aalthegither from the wan that julted Cameron.

'"What's the meanin' of that?" I whuspered to the mustress. 'That's no' the bride's-cake you had in the window."

'"No, says she, "but it's a far better one, isn't it?"

'"It's a better-lookin' wan, "I says, "but the other wan might have done the business."

'"Maybe it would," she said, "but I have all my wuts aboot me, and I wassna goin' to have the neighbours say that both the bride and bride's-cake were second hand." Oh! I'm tellin' you she's a smert wan the mustress!

'Well, I wish you and your good lady long life and happiness, Captain,' I said.

'Thanky, thanky,' said he. 'I'll tell the mustress. Could you no put a bit in the papers sayin', "The rale and only belle o' Captain Macfarlane's weddin' wass the young lady first in the grand merch, dressed in broon silk."'

'Who was the young lady dressed in brown?' I asked.

'What need you ask for?' he replied. 'Who would it be but the mustress?"

22 A NEW COOK

[The first story from the second Para collection 'In Highland Harbours with Para Handy, S.S. *Vital Spark*'.]

THE SS *Texa*[1] made a triumphal entry to the harbour by steaming in between two square-rigged schooners, the *Volant* and *Jehu*, of Wick, and slid silently, with the exactitude of long experience, against the piles of Rothesay quay, where Para Handy sat on a log of wood. The throb of her engine, the wash of her propeller, gave place to the strains of a melodeon, which was playing 'Stop yer ticklin, Jock', and Para Handy felt some sense of gaiety suffuse him, but business was business, and it was only for a moment he pemitted himself to be carried away on the divine wings of music.

'Have you anything for me, 'M'Kay?' he hailed the *Texa*'s clerk.

The purser cast a rapid glance over the deck, encumbered with planks, crates, casks of paraffin oil, and herring-boxes, and seeing nothing there that looked like a consignment for the questioner, leaned across the rail, and made a rapid survey of the open hold. It held nothing maritime — only hay-bales, flour-bags, soap-boxes, shrouded mutton carcases, rolls of plumbers' lead, two head-stones for Ardrishaig, and the dismantled slates, cushions, and legs of a billiard-table for Strachur.

'Naething the day for you, Peter,' said the clerk; 'unless it's yin o' the heid-stanes,' and he ran his eye down the manifest which he held in his hand.

'Ye're aawful smert, M'Kay,' said Para Handy. 'If ye wass a rale purser wi' brass buttons and a yellow-and-black strippit tie on your neck, there would be no haadin' ye in! It's no' luggage I'm lookin' for; it's a kind o' a man I'm expectin'. Maybe he's no' in your depairtment; he'll be traivellin' saloon. Look behind wan o' them herring-boxes, Lachie, and see if ye canna see a sailor.'

His intuition was right; the *Texa*'s only passenger that afternoon was discovered sitting behind the herring-boxes playing a melodeon, and smiling beatifically to himself, with blissful unconsciousness that he had arrived at his destination. He came to himself with a start when the purser asked him if he was going off here; terminated the melody of his instrument in a melancholy squawk, picked up a carelessly tied canvas bag that lay at his feet, and hurried over the plank to the quay, shedding from

1. *The* Texa *was acquired by Messrs David MacBrayne in 1889 and, like the* Cygnet, *was used on the Glasgow to Inveraray cargo service.*

the bag as he went a trail of socks, shoes, collars, penny ballads, and seamen's biscuits, whose exposure in this awkward fashion seemed to cause him no distress of mind, for he only laughed when Para Handy called them to his attention, and left to one of the *Texa*'s hands the trouble of collecting them, though he obligingly held the mouth of the sack open himself while the other restored the dunnage. He was a round, short, red-faced, clean-shaven fellow of five-and-twenty, with a thin serge suit, well polished at all the bulgy parts, and a laugh that sprang from a merry heart.

'Are you The Tar's kizzen?[2] Are you Davie Green?' asked Para Handy.

'Right-oh! The very chap,' said the stranger. 'And you'll be Peter? Haud my melodeon, will ye, till I draw my breath. Right-oh!'

'Are ye sure there's no mistake?' asked Para Handy as they movd along to the other end of the quay where the *Vital Spark* was lying. 'You're the new hand I wass expectin', and your name's Davie?'

'My name's Davie, richt enough,' said the stranger, 'but I seldom got it; when I was on the Cluthas[3] they always ca'd me Sunny Jim.'

'Sunny Jum!' said the Captain. 'Man! I've often heard aboot ye; you were namely for chumpin' fences?'[4]

'Not me!' said Davie. 'Catch me jumpin' onything if there was a hole to get through. Is that your vessel? She's a tipper! You and me'll get on A1. Wait you till ye see the fun I'll gie ye! That was the worst o' the Cluthas — awfu' short trips, and every noo and then a quay; ye hadn't a meenute to yerself for a baur at all. Whit sort o' chaps hae ye for a crew?'

'The very pick!' said Para Handy as they came alongside the *Vital Spark,* whose crew, as a matter of fact, were all on deck to see the new hand. 'That's Macphail, the chief enchineer, wan of Brutain's hardy sons, wi' the wan gallows;[5] and the other chap's Dougie, the first mate, a Cowal laad; you'll see him plainer efter his face iss washed for tea. Then there's me, myself, the Captain. Laads, this iss Colin's kizzen, Sunny Jum.'

2. *Cousin.*

3. *Small passenger ferries operating on the Clyde between Victoria Bridge and Whiteinch.*

4. *A reference to a well-known contemporary advertisement for the breakfast cereal, Force.*

'High o'er the hill leaps Sunny Jim,
Force is the stuff that raises him.'

5. *Not a reference to the scaffold but to the engineer's obviously defective trouser braces or 'galluses'*

Sunny Jim stood on the edge of the quay, and smiled like a sunset on his future shipmates. 'Hoo are yez, chaps?' he cried genially, waving his hand.

'We canna compleen,' said Dougie solemnly. 'Are ye in good trum yersel'? See's a grup o' your hold-aal, and excuse the gangway.'

Sunny Jim jumped on board, throwing his dunnage-bag before him, and his feet had no sooner touched the deck than he indulged in a step or two of the sailor's hornpipe with that proficiency which only years of practie in a close-mouth[6] in Crown Street, SS,[7] could confer. The Captain looked a little embarrassed; such conduct was hardly business-like, but it was a relief to find that The Tar's nominee and successor was a cheery chap at any rate. Dougie looked on with no disapproval, but Macphail grunted and turned his gaze to sea, disgusted at such free-and-easy informality.

'I hope ye can cook as weel's ye can dance,' he remarked coldly.

Sunny Jim stopped immediately. 'Am I supposed to cook?' he asked, concealing his surprise as he best could.

'Ye are that!' said Macphail. 'Did ye think ye were to be the German band on board, and go roon' liftin' pennies? Cookin's the main thing wi' the second mate o' the *Vital Spark*, and I can tell ye we're gey particular; are we no', Dougie!'

'Aawful!' said Dougie sadly. 'Macphail here hass ben cookin' since The Tar left; he'll gie ye his receipt for haddies made wi' enchine-oil.'

The *Vital Spark* cast off from Rothesay quay on her way for Bowling, and Sunny Jim was introduced to several pounds of sausages to be fried for dinner, a bag of potatoes, and a jar of salt, with which he was left to juggle as he could, while the others, with expectant appetites, performed their respective duties. Life on the open sea, he found, was likely to be as humdrum as it used to be on the Cluthas, and he determined to initiate a little harmless gaiety. With some difficulty he extracted all the meat from the uncooked sausages, and substituted salt. Then he put them on the frying-pan. They had no sooner heated than they began to dance in the pan with curious little cracking explosions. He started playing his melodeon, and cried on the crew, who hurried to see this unusual phenomnon.

6. *Common entrance to a block of tenement flats.*

7. *Crown Street, Gorbals, a working-class area of Glasgow on the south side of the Clyde.*

'Well, I'm jeegered,' said the Captain; 'what in aal the world iss the matter wi' them?'

'It's a waarnin',' said Dougie lugubriously, with wide-staring eyes.

'Warnin', my auntie!' said Sunny Jim, playing a jig-tune. 'They started jumpin' like that whenever I begood to play my bonnie wee melodeon.'

'I daarsay that,' said Para Handy; 'for you're a fine, fine player, Jum, but — but it wassna any invitation to a baal I gave them when I paid for them in Ro'sa'.'

'I aye said sausages werena meat for sailors,' remarked the engineer, with bitterness, for he was very hungry. 'Ye'll notice it's an Irish jig they're dancin' to,' he added with dark significance.

'I don't see myslf,' said the Captain, 'that it maitters whether it iss an Irish jeeg or the Gourock Waltz and Circassian Circle.'

'Does it no'?' retorted Macphail. 'I suppose ye'll never hae heard o' Irish terrier dugs?' I've ett my last sausage onywye! Sling us ower that pan-loaf,' and seizing the bread for himself he proceeded to make a spartan meal.

Sunny Jim laughed till the tears ran down his jovial countenance. 'Chaps,' he exclaimed, with firm conviction, 'this is the cheeriest ship ever I was on; I'm awful gled I brung my music.'

Dougie took a fork and gingerly investigated. 'As hard as whun-stanes! he proclaimed; 'they'll no be ready by the time we're at the Tail o' the Bank. Did you ever in your mortal life see the like of it?' and he jabbed ferociously with the fork at the bewitched sausages.

'That's richt!' said Macphail. 'Put them oot o' pain.'

'Stop you!' said Para Handy. 'Let us pause and consuder. It iss the first time ever I saw sausages with such a desperate fine ear for music. If they'l no' fry, they'll maybe boil. Put them in a pot, Jum.'

'Right-oh!' said Sunny Jim, delighted at the prospect of a second scene to his farce, and the terpsichorean sausages were consigned to the pot of water which had boiled the potatoes. The crew sat round, staving off the acuter pangs of hunger with potatoes and bread

'You never told us what for they called you Sunny Jum, Davie,' remarked the Captain. 'Do you think it would be for your complexion?'

'I couldna say,' replied the new hand, 'but I think mysel' it was because I was aye such a cheery wee chap. The favourite Clutha on the Clyde, when the Cluthas was rinnin', was the yin I was on; hunners o' trips used to come wi' her on the Setturdays on the aff-chance that I was maybe gie them a baur. Mony a pant we had! I could hae got a job at the Finnieston

Ferry[8] richt enough, chaps, but they wouldna alloo the melodeon, and I wad sooner want my wages.'

'A fine, fine unstrument!' said Para Handy agreeably. 'Wi' it and Dougie's trump we'll no' be slack in passin' the time.'

'Be happy! — that's my motto,' said Sunny Jim, beaming upon his auditors like one who brings a new and glorious evangel. "Whatever happens, be happy, and then ye can defy onything. It's a' in the wye ye look at things. See?

'That's what I aalways say mysel' to the wife,' said Dougie in heart-broken tones, and his eye on the pot, which was beginning to boil briskly.

'As shair as daith, chaps, I canna stand the Jock o' Hazeldean[9] kind of thing at a' — folk gaun aboot lettin' the tear doon-fa' a' the time. Gie me a hearty laugh and it's right-oh! BE HAPPY! — that's the Golden Text for the day, as we used to say in the Sunday School.'

'I could be happy easy enough if it wassna that I wass so desperate hungry,' said Dougie in melancholy accents, lifting the lid to look into the pot. He could see no sign of the sausages, and with new forebodings he began to feel for them with the stick. They had disappeared! 'I said from the very first it wass a warnin'!' he exclaimed, resigning the stick to the incredulous engineer.

'This boat's haunted,' said Macphail, who also failed to find anything in the pot. 'I saw ye puttin' them in wi' my ain eyes, and noo they're no' there.'

Para Handy grabbed the spirtle,[10] and feverishly explored on his own account, with the same extraordinary results.

'My Chove!' he exclaimed. 'Did you ever see the like of that, and I

---

8. *Vehicular ferry across the Clyde in Glasgow.*

9. *A reference to the poem of this name by Sir Walter Scott which opens with the lines:*
    'Why weep ye by the tide, ladye?
    Why weep ye by the tide?
    I'll wed ye to my youngest son,
    And ye sall be his bride;
    And ye sall be his bride, ladye,
    Sae comely to be seen:
    But aye she loot the tears down fa'
    For Jock o' Hazeldean.

10. *Wooden spoon*

havena tasted wan drop of stimulants since last Monday. Laads! I don't know what you think aboot it, but it's the church twice for me tomorrow!

. . . . .

Sunny Jim quite justified his nickname by giving a pleasant surpise to his shipmates in the shape of a meat-tea later in the afternoon.

Rothesay Pier *Argyll & Bute District Libraries*

23   PENSION FARMS

THE *Vital Spark* was making for Lochgoilhead, Dougie at the wheel, and the Captain straddled on a water-breaker, humming Gaelic songs, because he felt magnificent after his weekly shave. The chug-chug-chug of the engines was the only other sound that broke the silence of the afternoon, and Sunny Jim deplored the fact that in the hurry of embarking early in the morning he had quite forgotten his melodeon — those peaceful days at sea hung heavy on his urban spirit.

'That's Ardgoil,' remarked Macphail, pointing with the stroup of an oil-can at the Glasgow promontory,[1] and Para Handy gazed at the land with affected interest.

'So it iss, Macphail,' he said ironically. 'That wass it the last time we were here, and the time before, and the time before that again. You would think it would be shifted. It's wan of them guides for towerists you should be, Macphail, you're such a splendid hand for information. What way do you spell it?'

'Oh, shut up!' said the engineer with petulance; 'ye think ye're awfu' clever. I mind when that wee hoose at the p'int was a hen farm, and there's no' a road to't. Ye could only get near the place wi' a boat.'

'If that wass the way of it,' said Dougie, 'ducks would suit them better, they could swim. It's a fine thing a duck.'

'But a goose is more extraordinar',' said Macphail with meaning. 'Anyway it was hens, and mony a time I wished I had a ferm for hens.'

'You're better where you are,' said the Captain, 'oilin' engines like a chentleman. A hen ferm is an aawful speculation, and you need your wuts aboot you if you start wan. All your relations expect their eggs for nothing, and the very time o' the year when eggs iss dearest, hens takes a tirrievee[2] and stop layin'. Am I no' tellin' the truth, Dougie?'

---

1. *The 9,000 acres of the Ardgoil Estate were presented to the City of Glasgow by A. Cameron Corbett, M.P. for Glasgow Tradeston. In his letter to Lord Provost John Ure Primrose announcing the gift he wrote 'My general object is to preserve a grand rugged region for the best use of those who love the freedom of the mountains and wild natural beauty . . .'. The area is sometimes known as Argyll's Bowling Green, popularly thought to be an ironic reference to its extremely rugged terrain; however other sources claim Bowling Green as a corruption of the Gaelic Buaile na Greine—the Sunny Cattle Fold. The estate was used for country holidays for underprivileged children and was a popular destination for trips and excursions. In 1965 after a number of years of substantial financial losses it was feued to the Forestry Commission.*

2. *A fit or tantrum. Variant spelling of 'tirrivee'*

'You are that!' said the mate agreeably; 'I have noticed it mysel'.'

'If ye didna get eggs ye could live aff the chickens,' suggested Sunny Jim. 'I think a hen ferm would be top, richt enough!'

'It's not the kind o' ferm I would have mysel' whatever o't,' said Para Handy; 'there's far more chance o' dacent livin' oot o' rearin' pensioners.'

'Rearin' pensioners?' remarked Macphail; 'ye would lie oot o' your money a lang while rearin' pensioners; ye micht as weel start growin' trees.'

'Not at aal! not at aal!' said Para Handy; 'there's quick returns in pensioners if you put your mind to the thing and use a little caation. Up in the Islands, now, the folks iss givin' up their crofts[3] and makin' a kind o' ferm o' their aged relations. I have a cousin yonder oot in Gigha wi' a stock o' five fine healthy uncles — no' a man o' them under seventy. There's another frien' o' my own in Mull wi' thirteen heid o' chenuine old Macleans. He gaithered them aboot the islands wi' a boat whenever the rumours o' the pensions started.[4] Their frien's had no idea what he wanted wi' them, and were glad to get them off their hands. "It's chust a notion that I took," he said "for company; they're great amusement on a winter night," and he got his pick o' the best o' them. It wassna every wan he would take; they must be all Macleans, for the Mull Macleans never die till they're centurions, and he wouldna take a man that wass over five and seventy. They're yonder, noo, in Loch Scridain, kept like fightin' cocks; he puts them oot on the hill each day for exercise, and if wan o' them takes a cough they dry his clothes and give him something from a bottle.'

'Holy smoke!' said Dougie, 'where's the profits comin' from?'

'From the Government,' said Para Handy. 'Nothing simpler! He gets five shillings a heid in the week for them, and that's £169 in the year for the whole thirteen — enought to feed a regiment! Wan pensioner maybe wadna pay you, but if you have a herd like my frien' in Mull, there's money in it. He buys their meal in bulk from Oban, and they'll grow their own potatoes; the only thing he's vexed for iss that they havena wool, and he canna clip them. If he keeps his health himsel', and doesna lose his heid for a year or twa, he'll have the lergest pension ferm in Scotland, and be

---

3. *Smallholdings in the Highlands and Islands.*

4. *In 1908 David Lloyd George, as Chancellor of the Exchequer in Asquith's Liberal Government, introduced the first state Old Age Pension scheme into Britain. This paid the sum of five shillings (25 pence) per week to single people aged 70 and over and seven shillings and sixpence (37 pence) per week to married couples.*

able to keep a gig. I'm no' a bit feared for Donald, though; he's a man o' business chust ass good ass you'll get on the streets o' Gleska.'

'Thirteen auld chaps like that aboot the hoose wad be an awfu' handful,' suggested Sunny Jim.

'Not if it's at Loch Scridain,' answered Para Handy; 'half the time they're on the gress, and there's any amount o' fanks.[5] They're quite delighted swappin' baurs wi' wan another aboot the way they could throw the hammer fifty years ago, and they feel they're more important noo than ever they were in a' their lives afore. When my frien' collected them, they hadna what you would caal an object for to live for except it wass their own funerals; noo they're daft for almanacs, and makin' plans for living to a hundred, when the fermer tells them that he'll gie them each a medal and a uniform. Oh'! a smert, smert laad, Donal'. Wan o' Brutain's hardy sons! Nobody could be kinder!'

'It's a fine way o' makin' a livin',' said Macphail. 'I hope they'll no' go wrang wi' him.

'Fine enough,' said Para Handy, 'but the chob iss not withoot responsibilities. Yonder's my cousin in Gigha wi' his stock o' five, and a nice bit ground for them, and you wouldna believe what it needs in management. He got two of them pretty cheap in Salen, wan o' them over ninety, and the other eight-six; you wouldna believe it, but they're worse to manage than the other three that's ten years younger. The wan over ninety's very cocky of his age, and thinks the other wans iss chust a lot o' boys. He says it's a scandal givin' them a pension; pensions should be kept for men that's up in years, and then it should be something sensible — something like a pound. The wan that iss eighty-six iss desperate dour, and if my cousin doesna please him, stays in his bed and says he'll die for spite.'

'That's gey mean, richt enough!' said Sunny Jim; 'efter your kizzen takin' a' that trouble!'

'But the worst o' the lot's the uncle that he got in Eigg; he's seventy-six, and talkin' aboot a wife!'

'Holy smoke!' said Dougie, 'isn't that chust desperate!'

'Ay; he hass a terrible conceity notion o' his five shillin's a-week; you would think he wass a millionaire. "I could keep a wife on it if she wass young and strong," he tells my cousin, and it takes my cousin and the mustress aal their time to keep him oot o' the way o' likely girls. They don't ken the day they'll lose him.'

5. *Sheep pens*

109

'Could they no' put a brand on him?' asked Dougie.

'Ye daurna brand them,' said the Captain, 'nor keel[6] them either. The law'll no allo' it. So you see yersel's there's aye a risk, and it needs a little capital. My cousin had a bit of a shop, and he gave it up to start the pension ferm; he'll be sayin' sometimes it wass a happier man he wass when he wass a merchant, but he's awfu' prood that noo he hass a chob, as you might say, wi' the Brutish Government.'

6. *To keel: to put a painted mark of ownership on a sheep.*

R.M.S. Davaar *Argyll & Bute District Libraries*

24 TREASURE TROVE

SUNNY JIM proved a most valuable acquisition to the *Vital Spark*. He was a person of humour and resource, and though they were sometimes the victims of his practical jokes, the others of the crew forgave him readliy because of the fun he made. It is true that when they were getting the greatest entertainment from him they were, without thinking it, generally doing his work for him — for indeed he was no sailor, only a Clutha mariner — but at least he was better value for his wages than The Tar, who would neither take his fair share of the work nor tell a baur. Sunny Jim's finest gift was imagination; the most wonderful things in the world had happened to him when he was on the Cluthas — all intensely interesting, if incredible: and Para Handy, looking at him with admiration and even envy, after a narrative more extraordinary than usual, would remark. 'Man! it's a peety listenin' to such d — d lies iss a sin, for there iss no doubt it iss a most pleasant amusement!'

Macphail the engineer, the misanthrope, could not stand the new hand. 'He's no' a sailor at a'!' he protested; he's a clown; I've see'd better men jumpin' through girrs¹ at a penny show.'

'Weel, he's maybe no' aawful steady at the wheel, but he hass a kyind, kyind he'rt!' Dougie said.

'He's chust sublime!' said Para Handy. 'If he wass managed right there would be money in him!'

Para Handy's conviction that there was money to be made out of Sunny Jim was confirmed by an episode at Tobermory, of which the memory will be redolent in Mull for years to come.

The *Vital Spark*, having discharged a cargo of coal at Oban, went up the Sound to load with timber, and on Calve Island, which forms a natural breakwater for Tobermory harbour, Dougie spied a stranded whale. He was not very much of a whale as whales go in Greenland, being merely a tiny fellow of about five-and-twenty tons, but as dead whales here are as rarely to be seen as dead donkeys, the *Vital Spark* was steered close in to afford a better view, and even stopped for a while that Para Handy and his mate might land with the punt on the islet and examine the unfortunate cetacean.

'My Chove! he's a whupper!' was Dougie's comment, as he reached up and clapped the huge mountain of sea-flesh on its ponderous side. 'It wass

---

1. *Hoops.*

right enough, I can see, Peter, aboot yon fellow Jonah;[2] chust look at the accommodation!'

'Chust waste, pure waste,' said the skipper; 'you can make a meal off a herrin', but whales iss only lumber, goin' aboot ass big as a land o' hooses, blowin' aal the time, and puttin' the fear o' daith on aal the other fushes. I never had mich respect for them.'

'If they had a whale like that aground on Clyde,' said Dougie, as they returned to the vessel, 'they would stick bills on't; it's chust thrown away on the Tobermory folk.'

Sunny Jim was enchanted when he heard the whale's dimensions. 'Chaps,' he said with enthusiasm, 'there's a fortune in't; right-oh! I've see'd them chargin' tuppence to get into a tent at Vinegar Hill,[3] whaur they had naethin' fancier nor a sea-lion or a seal.'

'But they wouldna be deid,' said Para Handy; 'and there's no' much fun aboot a whale's remains. Even if there was, we couldna tow him up to Gleska, and if we could, he wouldna keep.'

'Jim'll be goin' to embalm him, rig up a mast on him, and sail him up the river; are ye no', Jim?' said Macphail with irony.

'I've a faur better idea than that,' said Sunny Jim. 'Whit's to hinder us clappin' them tarpaulins roon' the whale whaur it's lyin', and showin' 't at a sixpence a heid to the Tobermory folk? Man! ye'll see them rowin' across in hunners, for I'll bate ye there's no much fun in Tobermory in the summer time unless it's a Band o' Hope[4] soiree.[5] Give it a fancy name — the "Tobermory Treasure"; send the bellman roond the toon, sayin' it's on view tomorrow from ten till five, and then goin' on to Oban; Dougie'll lift the money, and the skipper and me'll tell the audience a' aboot the customs o' the whale when he's in life. Macphail can stand by the ship at Tobermory quay.'

'Jist what I said a' along,' remarked Macphail darkly. 'Jumpin' through girrs! Ye'll need a big drum and a naphtha lamp.'

'Let us first paause and consider,' remarked Para Handy, with his usual caution; 'iss the whale oors?'

'Wha's else wad it be?' retorted Sunny Jim. 'It was us that fun' it, and

---

2. *Dougie is of course referring to the story of Jonah and the whale recounted in the Old Testament (Jonah Ch. 1. v.17—Ch.2. v.10).*

3. *An area in the East End of Glasgow, near the Gallowgate, used by circuses and fairs.*

4. *The Band of Hope was a juvenile religious and temperance organisation.*

5. *An evening entertainment*

naebody seen it afore us, for it's no' mony oors ashore.'

'Everything cast up on the shore belangs to the Crown; it's the King's whale,' said Macphail.

'Weel, let him come for 't,' said Sunny Jim; 'by the time he's here we'll be done wi' t.'

The presumption that Tobermory could be interested in a dead whale proved quite right; it was the Glasgow Fair week, and the local boat-hirers did good business taking parties over to the island where an improvised enclosure of oars, spars, and tarpaulin and dry sails concealed the 'Tobermory Treasure' from all but those who were prepared to pay for admission. Para Handy, with his hands in his pockets and a studied air of indifference, as if the enterprise was none of his, chimed in at intervals with facts in the natural history of the whale, which Sunny Jim might overlook in the course of his introductory lecture.

'The biggest whale by three feet that's ever been seen in Scotland.' Sunny Jim announced. 'Lots o' folk thinks a whale's a fish, but it's naething o' the kind; it's a hot-blooded mammoth, and couldna live in the watter mair nor a wee while at a time without comin' up to draw its breath. This is no' yin of thae common whales that chases herrin', and goes pechin' [6] up and doon Kilbrannan Sound; [7] it's the kind that's catched wi' the harpoons and lives on naething but roary borealises and icebergs.'

'They used to make umbrella-rubs wi' this parteecular kind,' chimed in the skipper diffidently; 'forbye, they're full o' blubber. It's an aawful useful thing a whale, chentlemen.' he had apparently changed his mind about the animals, for which the previous day he had said he had no respect.

'Be shair and tell a' your friends when ye get ashore that it's maybe gaun on to Oban tomorrow,' requested Sunny Jim. 'We'll hae it up on the Esplanade there and chairge a shillin' a heid; if we get it the length o' Gleska, the price'll be up to hauf-a-croon.'

'Is it a "right" whale?' asked one of the audience in the interests of exact science.

'Right enough, as shair's onything; isn't it, Captain?' said Sunny Jim.

'What else would it be?' said Para Handy indignantly. 'Does the chentleman think there iss onything wrong with it? Perhaps he would like

6. *Panting, breathing heavily.*

7. *The Kilbrannan Sound lies between the Island of Arran and the peninsula of Kintyre.*

to take a look through it; eh, Jum? Or maybe he would want a doctor's certeeficate that it's no a dromedary.'

The exhibition of the 'Tobermory Treasure' proved so popular that its discoverers determined to run their entertainment for about a week. On the third day passengers coming into Tobermory with the steamer *Claymore*[8] sniffed with appreciation, and talked about the beneficial influence of ozone, the English tourists debated whether it was due to peat or heather. In the afternoon several yachts in the bay hurriedly got up their anchors and went up Loch Sunart, where the air seemed fresher. On the fourth day the residents of Tobermory overwhelmed the local chemist with demands for camphor, carbolic powder, permanganate of potash, and other deodorants and disinfectants; and several plumbers were telegraphed for to Oban. The public patronage of the exhibition on Calve Island fell off.

'If there's ony mair o' them wantin' to see this whale,' said Sunny Jim, 'they'll hae to look slippy.'

'It's no' that bad to windward,' said Para Handy. 'What would you say to coverin' it up wi' more tarpaulins?'

'You might as weel cover't up wi' crape or muslin,' was Dougie's verdict. 'What you would need iss armour-plate, he same ass they have roond the cannons in the man-o'-wars. If this wind doesn't change to the west, half the folk in Tobermory'll be goin' to live in the cellar o' the Mishnish Hotel.'

Suspicion fell on the 'Tobermory Treasure' on the following day, and an influential deputation waited on the police sergeant, while the crew of the *Vital Spark,* with much discretion, abandoned their whale, and kept to their vessel's fo'c'sle. The sergeant informed the deputation that he had a valuable clue to the source of these extraordinary odours, but that unfortunately he could take no steps without a warrant from the Sheriff, and the Sheriff was in Oban. The deputation pointed out that the circumstances were too serious to permit of any protracted legal forms and ceremonies; the whale must be removed from Calve Island by its owners immediately, otherwise there would be a plague. With regret the police sergeant repeated that he could do nothing without authority, but he added casually that if the deputation visited the owners of the whale and scared the life out of them, he would be the last man to interfere.

---

8. *A famous steamer built by William Denny & Bros. at Dumbarton in 1881 for David MacBrayne's West Highland services.* Claymore *was famed, both for her striking looks and her fifty years of service on the West Coast.*

'Hullo, chaps! pull the hatch efter yez, and keep oot the cold air!' said Sunny Jim, as the spokesman of the deputation came seeking for the crew in the fo'c'sle. 'Ye'd be the better o' some odecolong on your hankies.'

'We thought you were going to remove your whale to Oban before this,' said the deputation sadly.

'I'm afraid,' said Para Handy, 'that whale hass seen its best days, and wouldna be at aal popular in Oban.'

'Well, you'll have to take it out of here immediately anyway,' said the deputation. 'It appears to be your property.'

'Not at aal, not at aal!' Para Handy assured him; 'it belongs by right to His Majesty, and we were just takin' care of it for him till he would turn up, chairgin' a trifle for the use o' the tarpaulins and the management. It iss too great a responsibility now, and we've given up the job; aren't we, Jum?'

'Right-oh!' said Sunny Jim, reaching for his melodeon; 'and it's time you Tobermory folk were shiftin' that whale.'

'It's impossible,' said the deputation, 'a carcase weighing nearly thirty tons — and in such a condition!'

'Indeed it is pretty bad,' said Para Handy; 'pehaps it would be easier to shift the toon o' Tobermory.'

But that was, luckily, not necessary, as a high tide restored the 'Tobermory Treasure' to its natural element that very afternoon.

Tobermory

Valentines Series

Tobermory *Argyll & Bute District Libraries*

115

25 PARA HANDY HAS AN EYE TO BUSINESS

IT was a lovely day, and the *Vital Spark,* without a cargo, lay at the pier of Ormidale,[1] her newly painted under-strakes reflected in a loch like a mirror, making a crimson blotch in a scene that was otherwise winter-brown. For a day and a half more there was nothing to be done. 'It's the life of a Perfect Chentlemen,' said Dougie. The engineer, with a novelette he had bought in Glasgow, was lost in the love affairs of a girl called Gladys, who was excessively poor, but looked, at Chapter Five, like marrying a Colonel of Hussars who seemed to have no suspicion of the fate in store for him; and Sunny Jim, with the back of his head showing at the fo'c'sle scuttle, was making with his melodeon what sounded like a dastardly attack on 'The Merry Widow'.

'I wass thinkin', seein' we're here and nothing else doin', we might be givin' her the least wee bit touch o' the tar-brush,' remarked Para Handy, who never cared to lose a chance of beautifying his vessel.

'There it is again!' exclaimed Macphail, laying down his novelette in exasperation. 'A chap canna get sittin' doon five meenutes in this boat for a read to himsel' withoot somebody breakin' their legs to find him a job. Ye micht as weel be in a man-o'-war.' Even Dougie looked reproachfully at the Captain; he had just been about to pull his cap down over his eyes and have a little sleep before his tea.

'It wass only a proposeetion,' said the Captain soothingly. 'No offence! Maybe it'll do fine when we get to Tarbert. It's an awfu' peety they're no' buildin' boats o' this size wi' a kind of study in them for the use o' the enchineers,' and he turned for sympathy to the mate, who was usually in the mood to rag Macphail. But this time Dougie was on Macphail's side.

'There's some o' your jokes like the Carradale funerals — there's no' much fun in them,' he remarked. 'Ye think it's great sport to be tar-tar-tarring away at the ship; ye never consult either oor healths or oor inclinations. Am I right, Macphail?'

'Slave-drivin'! that's whit I ca't,' said Macphail emphatically. 'If Lloyd George kent aboot it, he would bring it before the Board o' Tred.'[2]

The Captain withdrew, moodily, from his crew, and ostentatiously scraped old varnish off the mast. This business engaged him only for a

---

1. *An isolated pier on Loch Riddon in the Kyles of Bute.*

2. *As this story comes after 'Pension Farms' in the Para Handy canon and as Mr Lloyd George had moved on from the Board of Trade to be Chancellor of the Exchequer and creator of Old Age Pensions in 1908 we must assume that Macphail had not been keeping up with recent Cabinet changes.*

little; the weather was so plainly made for idleness that he speedily put the scraper aside and entered into discourse with Sunny Jim.

'Whatever you do, don't be a Captain, Jum,' he advised him.

'I wisht I got the chance!' said Sunny Jim.

'There's nothing in't but the honour o' the thing, and a shilling or two extra; no' enough to pay the drinks to keep up the poseetion. Here am I, and I'm anxious to be frien'ly wi' the chaps, trate them the same's I wass their equal, and aalways ready to come-and-go a bit, and they go and give me the name o' a slave-driver! Iss it no' chust desperate?'

'If I was a Captain,' said Sunny Jim philosophically, 'I wad dae the comin' and mak' the ither chaps dae the goin', and d — d smert aboot it.'

'That't aal right for a Gleska man, but it's no' the way we're brocht up on Loch Long; us Arrochar folk, when we're Captains, believe in a bit o' compromise wi' the crews. If they don't do a thing when we ask them cuvilly, we do't oorsel's, and that's the way to vex them.'

'Did ye never think ye wad like to change your job and try something ashore?' asked Sunny Jim.

'Many a time!' confessed the Captain. 'There's yonder jobs that would suit me fine. I wass nearly, once, an innkeeper. It wass at a place called Cladich;[3] the man came into a puckle money wi' his wife, and advertised the goodwull at a great reduction. I left the boat for a day and walked across to see him. He wass a man they caalled MacDiarmid, and he was yonder wi' his sleeves up puttin' corks in bottles wi' a wonderful machine. Did you ever see them corkin' bottles, Jum?'

'I never noticed if I did,' said Sunny Jim; 'but I've seen them takin' them oot.'

'Chust that! This innkeeper wass corkin' away like hey-my-nanny.

'"You're sellin' the business?" says I.

'"I am," says he; and him throng corkin' away at the bottles.

'"What's your price?" says I.

'"A hundred and fifty pounds for the goodwull and the stock the way it stands," says he.

'"What aboot the fixtures?" then says I.

'"Oh, they're aal right!" said the innkeeper, cork-cork-corkin' away at the bottles: "the fixtures goes along with the goodwull."

'"What fixtures is there?" says I.

'"There's three sheep fermers, the shoemaker doon the road, and

3. *Village on Loch Awe-side.*

Macintyre the mail-driver, and that's no' coontin' a lot o' my Sunday customers,"[4] said the innkeeper.'

'You didna tak' the business, then?' said Sunny Jim.

'Not me!' said Para Handy. 'To be corkin' away at bottles aal my lone yonder would put me crazy. Forbye, I hadna the half o' the hunder-and-fifty. There wass another time I went kind o' into business buyin' eggs —'

'Eggs!' exclaimed Sunny Jim with some astonishment — 'whit kin' o' eggs?'

'Och! chust egg eggs,' said the Captain. 'It wass a man in Arran said there wass a heap o' money in them if you had the talent and a wee bit powney[5] to go roond the countryside. To let you ken: it wass before the *Fital Spark* changed owners; the chentleman that had her then wass a wee bit foolish; nothing at aal against his moral and releegious reputation, mind, but apt to go over the score with it, and forget where-aboots the vessel would be lying. This time we were for a week or more doin' nothin' in Loch Ranza, and waitin' for his orders. He couldna mind for the life o' him where he sent us, and wass telegraphin' aal the harbour-masters aboot the coast to see if they kent the whereaboots o' the *Fital Spark,* but it never came into his heid that we might be near Loch Ranza, and there we were wi' the best o' times doin' nothing.'

'Could ye no' hae sent him a telegraph tellin' him where ye wiz?' asked Sunny Jim.

'That's what he said himsel', but we're no' that daft, us folk from Arrochar; I can tell you we have aal oor faculties. Dougie did better than that; he put a bit o' paper in a bottle efter writin' on't a message from the sea — "s.s. *Fital Spark* stranded for a fortnight in a fit o' absent-mind; aal hands quite joco, but the owner lost."

"We might have been lyin' in Loch Ranza yet if it wassna that I tried Peter Carmichael's business. "When you're doin' nothing better here," he said to me, "you micht be makin' your fortune buyin' and sellin' eggs, for Arran's fair hotchin' wi' them.""

4. *Sabbatarian and temperance pressures in Victorian Scotland had resulted in the passing of the Public Houses (Scotland) Act of 1853, the so-called Forbes-MacKenzie Act. This not only introduced the novelty of an official closing time for public houses (11.00 p.m.) but completely shut pubs on a Sunday. However hotels, like the Inn at Cladich in this story, were permitted to serve bona fide travellers. As a result the thirsty from one village went two or three miles to the next and thus qualified for the privilege.*

5. *Pony.*

"'What way do you do it?" says I.

"'You need a wee cairt and a powney," said Peter Carmichael, "and I've the very cairt and powney that would suit you. You go roond the island gatherin' eggs from aal the hooses, and pay them sixpence a dozen — champion eggs ass fresh ass the mornin' breeze. Then you pack them in boxes and send them to Gleska and sell them at a profit."

"'What profit do you chenerally allow yoursel'?" I asked Peter.

"'Oh! chust nate wan per cent," said Peter; "you chairge a shillin' in Gleska for the eggs; rale Arran eggs, no' foreign rubbadge. Folk'll tell you to put your money in stone and lime; believe me, nothing bates the Arran egg for quick returns. If the people in Gleska have a guarantee that any parteecular egg wass made in Arran, they'll pay any money for it; it's ass good ass a day at the coast for them, poor craturs!'

'Seein' there wass no prospeck o' the owner findin' where we were unless he sent a bloodhound oot to look for us, I asked Carmichael hoo long it would take to learn the business, and he said I could pick it up in a week. I agreed to buy the cairt and powney and the goodwull o' the business if the chob at the end o' the week wass like to bring in a pleasin' wage, and Dougie himsel' looked efter the shup. You never went roond the country buyin' eggs? It's a chob you need a lot o' skill for. Yonder wass Peter Carmichael and me goin' roon by Pirnmill, Machrie, and Blackwaterfoot, Sliddery and Shiskine —'

'Ach! ye're coddin'!' exclaimed Sunny Jim; 'There's no such places.'

'It's easy seen you were a' your days on the Clutha steamers,' said the Captain patiently; 'I'll assure you that there's Slidderys and Shiskines oot in Arran. Full o' eggs! The hens oot yonder's no puttin' bye their time!

'Three days runnin' Peter and me and the powney scoured the country and gaithered so many eggs that I began to get rud in the face whenever I passed the least wee hen. We couldna get boxes enough to hold them in Loch Ranza, so we got some bales o' hay and packed them in the hold of the *Fital Spark,* and then consudered. "There's nothing to do noo but to take them to the Broomielaw and sell them quick at a shillin'," said Carmichael. "The great thing iss to keep them on the move and off your hands before they change their minds and start for to be chuckens. Up steam, smert, and off wi' ye! And here's the cairt and powney — fifteen pounds.'

"'Not at aal, Carmichael!" I said to him; "I'll wait till I'll see if you wass right aboot the wan per cent of profits. Stop you here till I'll come back."

'I telegraphed that day to the owner o' the vessel, sayin' I was comin' into the Clyde wi' a cargo, and when we got to Gleska he wass standin' on the quay, and not in the best o' trum.

'"Where in a' the world were you?' says he; "and me lookin' high and low for you! What's your cargo?"

'"Eggs from Arran, Mr. Smith," says I, "and a bonny job I had gettin' them at sixpence the dozen."

'"Who are they from?" he asked glowerin' under the hatches.

'"Chust the cheneral population, Mr. Smith," says I.

'"Who are they consigned to?" he asked then — and man he wassna in trum at aal, at aal!

'"Anybody that'll buy them, sir," said I; "it's a bit of a speculation."

'He scratched his heid and looked at me. "I mind o' orderin' eggs," says he, "but I never dreamt I wass daft enough to send for a boat-load o' them. But noo they're here I suppose we'll have to make the best o' them." So he sold the eggs, and kept the wan per cent for freight and responsibeelity, and I made nothin' off it except that I shifted my mind aboot takin' a chob ashore, and didn't buy Carmichael's cairt and powney.'

Carradale *Argyll & Bute District Libraries*

26 AN OCEAN TRAGEDY

IT was a lovely afternoon at the end of May, and the *Vital Spark* was puffing down Kilbrannan Sound with a farmer's flitting. Macphail, the engineer, sat 'with his feet among the enchines and his heid in the clouds', as Dougie put it — in other words, on the ladder of his engine-room, with his perspiring brow catching the cool breeze made by the vessel's progress, and his emotions rioting through the adventures of a governess in the *Family Herald Supplement*. Peace breathed like an exhalation from the starboard hills; the sea was like a mirror, broken only by the wheel of a stray porpoise, and Sunny Jim indulged the Captain and the mate with a medley on his melodeon.

'You're a capital player, Jum,' said the Captain in a pause of the entertainment. 'Oh, yes, there's no doot you are cluver on it; it's a gift, but you havena the selection, no, you havena the selection, and if you havena the selection where are you?'

'He's doin' his best,' said Dougie sympathetically, and then, in one of those flashes of philosophy that come to the most thoughtless of us at times — 'A man can do no more.'

'Whit selections was ye wantin'?' asked the musician, with a little irritation; 'if it's Gaelic sangs ye're meanin' I wad need a drum and the nicht aff.'

'No, I wassna thinkin' aboot Gaalic sangs,' explained Para Handy; 'when we're consuderin' them we're consuderin' music; I was taalkin' of the bits of things you put on the melodeon; did you ever hear "Napoleon"?' and clearing his throat he warbled —

> 'Wa-a-an night sad and dree-ary
>   Ass I lay on my bed,
> And my head scarce reclined on the pillow;
> A vision surprisin' came into my head,
> And I dreamt I wass crossin' the billow,
> And ass my proud vessel she dashed o'er the deep –'

'It wasna the *Vital Spark*, onywye,' remarked Macphail cynically; 'afore I got her biler sorted she couldna dash doon a waterfall —'
> 'I beheld a rude rock, it was craggy and steep,'

(proceeded the vocalist, paying no attention),

> 'Twas the rock where the willow iss now seen to weep,
> O'er the grave of the once-famed Napo-o-ole-on!'

'I never heard better, Peter,' said the mate approvingly. 'Take your breath and give us another touch of it. There's nothing bates the old songs.'

'Let me see, noo, what wass the second verse?' asked the Captain, with his vanity as an artist fully roused; 'It was something like this —

> 'And ass my proud vessel she near-ed the land,
> I beheld clad in green, his bold figure;
> The trumpet of fame clasped firm in his hand,
> On his brow there wass valour and vigour.'

"Balloons! balloons!' cried Macphail, imitating some Glasgow street barrow-vendor. 'Fine balloons for rags and banes.'

'Fair do! gie the Captain a chance,' expostulated Sunny Jim. 'Ye're daein' fine, Captain; Macphail's jist chawed because he canna get readin'.'

> "'Oh, stranger," he cried, "dost thou come unto me,
> From the land of thy fathers who boast they are free;
> Then, if so, a true story I'll tell unto thee
> Concerning myself – I'm Napo-o-o-ole-on,"'

proceeded the Captain, no way discouraged, and he had no sooner concluded the final doleful note than a raucous voice from the uncovered hold cried 'Co-co-coals!'

Even Dougie sniggered; Macphail fell into convulsions of laughter, and Sunny Jim showed symptoms of choking.

'I can stand Macphail's umpudence, but I'll no' stand that nonsense from a hoolit[1] on my own shup,' exclaimed the outraged vocalist, and, stretching over the coamings, he grabbed from the top of a chest of drawers in the hold a cage with a cockatoo. 'Come oot like a man,' said he, 'and say't again.'

'Toots! Peter, it's only a stupid animal; I wouldna put myself a bit aboot,' remarked Dougie soothingly. 'It's weel enough known them cockatoos have no ear for music. Forbye, he wasna meanin' anything when he cried "Coals!" he was chust in fun.'

'Fun or no,' said Macphail, 'a bird wi' sense like that's no' canny. Try him wi' another verse, Captain, and see if he cries on the polis.'

---

1. *Owl. Captain Macfarlane's grasp of ornithology is clearly breaking down under the strain!*

'If he says another word I'll throw him over the side,' said Para Handy. 'It's nothing else but mutiny,' and with a wary eye on the unsuspecting cockatoo he sang another verse —

> *"'You remember that year so immortal," he cried,*
> *"When I crossed the rude Alps famed in story,*
> *With the legions of France, for her sons were my pride,*
> *And I led them to honour and glory –"'*

'Oh, crickey! Chase me, girls!' exclaimed the cockatoo, and the next moment was swinging over the side of the *Vital Spark* to a watery grave.

The fury of the outraged Captain lasted but a moment; he had the vessel stopped and the punt out instantly for a rescue; but the unhappy bird was irrecoverably gone, and the tea-hour on the *Vital Spark* that afternoon was very melancholy. Macphail, particularly, was inexpressibly galling in the way he over and over again brought up the painful topic.

'I canna get it oot o' my heid,' he said; 'the look it gied when ye were gaun to swing it roon' your heid and gie't the heave! I'll cairry that cockatoo's last look to my grave.'

'Whit kin' o' look was it?' asked Sunny Jim, eager for details; 'I missed it.'

'It was a look that showed ye the puir bird kent his last oor was come,' explained the engineer. 'It wasna anger, and it wasna exactly fricht; it was — man! I canna picture it to ye; but efter this ye needna tell me beasts have nae sowls; it's a' my aunty. Yon bird —'

'I wish I hadna put a finger on him,' said the Captain, sore stricken with remorse. 'Change the subject.'

'The puir bird didna mean ony hairm,' remarked Sunny Jim, winking at the engineer. '"Coals! or "Chase me girls!" is jist a thing onybody would say if they heard a chap singin' a sang like yon; it's oot o' date. Fair do! ye shouldna hae murdered the beast; the man it belangs to 'll no' be awfu' weel pleased.'

'Murdered the beast!' repeated the conscience-stricken Captain, 'it's no' a human body you're talkin' aboot,' and the engineer snorted his amazement.

'Michty! Captain, is that a' ye ken?' he exclaimed. 'If it's no' murder, it's manslaughter; monkeys, cockatoos, and parrots a' come under the Act o' Parliament. A cockatoo's no' like a canary; it's able to speak the language and give an opeenion, and the man that wad kill a cockatoo wad kill a wean.'

'That's right enough, Peter,' said Dougie pathetically; 'everybody kens it's manslaughter. I never saw a nicer cockatoo either; no' a better behaved bird; it's an awful peety. Perhaps the polis at Carradale will let the affair blow bye.'

'I wasna meanin' to herm the bird,' pleaded Para Handy. 'It aggravated me. Here wass I standin' here singin' "Napoleon", and the cockatoo wass yonder, and he hurt my feelin's twice; you would be angry yoursel' if it wass you. My nerves got the better o' me.'

'If the polis cross-examine me,' said the engineer emphatically, 'I'll conceal naething. I'll no' turn King's evidence or onything like that, mind, but if I'm asked I'll tell the truth, for I don't want to be mixed up wi' a case o' manslaughter and risk my neck.'

Thus were the feelings of the penitent Para Handy lacerated afresh every hour of the day, till he would have given everything he possessed in the world to restore the cockatoo to life. The owner's anger at the destruction of his bird was a trifle to be anticipated calmly; the thought that made Para Handy's heart like lead was that cockatoos DID speak, that this one even seemed to have the gift of irony, and that he had drowned a fellow-being; it was, in fact, he admitted to himself, a kind of manslaughter. His shipmates found a hundred ways of presenting his terrible deed to him in fresh aspects.

'Cockatoos iss mentioned in the Scruptures,'[2] said Dougie; 'I don't exactly mind the place, but I've seen it.'

'They live mair nor a hundred years if they're weel trated,' was Sunny Jim's contribution to the natural history of the bird.

'Naebody ever saw a deid cockatoo,' added the engineer.

'I wish you would talk aboot something else,' said the Captain piteously; I'm troubled enough in mind withoot you bringin' that accursed bird up over and over again,' and they apologized, but always came back to the topic again.

'I wid plead guilty and throw mysel' on the mercy o' the coort,' was Macphail's suggestion. 'At the maist it'll no' be mair nor a sentence for life.'

2. *Sadly, but perhaps unsurprisingly, Dougie is mistaken. The cockatoo comes from Australia and New Guinea, not the Holy Land. What the mate is perhaps thinking of (if he is not simply persecuting the hapless skipper) is the cockatrice. This is a bird of a very different feather, being generally considered as some sort of venomous snake and there are indeed four references to this unpleasant beast in the 'Scruptures'*

'Ye could say ye did it in self-defence,' recommended Sunny Jim. 'Thae cockatoos bites like onything.'

'A great calamity!' moaned Dougie, shaking his head.

When the cargo of furniture was discharged and delivered, the farmer discovered the absence of his cockatoo, and came down to make inquiries.

'He fell over the side,' was the Captain's explanation. 'We had his cage hanging on the shrouds, and a gale struck us and blew it off. His last words wass, "There's nobody to blame but myself."'

'There was no gale aboot here,' said the farmer, suspecting nothing. 'I'm gey sorry to lose that cage. It was a kind o' a pity, too, the cockatoo bein' drooned.'

'Say nothing aboot that,' pleaded the Captain. 'I have been mournin' about that cockatoo all week; you wouldna believe the worry it has been for me, and when all iss said and done I consider the cockatoo had the best of it.'

Campbeltown Harbour *Argyll & Bute District Libraries*

POLITICS, INTERNATIONAL AFFAIRS AND THE CREW OF THE *VITAL SPARK*

A steam-lighter, whether or not 'the smertest boat in the tred', going about her routine business on the peaceful waters of the Clyde and in remote West Highland harbours would seem comfortably removed from the troubles of the wider world. However, as we shall see, the problems of the outside world increasingly impinge on the *Vital Spark* and her crew.

Nowhere does this happen more dramatically than in the next story 'Para Handy and the Navy'. The tale starts off with the crew being lectured by Macphail on the plight of the Royal Navy. This was a highly topical issue of the day. German—British naval rivalry, on the increase since the German Naval Act of 1898 had laid the foundations for a German battle fleet, came to a head in 1906.

In that year the Royal Navy launched the first of a new and powerful class of battleships, H.M.S. *Dreadnought*. This ship represented a major qualitative leap in warship design and mounting ten 12inch guns was both more powerful, faster and better protected than any contemporary warship. Germany responded with the 1906 Naval Act which committed her to matching British battleship production both in quantity and quality. In 1909 British Naval Estimates were considerably increased and the new construction programme was publicly justified by reference to the German naval threat.

Feelings in Britain became raised, as this story indicates, and a popular Jingoistic slogan of the day was 'We want eight and we wont wait!' The eight in question being battleships of the Dreadnought class.

A later story 'The Stowaway' deals with the German spy scare. In the years before the First World War there was consisderable concern about German espionage, war plans and preparations. This led, among other things, to the passing of the Official Secrets Act in 1911. A substantial body of literature was published on the theme of a future war between Britain and Germany, the best known example of this genre being Erskine Childers' 'The Riddle of the Sands', published in 1903.

As we have seen from 'Pension Farms' the crew generally keep abreast of national politics and home affairs as well as being alert to the latest developments on the international scene. In, 'The Goat',(a story not included in this volume) Para's account of Wully Crawford, Tarbert's first 'polisman' is initiated by a discussion of the conduct of the Metropolitan Police and Home Secretary Winston Churchill at the 'Siege of Sidney Street'—the incident in Stepney in 1911 with a gang of Latvian anarchists and criminals led, it was thought, by the mysterious figure of Peter Piaktow, 'Peter the Painter'. While Para had nothing but praise for the Home Secretary (who Macphail the engineer, with a degree of exaggeration, describes as shaking 127 bullets out of his Astrakan coat) 'Man, he must be a tough young fellow, Wunston! Them bullets give you an awfu' bang.'; his view of the London police was not entirely complimentary '. . . the London polisman iss greatly wantin' in agility . . .'. He suggests that they could take lessons from the Tarbert 'polisman' who managed to keep law and order among the unruly Tarbert trawlermen by virtue of his agility.

Tarbert *Argyll & Bute District Libraries*

127

27 PARA HANDY AND THE NAVY

MACPHAIL the engineer sat on an upturned bucket reading the weekly paper, and full of patriotic alarm at the state of the British Navy.

'What are you groanin' and sniffin' at?' asked the Captain querolously. 'I should think mysel, that by this time you would be tired o' Mrs. Atherton. Whatna prank iss she up to this time?'

'It's no' Mrs. Atherton,' said the reader, 'it's something mair important; it's the Germans.'

'Holy smoke!' said Para Handy, 'are they findin' them oot, noo? Wass I not convinced there wass something far, far wrong wi' them? Break the full parteeculars to me chently, Mac, and you, Jim, go and get the dinner ready; you're far too young to hear the truth aboot the Chermans. Which o' the Chermans iss it, Mac? Some wan in a good poseetion, I'll be bound! It's a mercy that we're sailors; you'll no' find mich aboot the wickedness o' sailors in the papers.'

'The British Navy's a' to bleezes! said Macphail emphatically. 'Here's Germany buildin' Dreadnought men-o'-war as hard's she can, and us palaverin'[1] awa' oor time.'

Para Handy looked a little disappointed. 'It's politics you're on,' said he; 'And I wass thinkin' it wass maybe another aawful scandal in Society. That's the worst o' the newspapers — you never knew where you are wi' them; a week ago it wass nothing but the high jeenks of the beauteous Mrs. Atherton. Do you tell me the Brutish Navy's railly done?'

'Complete!' said the engineer.

'Weel, that's a peety!' said Para Handy sympathetically; 'it'll put a lot o' smert young fellows oot o' jobs; I know a Tarbert man called Colin Kerr that had a good poseetion on the *Formidable*.[2] I'm aawful sorry aboot Colin.'

The engineer resumed his paper, and the *Vital Spark* chug-chugged her sluggish way between the Gantocks[3] and the Cloch,[4] with Dougie at the wheel, his nether garments hung precariously on the half of a pair of braces. 'There's nothing but dull tred everywhere,' said he. 'They're stoppin' a lot o' the railway steamers, too.'

1. *Fussing or trifling.*

2. *Pre-Dreadnought battleship built in 1898 and torpedoed in the Channel on 1st. January 1915 with extensive loss of life.*

3. *A notoriously dangerous shelf of barely submerged rocks off Dunoon.*

4. *Lighthouse on the Renfrewshire coast South-West of Gourock.*

'The state o' the British Navy's mair important than the stoppage o' a wheen passenger steamers,' explained the engineer. 'If you chaps read the papers ye would see this country's in a bad poseetion. We used to rule the sea —'

'We did that!' said the Captain heartily; 'I've seen us doin' it! Brutain's hardy sons!'

'And noo the Germans is gettin' the upper hand o' us; they'll soon hae faur mair Dreadnoughts than we hae. We're only buildin' four. Fancy that! Four Dreadnoughts at a time like this, wi' nae work on the Clyde, and us wi' that few Territorials we hae to go to the fitba matches and haul them oot to jine by the hair o' the heid. We've lost the two-Power standard.' [5]

'Man, it's chust desperate! said the Captain. 'We'll likely advertise for 't. What's the — what's the specialty aboot the Dreadnoughts?'

'It's the only cless o' man-o'-war that's coonted noo,' said the engineer, 'a tip-top battle-winner. If ye havena Dreadnoughts ye micht as weel hae dredgers.'

'Holy smoke! what a lot o' lumber aal the other men-o'-war must be!' remarked the Captain. 'That'll be the way they're givin' them up and payin' off the hands.'

'Wha said they were givin' them up?'' asked the engineer snappishly.

'Beg pardon! beg pardon! I thocht I heard you mention it yon time I remarked on Colin Kerr. I thocht that maybe aal the other boats wass absolute, and we would see them next week lyin' in the Kyles o' Bute wi' washin's hung oot on them.'

'There's gaun to be nae obsolete boats in the British Navy efter this,' said the engineer; 'we're needin' every man-o'-war that'll haud thegither. The Germans has their eye on us.'

'Dougie,' said the Captain firmly, with a glance at the deshabille of his mate, 'go doon this instant and put on your jecket! The way you are, you're not a credit to the boat.'

A terrific bang broke upon the silence of the Firth; the crew of the *Vital Spark* turned their gaze with one accord towards the neighbourhood of

5. *The two-Power standard was a well-established target for British naval strength. The aim was to have a fleet to match those of any two possible combined adversaries. As Macphail observes, in his somewhat unaccustomed role as naval strategist, the advent of the Dreadnought type in Britain and Germany had eroded Britain's naval superiority. 'If ye havena Dreadnoughts ye micht as weel hae dredgers.' While this is a somewhat extravagant way of expressing the matter the fact remains that the Dreadnought type so outperformed earlier capital ships as to make them of very limited utility.*

Kilcreggan, whence the report seemed to have proceeded, and were frightfully alarmed a second or two afterwards when a shell burst on the surface of the sea a few hundred yards or so from them, throwing an enormous column of water into the air.

'What did I tell ye!' cried Macphail, as he dived below to his engine-room.

'Holy smoke!' exclaimed Para Handy; 'did ye notice anything, Dougie?'

'I think I did!' said the mate, considerably perturbed; There must be some wan blastin'.'

'Yon wassna a blast,' said the Captain; 'their firin' cannons at us from Portkill.'[6]

'There's a pant for ye!' exclaimed Sunny Jim, dodging behind the funnel.

'What for would they be firin' cannons at us?' asked the mate, with a ludicrous feeling that even the jacket advised a minute or two ago by the Captain would now be a most desirable protection.

Another explosion from the fort at Portkill postponed the Captain's answer, and this time the bursting shell seemed a little closer.

'Jim,' said the mate appealingly, 'would ye mind takin' haud o' this wheel till I go down below and get my jacket? If I'm to be shot, I'll be shot like a Hielan' chentleman and no' in my shirt-sleeves.'

'You'll stay where you are!' exclaimed the Captain, greatly excited; 'you'll stay where you are, and die at your post like a Brutish sailor. This is WAR. Port her heid in for Macinroy's Point,[7] Dougald, and you, Macphail, put on to her every pound of steam she'll cairry. I wish to Providence I had chust the wan wee Union Jeck.'

'Whit would ye dae wi' a Union Jeck?' asked the engineer putting up his head and ducking nervously as another shot boomed over the Firth.

'I would nail it to the mast!' said Para Handy, buttoning his coat. 'It would show them Cherman chentlemen we're the reg'lar he'rts of oak.'

'Ye don't think it's Germans that's firin', dae ye?' asked the engineer, cautiously putting out his head again. 'It's the Garrison Arteelery that's firin' frae Portkill.'

'Whit are the silly duvvles firin' at us for, then?' asked Para Handy; 'I'm sure we never did them any herm.'

6. *Fort, manned by Territorials of the Royal Garrison Artillery, on Rosneath Point.*

7. *Our hero is, despite his bold words, steaming for the shelter of the Renfrewshire coast. Macinroy's Point is just beyond Gourock.*

'I ken whit for they're firin',' said the engineer maliciously; 'they're takin' the *Vital Spark* for yin o' them German Dreadnoughts. Ye have nae idea o' the fear o' daith that's on the country since it lost the two-Power standard.'

This notion greatly charmed the Captain, being distinctly complimentary to his vessel; but his vanity was soon dispelled, for Sunny Jim pointed out that the last shot had fallen far behind them, in proximity to a floating target now for the first time seen. 'They're jist at big-gun practice,' he remarked with some relief, 'and we're oot o' the line o' fire.'

'Of course we are!' said Para Handy. 'I kent that aal along. Man, Macphail, but you were tumid, tumid! You're losin' aal your nerve wi' readin' aboot the Chermans.'

Kyles of Bute *Argyll & Bute District Libraries*

28 AMONG THE YACHTS

MACPHAIL was stoking carefully and often, like a mother feeding her first baby; keeping his steam at the highest pressure short of blowing off the safety valve, on which he had tied a pig-iron bar; and driving the *Vital Spark* for all she was worth past Cowal. The lighter's bluff bows were high out of water, for she was empty, and she left a wake astern of her like a liner.

'She hass a capital turn of speed when you put her to it,' said the Captain, quite delighted; 'it's easy seen it's Setturday, and you're in a hurry to be home, Macphail. You're passin' roond that oil-can there the same ass if it wass a tea-pairty you were at, and nobody there but women. It's easy seen it wass a cargo of coals we had the last trip, and there's more in your bunkers than the owner paid for. But it's none o' my business; please yoursel'!'

'We'll easy be at Bowlin' before ten,' said Dougie, consulting his watch. 'You needna be so desperate anxious.'

The engineer mopped himself fretfully with a fistful of oily waste and shrugged his shoulders. 'If you chaps like to palaver awa' your time,' said he, 'it's all the same to me, but I was wantin' to see the end o' the racin'.'

'Whatna racin'?' asked the Captain.

'Yat-racin',' said the engineer, with irony. 'Ye'll maybe hae heard o't. If ye havena, ye should read the papers. There's a club they ca' the Royal Clyde[1] at Hunter's Quay, and a couple o' boats they ca' the *Shamrock*[2] and the *White Heather*[3] are sailin' among a wheen o' ithers for a cup. I wouldna care if I saw the feenish; you chaps needna bother; just pull doon the skips o' your keps on your e'en when ye pass them, and ye'll no' see onything.'

'I don't see much in aal their yat-racin',' said Para Handy.

1. *The Royal Clyde Yacht Club, with its base at Hunter's Quay, near Dunoon, was founded in 1871, though its origins go back to the Clyde Model Yacht Club of 1856. This was a club formed to cater for owners of smaller yachts, not model yachts in the modern sense, who were excluded from membership of the prestigious Royal Northern Yacht Club (founded in 1824) which had its headquarters at Rothesay. In recent years the two clubs have merged and have their Headquarters at Rhu on the Gareloch.*

2. *Sir Thomas Lipton's famous 23 metre cutter designed and built in 1908 by the famous Clyde yacht building firm of W. Fife & Son of Fairlie.*

3. *Another of the classic Fife designed yachts—this time a 151 tons (Thames Measurement) yawl built in 1904 in Southampton and owned at this time by Myles B Kennedy.*

'If I was you, then, I would try the Eye Infirmary,' retorted the engineer, 'or wan o' them double-breisted spy-glesses.[4] Yonder the boats; we're in lots o' time —' and he dived again among his engines, and they heard the hurried clatter of his shovel.

'Anything wi' Macphail for sport!' remarked the Captain sadly. 'You would think at his time o' life, and the morn Sunday, that his meditaations would be different ... Give her a point to starboard, Dougie, and we'll see them better. Yonder's the *Ma'oona;*[5] if the duvvle wass wise he would put aboot at wance or he'll hit that patch o' calm.'

'There's an aawful money in them yats!' said the mate, who was at the wheel.

'I never could see the sense o't,' remarked the Captain ... 'There's the *Hera*[6] tacking; man, she's smert! smert! Wan o' them Coats's boats;[7] I wish she would win; I ken a chap that plays the pipes on her.'

Dougie steered as close as he could on the racing cutters with a sportsman's scrupulous regard for wind and water. 'What wan's that?' he asked, as they passed a thirty-rater which had struck the calm.

'That's the *Pallas,*'[8] said the Captain, who had a curiously copious knowledge of the craft he couldn't see the sense of. 'Another wan o' the Coats's; every other wan you see belongs to Paisley. They buy them by the gross, the same ass they were pirns,[9] and distribute them every noo and then among the faimely. If you're a Coats you lose a lot o' time makin' up your mind what boat you'll sail tomorrow; the whole o' the Clyde below the Tail o' the Bank[10] is chock-a-block wi' steamboat-yats and cutters the

4. *The sardonic engineer is referring to binoculars or field- glasses, still at this period something of a novelty.*

5. *Almeric Paget M.P.'s 15 metre cutter, built in 1888 by R. McAllister & Son at Dumbarton.*

6. *A 12 metre cutter built in 1908 by McAllister and owned by J.H. Gubbins*

7. *The Coats family of Paisley textile magnates were prominent in yacht racing circles.*

8. *A smallish (35.6' cutter) owned by A.II. Glen Coats*

9. *A bobbin or spool. The Coats, as threadmakers, would be large scale buyers of pirns—hence the point of Para's allusion. Some idea of the family interest in yachting may be gained from a perusal of the Lloyd's Register of Yachts which, in 1910, listed James Coats Jnr. of Ferguslie House, Paisley as the owner of 6 yachts, ranging in size from the 3 ton Sprite to the 498 ton Gleniffer. The same edition lists another 6 vessels owned by members of the Coats or Glen-Coats family.*

10. *Stretch of the Clyde off Greenock, used as an anchorage for trans-Atlantic liners or for ships waiting for appropriate conditions to pass up-river.*

Coats's canna hail a boat ashore from to get a sail, for they canna mind their names. Still-and-on, there's nothing wrong wi' them — tip-top sportin' chentlemen!'

'I sometimes wish, mysel', I had taken to the yats,' said Dougie; 'it's a suit or two o' clothes a year, and a pleasant occupaation. Most o' the time in canvas sluppers.'

'You're better the way you are,' said Para Handy; 'there's nothing bates the mercantile marine for makin' sailors. Brutain's hardy sons! We could do withoot yats, but where would we be withoot oor coal-boats? Look at them chaps sprauchlin'[11] on the deck; if they saw themsel's they would see they want another fut on that main-sheet. I wass a season or two in the yats mysel' — the good old *Marjory*.[12] No' a bad job at aal, but aawful hurried. Holy smoke! the way they kept you jumpin' here and there the time she would be racin'! I would chust as soon be in a lawyer's office. If you stopped to draw your breath a minute you got yon across the ear from a swingin' boom. It's a special breed o' sailor-men you need for racin'-yats, and the worst you'll get iss off the Islands.'

'It's a cleaner job at any rate than carryin' coals,' remarked the mate, with an envious eye on the spotless decks of a heeling twenty-tonner.

'Clean enough, I'll alloo, and that's the worst of it,' said Para Handy. 'You might ass weel be a chamber-maid — up in the mornin' scourin' brass and scrubbin' floors, and goin' ashore wi' a fancy can for sixpenceworth o' milk and a dozen o' syphon soda. Not much navigation there, my lad! . . . If I wass that fellow I would gybe her there and set my spinnaker to starboard; what do you think yoursel', Macphail?'

'I thocht you werena interested,' said the engineer, who had now reduced his speed.

'I'm not much interested, but I'm duvellish keen,' said Para Handy. 'Keep her goin' chust like that, Macphail; we'll soon be up wi' the *Shamrock* and the *Heather;* they're yonder off Loch Long.'

A motor-boat regatta was going on at Dunoon; the *Vital Spark* seemed hardly to be moving as some of the competitors flashed past her, breathing petrol fumes.

'You canna do anything like that,' said Dougie to the engineer, who snorted.

'No,' said Macphail contemptuously, 'I'm an engineer; I never was

11. *Sprawling*

12. *A popular yacht name and it is sadly impossible to establish which vessel Para crewed on.*

much o' a hand at the sewin'-machine. I couldna lower mysel' to handle engines ye could put in your waistcoat pocket.'

'Whether you could or no',' said Para Handy, 'the times iss changin', and the motor-launch iss coming for to stop.'

'That's whit she's aye daein',' retorted the engineer; 'stoppin's her strong p'int; gie me a good substantial compound engine; nane o' your hurdy-gurdies! I wish the wind would fresh a bit, for there's the *Shamrock,* and her mainsail shakin'.' He dived below, and the *Vital Spark* in a little had her speed reduced to a crawl that kept her just abreast of the drifting racers.

'Paddy's hurricane — up and doon the mast,' said Dougie in a tone of disappointment. 'I would like, mysel', to see Sir Thomas Lipton[13] winnin', for it's there I get my tea.'

Para Handy extracted a gully-knife from the depths of his trousers pockets, opened it, spat on the blade for luck, and, walking forward, stuck it in the mast, where he left it. 'That's the way to get wind,' said he; 'many a time I tried it, and it never fails. Stop you, and you'll see a breeze immediately, Them English skippers, Sycamore and Bevis,[14] havena the heid to think o't.'

'Whit's the use o' hangin' on here? said the engineer, with a wink at Dougie; 'it's time we were up the river; I'll better get her under weigh again.'

The Captain turned on him with a flashing eye. 'You'll do nothing o' the kind, Macphail,' said he; 'we'll stand by here and watch the feenish, if it's any time before the Gleska Fair.'

Shamrock, having split tacks off Kilcreggan, laid away to the west, while *White Heather* stood in for the Holy Loch, seeking the evening breeze that is apt to blow from the setting sun. It was the crisis of the day, and the crew of the *Vital Spark* watched speechlessly for a while the yachts manoeuvring. For an hour the cutter drifted on this starboard leg, and Sunny Jim, for reasons of his own, postponed the tea.

---

13. *Thomas Johnstone Lipton (1850-1931), born in humble circumstances in Glasgow, established a chain of stores through an original and dynamic approach to food retailing—he made his first million by the age of 30. Noted for his gifts to charity he also spent a fortune on attempts to win back the America's Cup from the United States with a series of yachts called (in tribute to his Irish ancestry) Shamrock. Knighted in 1898, he was made a baronet in 1902 by King Edward VII—another keen yachtsman.*

14. *The professional skippers of the great rivals* Shamrock *(Sycamore) and* White Heather *(Bevis).*

'It wants more knifes,' sid Para Handy; 'have you wan, Dougie?' but Dougie had lost his pocket-knife a week ago, and the engineer had none either.

'If stickin' knifes in the mast would raise the wind,' said Sunny Jim, 'there would be gales by this time, for I stuck the tea-knife in an oor ago.'

'Never kent it to fail afore!' said Para Handy . . . 'By George! It's comin'. Yonder's Bevis staying!'

White Heather, catching the wind, reached for the closing lap of the race with a bone in her mouth, and Para Handy watched her, fascinated, twisting the buttons off his waistcoat in his intense excitement. With a turn or two of the wheel the mate put the *Vital Spark* about and headed for the mark; Macphail deserted his engine and ran forward to the bow.

'*The Heather* hass it, Dougald,' said the Captain thankfully; 'I'm vexed for you, considerin' the place you get our tea.'

'Hold you on, Peter,' said the mate; 'there's the *Shamrock* fetchin''; a race is no' done till it's feenished.' His hopes were justified. *Shamrock,* only a few lengths behind, got the same light puff of wind in her sails, and rattled him a winner by half a minute.

'Macphail!' bawled the Captain, 'I'll be much obleeged if you take your place again at your bits of engines, and get under weigh; it's any excuse wi' you for a diversion, and it's time we werena here.'

29 HERRING — A GOSSIP

'OF aal the fish there iss in the sea.' said Para Handy, 'nothing bates the herrin'; it's a providence they're plentiful and them so cheap!'

'They're no' in Loch Fyne, wherever they are,' said Dougie sadly; 'the only herrin' that they're gettin' there iss rud ones comin' up in barrels wi' the *Cygnet* or the *Minard Castle*.[1] For five years back the trade wass desperate.'

'I wouldna say but you're right,' agreeably remarked the Captain. 'The herrin' iss a great, great mystery. The more you will be catchin' o' them the more there iss; and when they're no' in't at aal they're no' there' — a great philosophic truth which the crew smoked over in silence for a few minutes.

'When I wass a hand on the gabberts,' continued the Captain, 'the herrin' fishin' of Loch Fyne wass in its prime. You ken yoursel' what I mean; if you don't believe me, Jum, there's Dougie himsel' 'll tell you. Fortunes! Chust simply fortunes! You couldna show your face in Tarbert then but a lot of the laads would gaither round at wance and make a jovial day of it. Wi' a barrel of nets in a skiff and a handy wife at the guttin', a man of the least agility could make enough in a month to build a land o' hooses, and the rale Loch Fyne was terrible namely over aal the world.'

'I mind o't mysel',' said Sunny Jim; 'they never sold onything else but the rale Loch Fyne in Gleska.'

'They did that whether or no',' explained Para Handy, 'for it wass the herrin's of Loch Fyne that had the reputation.'

'I've seen the Rooshians eatin' them raw in the Baltic,' said Macphail, the engineer, and Dougie shuddered. 'Eating them raw! said he; 'the dirty duvvles!'

'The herrin' wass that thick in Loch Fyne in them days,' recalled the Captain, 'that you sometimes couldna get your anchor to the ground, and the quality was chust sublime. It wassna a tred at aal so much as an amusement; you went oot at night when the weans wass in their beds, and you had a couple o' cran[2] on the road to Clyde in time for Gleska's

---

1. The Minard Castle *was launched in 1882 for the Lochfyne and Glasgow Steam Packet Company Ltd. and was intended to compete with MacBrayne's Loch Fyne cargo service. She later changed hands on a number of occasions but continued in service around the Clyde until 1926. Her opposite number in MacBrayne's service was the* Cygnet.

2. *The unit of measurement of herring; a barrel of 37.5 gallons capacity.*

breakfast. The quays wass covered wi' John O'Brian's boxes,[3] and man alive! but the wine and spirit tred wass busy. Loch Fyne wass the place for Life in them days — high jeenks and big hauls; you werena very smert if you werena into both o' them. If you don't believe me, Dougie himsel' 'll tell you.'

'You have it exact, Peter,' guaranteed the mate, who was thus appealed to; 'I wass there mysel'-'

'Of course I have it exact,' said Para Handy; 'I'll assure you it's no' a thing I read in the papers. Today there's no a herrin' in Loch Fyne or I'm mistaken.'

'If there's wan he'll be kind o' lonely,' said the mate. 'I wonder what in the muschief's wrong wi' them?'

'You might shot miles o' nets for a month and there's no' a herrin' will come near them.'

'Man! aren't they the tumid, frightened idiots!' said Dougie, with disgust.

'If ye ask me, I think whit spoiled the herrin' fishin in Loch Fyne was the way they gaed on writin' aboot it in the papers,' said Macphail. 'It was enough to scunner[4] ony self-respectin' fish. Wan day a chap would write that it was the trawlers that were daein' a' the damage; next day anither chap would say he was a liar, and that trawlin' was a thing the herrin' thrived on. Then a chap would write that there should be a close time so as to gie the herrin' time to draw their breaths for anither breenge[5] into the nets; and anither chap would write from Campbeltown and say a close time would be takin' the bread oot o' the mooths o' his wife and weans. A scientific man said herrin' came on cycles —'

'He's a liar, anyway,' said the Captain, with conviction. 'They were in Loch Fyne afore the cycle was invented. Are you sure, Macphail, it's no' the cod he means?'

'He said the herrin' fishin' aye missed some years noo and then in a' the herrin' places in Europe as weel's in Loch Fyne, and the Gulf Stream had something to dae wi't.'

3. *John O'Brian was a well-known West Coast fish merchant. Munro commented in The Brave Days p.62 on MacBrayne's & O'Brien's economic dominance. 'You could not . . . land at a quay but across red-painted gangways. MacBrayne and John O'Brian clearly shared the whole West Highland trade between them. Wherever was a gangway and a couple of bollards, there was also a pile of John O'Brian's herring boxes.'*

4. *Disgust.*

5. *Rush, plunge or dash.*

'That's the worst o' science,' said the Captain piously; 'it takes aal the credit away from the Creator. Don't you pay attention to an unfidel like that; when the herrin' wass in Loch Fyne they stayed there aal the time, and only maybe took a daunder[6] oot noo and then the length o' Ballantrae.'

'If it's no' the Gulf Stream, then ye'll maybe tell us whit it is?' said the engineer, with some annoyance.

'I'll soon do that,' said Para Handy; 'if you want to ken, it's what I said — the herrin' iss a mystery, chust a mystery!'

'I'm awfu' gled ye told me,' said the engineer ironically. 'I aye wondered. Whit's the parteecular mysteriousness aboot it?'

'It's a silly fish,' replied the Captain; 'it's fine for eatin', but it hasna the sagacity. If it had the sagacity it wouldna come lower than Otter Ferry, nor be gallivantin'[7] roond the Kyles o' Bute in daylight. It's them innovations that's the death o' herrin'. If the herrin' stayed in Loch Fyne attendin' to its business and givin' the drift-net crews encouragement, it would have a happier life and die respected.

'Whenever the herrin' of Loch Fyne puts his nose below Kilfinan, his character is gone. First the Tarbert trawlers take him oot to company and turn his heid; they there iss nothing for it for him but flying trips to the Kyles o' Bute, the Tail o' the Bank, the Gareloch. In Loch Fyne we never would touch the herrin' in the daytime, nor in winter; they need a rest, forbye we're none the worse o' one oorsel's; but the folk below Kilfinan have no regard for Chrustian principles, and they no sooner see an eye o' fish than they're roond aboot it with trawls, even if it's the middle o' the day or New-Year's mornin'. They never give the fish a chance; they keep it on the run till its fins get hot. If it ventures ass far ass the Tail o' the Bank, it gets that dizzy wi' the sight o' the shippin' traffic that it loses the way and never comes back to Loch Fyne again. A silly fish! If it only had sagacity! Amn't I right, Dougie?'

'Whatever you say yoursel', Captain; there's wan thing sure, the herrin's scarce.'

'The long and the short of it iss that they're a mystery,' concluded Para Handy.

---

6. *Stroll.*

7. *Gadding about, roaming around in search of pleasure.*

30 THE STOWAWAY

'DID you ever, ever, in your born days, see such umpidence?' said the mate of the smartest boat in the coasting trade, looking up from his perusal of a scrap of newspaper in which the morning's kippers had been brought aboard by Sunny Jim.

'What iss't, Dougald?' asked the Captain, sitting down on a keg to put on his carpet slippers, a sign that the day of toil on deck officially was over. 'You'll hurt your eyes, there, studyin' in the dark. You're gettin' chust ass bad ass the enchineer for readin'; we'll have to put in the electric light for you.'

'Chermans!' said Dougie. 'The country's crooded wi' them. They're goin' aboot disguised ass towerists,[1] drawin' plans o' forts and brudges.'

'Now, issn't that most desperate!' said Para Handy, poking up the fo'c'sle stove, by whose light his mate had been reading this disquieting intelligence. 'That's the way that British tred iss ruined. First it wass Cherman clocks, and then it wass jumpin'-jecks, and noo it's picture post-cairds.'[2]

'Criftens!' said Sunny Jim, who had come hurriedly down to put on a second waistcoat, for the night was cold: 'Whit dae ye think they're makin' the drawin's for?'

'Iss't no' for post-cairds?' asked the Captain innocently, and the cook uproariously laughed.

'Post-cairds my auntie!' he vulgarly exclaimed. 'It's for the German Airmy. As soon's they can get their bits o' things thegither, they're comin' ower here to fight us afore the Boy Scouts[3] gets ony bigger. They hae spies a' ower Britain makin' maps: I'll lay ye there's no' a beer-shop in the country that they havena dotted doon.'

'Holy smoke!' said Para Handy.

He watched the very deliberate toilet of Sunny Jim with some impatience. 'Who's supposed to be at the wheel at this parteecular meenute?' he asked, with apparent unconcern.

'Me,' said Sunny Jim. 'There's naething in sicht, and I left it a meenute just to put on this waistcoat. 'Ye're gettin' awfu' pernicketty wi' your

---

1. *Tourists.*

2. *German manufacturers had won a very large share of the fast- growing market for picture post cards. Many of the most popular series of views of picturesque British beauty spots were in fact produced in Germany.*

3. *The Boy Scout movement was founded by Robert Baden-Powell in 1908.*

wheel; it's no' the *Lusitania*.' [4]

'I'm no' findin' fault at aal, at aal, Jum, but I'm chust considerin',' said the Captain meekly. 'Take your time. Don't hurry, Jum. Would you no' give your hands a wash and put on a collar? It's always nice to have a collar on and be looking spruce if you're drooned in a collusion. Give a kind of a roar when you get up on deck if you see we're runnin' into anything.'

'Collusion!' said Sunny Jim contemptuously. 'Wi' a' the speed this boat can dae, she couldna run into a pend close [5] if it started rainin',' and he swung himself on deck.

'He hasna the least respect for the vessel,' said the Captain sadly. 'She might be a common gaabert for aal the pride that Jum hass in her.'

The *Vital Spark* had left Loch Ranza an hour ago, and was puffing across the Sound of Bute for the Garroch Head on her way to Glasgow. A pitch-black night, not even a star to be seen, and Sunny Jim at the wheel had occasionally a feeling that the Cumbrae Light for which he steered was floating about in space, detached from everything like a fire-balloon that winked every thirty seconds at the sheer delight of being free. He whistled softly to himself, and still very cold, in spite of his second waistcoat, envied Macphail the engineer, whom he could see in the grateful warmth of the furnace-door reading a penny novelette. Except for the wheeze and hammer of the engine, the propeller's churning, and the wash of the calm sea at the snub nose of the vessel, the night was absolutely still.

The silence was broken suddenly by sounds of vituperation from the fo'c'sle: the angry voices of the Captain and the mate, and a moment later they were on deck pushing a figure aft in front of them. 'Sling us up a lamp, Macphail, to see what iss't we have a haad o' here,' said the Captain hurriedly with a grasp on the stranger's coat-collar, and the engineer produced the light. It shone on a burly foreigner with coal-black hair, a bronze complexion, and a sack of onions [6] to which he clung with desperate tenacity.

4. *A famous trans-Atlantic liner launched from John Brown's Clydebank yard in 1906 for Cunard. The outrage caused by her sinking by a German submarine in May 1915 was one of the factors which brought about the United States' intervention in the First World War.*

5. *A passage or entry leading from the street to the rear of a tenement property.*

6. *Each year large numbers of Breton 'onion Johnnies' came on their bicycles to various parts of Britain selling strings of onions from door to door. Such travelling salesmen would have been perfectly familiar to Para and his crew and the obvious identification would have been made but for the spy hysteria of the Mate, Dougie.*

'Got him in Dougie's bunk, sound sleepin',' explained the Captain breathlessly, with the tone of an entomologist who has found a surprising moth. 'I saw him dandering aboot Loch Ranza in the mornin'. A stowaway! He wants to steal a trip to Gleska.'

'I'll bate ye he's gaun to the Scottish Exhibeetion,'[7] said Sunny Jim. 'We'll be there in time, but his onions'll gang wrang on him afore we get to Bowlin'. Whit dae they ca' ye for your Christian name, McCallum?'

'Onions,' replied the stranger. 'Cheap onions. No Ingles.'

'Oh, come aff it! We're no' such neds as to think that ony man could hae a Christian name like Onions,' said Sunny Jim. 'Try again, and tell us it's Clarence.'

'And what iss't your wantin' on my boat?' asked Para Handy sternly.

The foreigner looked from one to the other of them with large pathetic eyes from under a broad Basque bonnet. 'Onions. Cheap onions,' he repeated, extracting a bunch of them hastily from the bag. 'Two bob. Onions.'

'Gie the chap a chance,' said Sunny Jim ironically. 'Maybe he gie'd his ticket up to the purser comin' in.'

'He hasna a word o' English in his heid,' said Dougie. 'There's something at the bottom o't; stop you, and you'll see! It's no' for his health he's traivellin' aboot Arran wi' a bag o' onions, and hidin' himsel' on board a Christian boat. I'll wudger that he's Cherman.'

'It's no a German kep he's wearin' onyway,' said Macphail, with the confidence of a man who has travelled extensively and observed.

'That's a disguise,' said Dougie, no less confidently. 'You can see for yoursel' he hass even washed himsel'. Try him wi' a bit of the Cherman lingo, Macphail, and you'll see the start he'll get.'

Macphail, whose boast had always been that he could converse with fluency in any language used in any port in either hemisphere, cleared his throat and hesitatingly said, 'Parly voo francis?'

'Onions. Cheap onions,' agreeably replied the stranger.

'Francis! Francis! parly voo?' repeated the engineer, testily and loudly, as if the man were deaf.

'Maybe his name's no' Francis,' suggested Sunny Jim. 'Try him wi' Will Helm, or Alphonso; there's lots o' them no' called Francis.'

'He understands me fine, I can see by his eye,' said the engineer, determined to preserve his reputation as a linguist. 'But, man! he's cunnin'.'

7. *A large scale international exhibition was held in Glasgow in 1911*

142

'It's the wrong shup he hass come to if he thinks he iss cunnin' enough for us!' said the Captain firmly. 'It's the jyle in Greenock that we'll clap him in for breakin' on board of a well-known steamboat and spoilin' Dougald's bunk wi' onions.'

The stowaway sat nonchalantly down on a bucket, produced a knife and a hunk of bread, and proceeded to make a meal of it with onions. Immediately the crew was constituted into a court-martial, and treated the presence of their captive as if he were a deaf-mute or a harmless species of gorilla.

'What wass I tellin' you, Captain, at the very meenute I saw his feet stickin' oot o' my bunk?' inquired the mate. 'The country's overrun wi' Chermans. I wass readin' yonder that there's two hunder and fifty thousand o' them in Brutain.'

'What a lot!' said Para Handy. 'I never set eyes on wan o' them to my knowledge. What are they like, the silly duvvles?'

'They're chust like men that would be sellin' onions,' said Dougie. 'Lerge, big, heavy fellows like oor frien' here; and they never say nothing too nobody. You've seen hundreds o' them though you maybe didna ken. They're Chermans that plays the bands on the river steamers.'[8]

'Are they? are they?' said Para Handy with surprise; 'I always thought yon chaps wass riveters, or brass feenishers, that chust made a chump on board the boat wi' their instruments when she was passin' Yoker and the purser's back wass turned.'

'Germans to a man!' said Sunny Jim. 'There's no' a Scotchman among them; ye never saw yin o' them yet the worse o' drink.'

'Ye needna tell me yon chaps playin' awa' on the steamers iss makin' maps,' said Para Handy. 'Their eyes iss aalways glued on their cornucopias.'[9]

'They're goin' aboot ports and forts and battleships drawin' plans,' said the engineer. 'Whit did the Royal Horse Artillery find the ither day at Portsmouth? Yin o' them crawlin' up a gun to mak' a drawin' o' t, and they had to drag him oot by the feet.'

'Chust that!' said Para Handy, regarding their captive with greater interest. 'I can see mysel' noo; he looks desperate like a Cherman. Do you think he wass makin' plans o' the *Vital Spark?*'

8. *See above: No.4 'The Mate's Wife', note 5.*

9. *While the 'Cherman bands' might well have included a cornet, a member of the trumpet family, there is no evidence that their line-up included the cornucopia or horn of plenty.*

'That's whit I was askin' him in German!' said Macphail, 'and ye saw yersel' the suspicious way he never answered.'

'Jum,' said the Captain, taking the wheel himself, 'away like a smert lad and make a cup o' tea for the chap; it's maybe the last he'll ever get if we put him in the jyle[10] in Greenock or in Gleska.'

'Right-oh!' said Sunny Jim, gladly relinquishing the wheel. 'Will I set the table oot in the fore saloon? Ye'l excuse us bein' short o' floral decorations, Francis? Is there onything special ye would like in the way o' black breid or horse-flesh, and I'll order't frae the steward?'

'Onions,' said the stranger.

The foreigner spent the night imprisoned in the hold with the hatches down, and wakened with an excellent appetite for breakfast, while the vessel lay at a wharf on the upper river.

'There's money in't; it's like a salvage,' Dougie said to Para Handy, as they hurried ashore for a policeman.

'I canna see't,' said the Captain dubiously. 'What's the good o' a Cherman? If he wass a neegur bleck, you could sell him to the shows for a swallowin' swords, but I doot that this chap hassna got the right agility.'

'Stop, you!' said the mate with confidence. 'The Government iss desperate keen to get a haad o' them, and here's Mackay the polisman.'

'We have a kind o' a Cherman spy on board,' he informed the constable, who seemed quite uninterested.

'The Sanitary Depairtment iss up in John Street,' said the constable. 'It's not on my bate.' But he consented to come to the *Vital Spark* and see her stowaway.

'Toots, man! he's no' a Cherman, and he's no' a spy,' he informed them at a glance.

'And what iss he then?' asked the Captain.

'I don't ken what he iss, but he's duvvelish like a man that would be sellin' onions,' said Mackay, and on his advice the suspect was released.

It was somewhat later in the day that Dougie missed his silver watch, which had been hanging in the fo'c'sle.

10. *Jail.*

PARA AND THE WAR

The third collection of Para stories 'Hurricane Jack of the *Vital Spark*' is set in a world changed by the Great War. Some of the stories give the crew opportunities to tell highly coloured tales of deeds of daring to innocent 'towerists' after the War.

Other tales afford the opportunity for reflection on the changed ways which the War brought about. We learn of women wearing trousers ('Land Girls'); of the restrictions on the crew's natural instincts brought about by the legislation banning 'treating' in Clydeside pubs (a measure introduced to improve production in the shipyards and munitions works, and not Lloyd George's most popular enactment); of the horror of 'munition ale' a weak wartime brew made, Para surmised on the premises after the last washing-day ('The Mystery Ship'); of the inevitable confusion caused by the government 'tamperin' wi' the time o' day the way God made it' ('Summer-Time on the *Vital Spark*').

However despite the problems of war, with anti-submarine nets across the Clyde and Macphail being called up to join the Scottish Fusiliers (though Sunny Jim in the end goes in his place), the *Vital Spark* sails on its traditional routes and many of the stories could have been written at any point in the saga. Such tales include the splendid 'An Ocean Tragedy' (oddly enough the second time this title was used) which enables Para's vivid imagination to be displayed to best advantage. The only remotely military part of this story is Para's reference to his deck cargo of feather bonnets for the Territorials.

Seemingly unaffected by war is the classic 'Mudges'—perhaps the pick of the entire collection, with its account of the particular horrors of the Tighnabruaich midge—which can bite through corrugated iron roofs; the well-educated Gareloch midges '. . . ye'll see the old ones leadin' roond the young ones, learnin' them the proper grips' and the ferocious midges of Colonsay and their vicious attack on a 'chenuine English towerist'. Perhaps on reflection 'Mudges' is not an entirely un-warlike story!

31   THE LEAP-YEAR BALL

[Our first story from the 1923 collection 'Hurricane Jack of the *Vital Spark*]

SUNNY JIM, back again on one of his periodical short spells of long-shore sailoring, went ashore on Friday morning with a can of milk, and an old potato-sack for bread, and, such is the morning charm of Appin,[1] than he made no attempt to get either of them filled until he reached the inn at Duror. He wasn't a fellow who drank at any time excessively, but, Glasgow-born, he felt always homesick in foreign parts unless he could be, as Para Handy said, 'convenient and adjaacent to a licensed premise.' In a shop beside the inn he got his bread, and he might have got the milk a mile or two nearer Kintallen quay, from which he had come, but a sailor never goes to a farm for milk so long as he can get it at an inn.

'A quart,' he said to the girl at the bar, and pushed the can across the counter. As she measured out and filled his can with ale, he sternly kept an averted eye on a bill on the wall which spoke in the highest terms of Robertson's Sheep Dips.

'What in the world ye ca' this?' he exclaimed, regarding the can's contents with what to an unsophisticated child would look like genuine surprise. 'Michty! what thick cream! If the Gleska coos gave milk like that, the dairies would mak' their fortunes.'

'Was it not beer you wanted?' asked the girl, with sleeves rolled up on a pair of arms worth all the rest of the Venus de Medici, and a roguish eye.

'Nut at all!' said he emphaticlly. 'Milk. What ye sometimes put in tea.'

'Then it's the back of the house you should go to,' said the girl. 'This is not the milk department,' and she was about to empty the can again, but not with unreasonable celerity, lest the customer should maybe change his mind.

'Hold on!' said Sunny Jim, with a grasp at it. 'Seein' as it's there, I'll maybe can make use o't. See's a tumbler, Flora.'

For twenty minutes he leaned upon the counter and fleeted the time delightfully as in the golden world. He said he was off a yacht, and, if not officially, in every other sense the skipper. True, it was not exactly what might be called the yachting season, but the owners of the yacht were whimsical. Incidentally, he referred to his melodeon, and at that the girl declared he was the very man she had been looking for.

'Oh, come aff it, come aff it!' said Sunny Jim, with proper modesty, but

1. *The* Vital Spark *is in distant waters. Duror in Appin lies on Loch Linnhe to the north of Oban.*

yet with an approving glance at his reflection which was in the mirror behind her. 'I'm naething patent, but I'll admit there's no' a cheerier wee chap from here to Ballachulish.'

'Ye would be an awful handy man at a ball,' said the girl, 'with your melodeon. We're having a leap-year dance[2] tonight, and only a pair of pipers. What's a pair of pipers?'

'Two,' said Sunny Jim promptly.

'You're quite mistaken,' replied the girl with equal promptness; 'it's only two till the first reel's by, and then it's a pair o' bauchles no' able to keep their feet. You come with your melodeon, and i'll be your partner.'

He went back to the *Vital Spark* delighted, looked out his Sunday clothes and his melodeon, and chagrined his shipmates hugely by the narrative of his good fortune.

'What's a leap-year baal?' asked Para Handy. 'Iss there a night or two extra in it? No Chrustian baal should last over the week-end.'

'It's a baal where the women hae a' the say,' explained Macphail, the engineer, whose knowledge was encyclopaedic.

'Iss that it?' said Para Handy. 'It's chust like bein' at home! It's me that's gled I'm not invited. Take you something wise-like wi' ye in your pocket, Jum; I wouldna be in their reverence.'[3]

'I would like to see it,' said Dougie. 'Does the lady come in a kind of a cab for you?'

'It's only young chaps that's invited,' explained Sunny Jim, with brutal candour.

The Captain looked at him reproachfully. 'You shouldna say the like o' that to Dougie,' he remonstrated. 'Dougie's no' that terrible old.'

'I was sayin' it to baith o' you,' said Sunny Jim. 'It's no' a mother's meetin' this, it's dancin'.'

'There's no man in the shippin' tred wi' more agility than mysel',' declared the indignant skipper. 'I can stot[4] through the middle o' a dance like a tuppeny kahoochy ball. Dougie himsel' 'l tell you!'

'Yes, I've often seen you stottin',' agreed the mate, with great solemnity. Para Handy looked at him with some suspicion but he

2. *This, and an earlier story (not included in this edition) 'Leap Year on the* Vital Spark', *hinge on leap-year celebrations and may acordingly be dated to 1916.*

3. *Indebted to them.*

4. *Bounce. Stotting (in the sense that Dougie uses it in the next paragraph) can also mean being in an intoxicated condition.*

presented every appearance of a man with no intention to say anything offensive.

'You havena an extra collar and a bit o' a stud on you?' was the astonishing inquiry made by Dougie less than twenty minutes after Sunny Jim had departed for the Duror ball. 'I wass thinkin' to mysel' we might take a turn along the road to look at the life and gaiety.'

'Dougie, you're beyond redemption!' said Para Handy. 'A married man and nine or ten o' a family, and there you're up to all diversions like a young one!'

'I wassna going by the door o' the ball,' the mate exclaimed indignantly. 'You aye take me up wrong.'

'Oh, ye should baith gang,' suggested the engineer, with malicious irony. 'A couple o' fine young chaps! Gie the girls o' Appin a treat. Never let on you're mairried. They'll never suspect as lang's ye keep on your bonnets.'

'I think mysel' we should go Dougie, and we might be able to buy a penny novelle for Macphail to read on Sunday,' said the Captain. 'Anything fresh about Lady Audley, Macphail?'

Macphail ignored the innuendo. 'Noo's your chance,' he proceeded. 'Everything's done for ye by the fair sect: a lady MC to find ye pairtners; the women themsel's comin' up to see if your programme's full, and askin, every noo and then if ye care for a gless o' clairet-cup on draught. I wouldna say but ye would be better to hae a fan and a Shetland shawl to put ower your heads when you're comin' hame; everything's reversed at a leap-year ball.'

He would simply have goaded the Captain into going if the Captain had not made up his mind as soon as Dougie himself that he was going in any case.

'Two-and-six apiece for the tickets,' said the man at the door when Para Handy and his mate came drifting out of the bar and made a tentative attempt at slipping in unostentatiously.

'Not for a leap-year dance, Johnny,' said the Captain mildly. 'Everything is left to the ladies.'

'Except the payin'; that's ass usual,' said the doorkeeper, and the Captain and his mate regretfully paid for entrance. The room was crowded, and the masculine predominated to the extent that it looked as if every lady had provided herself with half-a-dozen partners that she might be assured of sufficient dancing. One of the pipers had already lapsed into the state so picturesquely anticipated by the girl whom Sunny Jim called Flora; the other leant on a window-sill, and looked with Celtic ferocity and disdain upon Sunny Jim, who was playing his melodeon for the Flowers of Edinburgh.

'You're playin' tip-top, Jum. I never heard you better,' said the Captain to him at the first interval; and the musician was so pleased that he introduced his shipmates to Flora.

'We're no' here for the baal at aal, at aal, but chust to put bye the time,' the Captain explained to her. 'I see you're no' slack for pairtners.'

'Not at present,' she replied; 'but just you wait till the supper's bye and you'll see a bonny difference.'

She was right, too. The masculine did certainly not predominate after midnight, being otherwise engaged. The fact that Flora was a wallflower seemed to distress Sunny Jim, who would gladly now relinquish his office of musician to the piper.

'That's a charmin' gyurl, and a desperate sober piper,' said the Captain to his mate, who spent most of the time looking for what he called the 'commytee', and had finally discovered, if not the thing itself, at all events what was as good. 'Jum's doin' capital at the melodeon, and it would be a peety if the piper took his job.'

They took out the piper, and by half an hour's intelligent administration of the committee's refreshments rendered him quite incapable of contributing any further music to the dancers.

'Now that's aal right,' said the Captain cheerfully returning to the hall. 'A piper's aal right if ye take him the proper way, but I never saw one wi' a more durable heid than yon fellow. Man, Jum's doin' capital! Hasn't he got the touch! It's a peety he's such a strong musician, for, noo that the pipers hass lost their reeds, he's likely to be kept at it till the feenish.'

'Lost their reeds!' said Dougie.

'Chust that!' replied the Captain calmly. 'I took them oot o' their drones, and I have them in my pocket. It's everyman for himsel' in Duror of Appin. You and me'll dance with Flora.'

Nothing could exceed the obvious annoyance of Sunny Jim when he saw his shipmates dance with Flora to the music of his own providing. Again and again he glanced with impatient expectancy towards the door for the relieving piper.

'The piper'll be back in a jiffy, Jum,' said Para Handy to him, sweeping past with Flora in a polka or a schottische. 'He's chust oot at the back takin' a drop of lemonade, and said he would be in immediately.'

'You're doing magnificent,' he said, coming round to the musician again as Dougie took the floor with Flora for the Haymakers. 'Ye put me awful in mind of yon chap, Paddy Roosky,[5] him that's namely for the fiddle. Man, if ye chust had a velvet jecket! Flora says she never danced to more becomin' music.'

'That's a' richt,' said the disgusted musician; 'but I'm gettin' fed up wi' playin' awa' here. I cam' here for dancin', and I wish the piper would look slippy.'

'He'll be in in wan meenute,' said Para Handy, with the utmost confidence, turning over the pipe reeds in his trousers pocket. 'It's a reel next time, Jum; you might have given us "Monymusk" and "Alister wears a cock't bonnet"; I'm engaged for it to Flora.'

Dance after dance went on, and, of course, there was no relieving piper. The melodeonist was sustained by the flattering comments of his shipmates on his playing and an occasional smile from Flora, who was that kind of girl who didn't care whom she danced with so long as she got dancing.

'Special request from Flora — would ye give us "The Full-Rigged Ship" the next one? That's a topper,' said the Captain to him. Or, 'Compliments of Flora, and would you mind the Garaka Waltz and Circassian Circle for the next, Jum? She says she likes my style o' dancin'.'

'I wish to goodness I'd never learned to play a bloomin' note,' said Sunny Jim.

But he played without cessation till the ball was ended, the fickle Flora dancing more often with his shipmates than with anybody else.

As they took the road to Kiltallen quay at six o'clock in the morning, Para Handy took some chanter reeds from his pocket and handed them to Sunny Jim.

'Ye should learn the pipes, Jum' he remarked. 'They're no' so sore on you as a melodeon. Man, but she wass a lovely dancer, Flora! Chust sublime! Am I no' right, Dougie?'

'A fair gazelle! The steps o' her!' said the mate poetically.

'And we were pretty smert on oor feet oursel's,' said Para Handy. 'It doesna do to have aal your agility in your fingers.'

---

5. *Para's familiarity with the world of classical music is somewhat suspect. Paddy Roosky (or somewhat more conventionally Ignace Jan Paderewski (1860-1941)) was a well-known Polish piano virtuoso, who became Prime Minister of Poland in 1919. He was, however, not in the least 'namely for the fiddle'.*

32 'MUDGES' [1]

'By Chove! but they're bad the night!' said Dougie, running a grimy paw across his forehead.

'Perfectly ferocious!' said Para Handy, slapping his neck. 'This fair beats Bowmore,[2] and Bowmore iss namely for its mudges. I never saw the brutes more desperate! You would actually think they were whustlin' on wan another, cryin', "Here's a clean sailor, and he hasna a collar on; gather about, boys!'

'Oh, criftens!' whimpered Sunny Jim, in agony, dabbing his face incessantly with what looked suspiciously like a dish-cloth; 'I've see'd midges afore this, but they never had spurs on their feet afore. Yah-h-h! I wish I was back in Gleska! They can say what they like aboot the Clyde, but anywhere above Bowlin' I'll guarantee ye'll no' be eaten alive. If they found a midge in Gleska, they would put it in the Kelvingrove Museum.'

Macphail, his face well lubricated, came up from among the engines, and jeered. 'Midges never bothered me,' said he contemptuously. 'If ye had been wi' me on the West Coast o' Africa, and felt the mosquitoes, it wouldna be aboot a wheen[3] o' gnats ye would mak' a sang. 'It's a' a hallucination aboot midges; I can only speak aboot them the way I find them, and they never did me ony harm. Perhaps it's no midges that's botherin' ye efter a'.'

'Perhaps no',' said Para Handy, with great acidity. 'Perhaps it's hummin'-birds, but the effect iss chust the same. Ye'll read in the Scruptures yonder aboot the ant goin' for the sluggard,[4] but the ant iss a perfect chentleman compared wi' the mudge. And from aal I ever heard o' the mosquito, it'll no' stab ye behind your back withoot a word o' warnin'. Look at them on Dougie's face — quite black! Ye would never think it wass the Sunday.'

It was certainly pretty bad at the quay of Arrochar. With the evening air had come out, as it seemed, the midges of all the Highlands. They hung in

1. *Midges. 'Almost everywhere in the Highlands below 2000 feet there are vast hordes of midges (Chironomidae) which affect the movements of mammalian life, including man, to a considerable extent. . . . The place of the midge in human ecology is such that a greatly increased tourist industry to the West Highlands could be encouraged if the midge could be controlled.' F.Fraser Darling & J. Morton Boyd: 'The Highlands and Islands'. London, Collins, 1964.*

2. *Port on the island of Islay.*

3. *An unspecified large number.*

4. *Proverbs Ch.6 v.6 'Go to the ant, thou sluggard; consider her ways and be wise:'*

clouds above the *Vital Spark,* and battened gluttonously on her distracted crew.

'When I was at the mooth o' the Congo River —' began the engineer; but Para Handy throttled the reminiscence.

'The Congo's no' to be compared wi' the West o' Scotland when ye come to insects,' said Para Handy. 'There's places here that's chust deplorable whenever the weather's the least bit warm. Look at Tighnabruaich! — they're that bad there, they'll bite their way through corrugated iron roofs to get at ye! Take Clynder, again, or any other place in the Gareloch, and ye'll see the old ones leadin' roond the young ones, learnin' them the proper grips. There iss a special kind of mudge in Dervaig, in the Isle of Mull, that hass aal the points o' a Poltalloch terrier,[5] even to the black nose and the cocked lugs, and sits up and barks at you. I wass once gatherin' cockles in Colonsay —'

'I could be daein' wi' some cockles,' sid Sunny Jim. 'I aye feel like a cockle when it comes near the Gleska Fair.'

'The best cockles in the country iss in Colonsay,' said the Captain. 'But the people in Colonsay iss that slow they canna catch them. I wass wance gatherin' cockles there, and the mudges were that large and bold, I had to throw stones at them.'

'It was a pity ye hadna a gun,' remarked Macphail, with sarcasm.

'A gun would be no' much wi' the mudges of Colonsay', replied the Captain; 'nothing would discourage yon fellows but a blast o' dynamite. What wass there on the island at the time but a chenuine English towerist, wi' a capital red kilt, and, man! but he was green! He was that green, the coos of Colonsay would go mooin' along the road efter him, thinkin' he wass gress. He wass wan of them English chentlemen that'll be drinkin' chinger-beer on all occasions, even when they're dry, and him bein' English, he had seen next to nothing aal his days till he took the boat from West Loch Tarbert. The first night on the island he went oot in his kilt, and came back in half an oor to the inns wi' his legs fair peetiful! There iss nothing that the mudges likes to see among them better than an English towerist with a kilt: the very tops wass eaten off his stockin's.'

'That's a fair streetcher, Peter!' exclaimed the incredulous engineer.

'It's as true ass I'm tellin' you,' said Para Handy. 'Anyone in Colonsay will tell you. He had wan of them names shed in the middle like

5. *An ancestor of the West Highland White Terrier, the Poltalloch terrier had a whitish coat, black-tipped ears and often a black nose. Poltalloch is in the heartland of the 'Para country', near Crinan.*

Fitz-Gerald or Seton-Kerr; that'll prove it to ye. When he came in to the inns wi' his legs chust fair beyond redemption, he didna even know the cause of it.

"'It's the chinger-beer that's comin' oot on you," says John Macdermott, that had the inns at the time. "There iss not a thing you can drink that iss more deliteerious in Colonsay. Nobody takes it here."

"'And what in all the world do they take?" said the English chentleman.

"'The water o' the mountain well," said John, "and whiles a drop of wholesome Brutish spirits. There's some that doesna care for water."

'But the English chentleman was eccentric, and nothing would do for him to drink but chinger, an' they took him doon to a shed where the fishermen were barkin' nets,[6] and they got him to bark his legs wi' catechu.[7] If it's green he wass before, he wass now ass brown's a trammel net.[8] But it never made a bit o' odds to the mudges oot in Colonsay! I tell you they're no' slack!'

'They're no' slack here neithers!' wailed Sunny Jim whose face was fairly wealed by the assailants. 'Oh, michty! I think we would be faur better ashore.'

'Not a bit!' said Dougie, furiously puffing a pipe of the strongest tobacco, in whose fumes the midges appeared to take the most exquisite pleasure. There's no' a place ashore where ye could take shelter from them — it being Sunday,' he significantly added.

'I'm gaun ashore anyway,' said Macphail, removing all superfluous lubricant from his countenance with a piece of waste. 'It wouldna be midges that would keep me lollin' aboot this auld hooker on a fine nicht. If ye had some experience o' mosquitoes! Them's the chaps for ye. It's mosquitoes that spreads the malaria fever.'

They watched him go jauntily up the quay, accompanied by a cloud of insects which seemed to be of the impression that he was leading them to an even better feeding-ground than the *Vital Spark*. He had hardly gone a hundred yards when he turned and came hurriedly back, beating the air.

'Holy frost!' he exclaimed, jumping on deck, 'I never felt midges like that in a' my days afore; they're in billions o' billions!'

'Tut, tut!' said Para Handy. 'Ye're surely getting awfu' turmid, Macphail. You that's so weel acquent wi' them mosquitoes! If I was a

6. *Coating nets with preservative.*

7. *A resin derived from a species of Acacia used in tanning and dyeing.*

8. *A type of fishing net.*

153

trevelled man like you, I wouldna be bate wi' a wheen o' Hielan' mudges. They're no' in't anyway. Chust imagination! Chust a hallucination! Ye mind ye told us?'

'There's no hallucination aboot them chaps,' said Macphail, smacking himself viciously.

'Nut at all!' said Sunny Jim. 'Nut at all! If there's ony hallucination aboot them, they have it sherpened. G-r-r-r! It's cruel; that's whit it is; fair cruel!'

'I promised I would go and see Macrae the nicht,' said the engineer. 'But it's no' safe to gang up that quay. This is yin o' the times I wish I was a smoker; that tobacco o' yours, Dougie, would shairly fricht awa' the midges,'

'Not wan bit of it!' said Dougie peevishly, rubbing the back of his neck, on which his tormentors were thickly clustered. 'I'm beginning to think mysel' they're partial to tobacco; it maybe stimulates the appetite. My! aren't they the brutes! Look at them on Jim!

With a howl of anguish Sunny Jim dashed down the fo'c'sle hatch, the back of his coat pulled over his ears.

'Is there naething at a' a chap could dae to his face to keep them aff?' asked the engineer, still solicitous about his promised visit to Macrae.

'Some people'll be sayin' paraffine-oil iss a good thing,' suggested the Captain. 'But that's only for Ro'sa' mudges; I'm thinkin' the Arrochar mudges would maybe consuder paraffine a trate. And I've heard o' others tryin' whisky — I mean rubbed on ootside. I never had enough to experiment wi't mysel'. Forbye, there's none.'

'I wadna care to gang up to Macrae's on a Sunday smellin' o' either paraffine-oil or whisky,' said Macphail.

'Of course no'!' said Para Handy. 'What wass I thinkin' of? Macrae's sister wouldna like it,' and he winked broadly at Dougie. 'Ye'll be takin' a bit of a daunder wi' her efter the church goes in. Give her my best respects, will ye? A fine, big bouncin' gyurl! A splendid form!'

'You shut up!' said Macphail to his commander, blushing, 'I think I'll gie my face anither syne wi' plenty o' saft soap for it, and mak' a breenge across to Macrae's afore the effect wears aff.'

He dragged a pail over the water-beaker, half filled it with water, added a generous proportion of soft soap from a tin can, and proceeded to wash himself without taking off his coat.

'Ye needna mind to keep on your kep,' said the Captain, grimacing to Dougie. 'Mima'll no' see ye. He's been callin' on Macrae a score o' times, Dougie, and the sister hasna found oot yet he's bald. Mercy on us! Did ye ever in your life see such mudges!'

'I'm past speakin' aboot them!' said the mate, with hopeless resignation. 'What iss he keepin' on his bonnet for?'

'He's that bald that unless he keeps it on when he's washin' his face he doesna know where to stop,' said Para Handy. 'The want o' the hair's an aawful depredaation!'

But even these drastic measures failed to render Macphail inviolate from the attack of the insects, whose prowess he had underestimated. For the second time he came running back from the head of the quay pursued by them, to be greeted afresh by the irony of his Captain.

'Isn't it annoyin'?' said the Captain, with fallacious sympathy. 'Mima will be weary waitin' on ye. If there wass a druggist's open, you might get something in a bottle to rub on. Or if it wassna the Sabbath, ye might get a can o' syrup in the grocer's.

'Syrup?' said the engineer inquiringly, and Para Handy slyly kicked Dougie on the shin.

'There's nothin' better for keepin' awa' the mudges, he explained. 'Ye rub it on your face and leave it on. It's a peety we havena any syrup on the boat.'

'Sunny Jim had a tin o' syrup last night at his tea,' said the engineer hopefully.

'But it must be the chenuine golden syrup,' said Para Handy. 'No other kind'll do.'

Sunny Jim was routed out from under the blankets in his bunk to produce syrup, which proved to be of the requisite golden character, as Para Handy knew very well it was, and five minutes later Macphail, with a shining countenance, went up the quay a third time attended by midges in greater myriads than ever. This time he beat no retreat.

'Stop you!' said Para Handy. 'When Mima Macrae comes to the door, she'll think it's no' an enchineer she has to caal on her, but a fly cemetery.'[9]

---

9. *A popular type of cake, a pastry slice made with dried fruit, is commonly known in Scotland as a 'fly cemetery' from the supposed resemblance of the filling of currants, raisins, etc. to an accumulation of dead insects.*

33 AN OCEAN TRAGEDY

GEORGE IV, being a sovereign of imagination, was so much impressed by stories of Waterloo that he began to say he had been there himself, and had taken part in it. He brought so much imagination to the narrative that he ended by believing it — an interesting example of the strange psychology of the liar. Quite as remarkable is the case of Para Handy, whose singular delusion of Sunday fortnight last is the subject of much hilarity now among seaman of the minor coasting-trade.

The first of the storm on Saturday night found the *Vital Spark* off Toward[1] on her way up-channel, timber-laden, and without a single light, for Sunny Jim, who had been sent ashore for oil at Tarbert, had brought back a jar of beer instead by an error that might naturally occur with any honest seaman.

When the lights of other ships were showing dangerously close the mate stood at the bow and lit matches, which, of course, were blown out instantly.

'It's not what might be called a cheneral illumination,' he remarked, 'but it's an imitation of the Gantock Light, and it no' workin' proper, and you'll see them big fellows will give us plenty o' elbow-room.'

Thanks to the matches and a bar of iron which Macphail had hung up on the lever of the steam-whistle, so that it lamented ceaselessly through the tempest like a soul in pain, the *Vital Spark* escaped collision, and some time after midnight got into Cardwell Bay,[2] with nothing lost except the jar, a bucket, and the mate's sou'-wester.

'A dirty night! It's us that iss weel out of it,' said Para Handy gratefully, when he had got his anchor down.

The storm was at its worst when the Captain went ashore on Sunday[3] to get the train for Glasgow on a visit to his wife, the farther progress of his vessel up the river for another day at least being obviously impossible. It was only then he realized that he had weathered one of the great gales that

1. *Toward Point, on the Cowal Peninsula south of Dunoon.*

2. *Part of Gourock Bay*

3. *Compare—'With those who have been born and bred upon the coast there is nearly always to be found a curious illusion that the greatest storms invariably take place on Sundays.' Neil Munro The Looker-On p.137. This piece first appeared in the News on Monday 6th November 1911, the day after the fiercest storm for twenty years. The Para story inspired by the storm appeared a fortnight later on 20th November.*

make history. At Gourock pierhead[4] shellbacks[5] of experience swore they had never seen the like of it; there were solemn bodings about the fate of vessels that had to face it. Para Handy, as a ship's commander who had struggled through it, found himself regarded as a hero, and was plied with the most flattering inquiries. On any other day the homage of the shellbacks might have aroused suspicion, but its disinterested nature could not be called in question, seeing all the public-houses were shut.

'Never saw anything like it in aal my born days,' he said. 'I wass the length wan time of puttin' off my sluppers and windin' up my watch for the Day of Chudgement. Wan moment the boat wass up in the air like a flyin'-machine, and the next she wass scrapin' the cockles off the bottom o' the deep. Mountains high — chust mountains high! And no' wee mountains either, but the very bens of Skye! The seas was wearin' through us fore and aft like yon mysterious river rides that used to be at the Scenic Exhibeetion, and the noise o' the cups and saucers clatterin' doon below was terrible, terrible! If Dougie wass here he could tell you.'

'A dog's life, boys!' said the shellbacks. 'He would be ill-advised that would sell a farm and go to sea. Anything carried away, Captain?'

A jar, a bucket, and a sou'wester seemed too trivial a loss for such a great occasion. Para Handy hurriedly sketched a vision of bursting hatches, shuttered bulwarks, a mate with a broken leg, and himself for hours lashed to the wheel.

It was annoying to find that these experiences were not regarded by the shellbacks as impressive. They seemed to think that nothing short of tragedy would do justice to a storm of such unusual magnitude.

Para Handy got into the train, and found himself in the company of some Paisley people, who seemed as proud of the superior nature of the storm as if they had themselves arranged it.

'Nothing like it in history, chentlemen,' said Para Handy, after borrowing a match. 'It's me that should ken, for I wass in it, ten mortal hours, battlin' wi' the tempest. A small boat carried away and a cargo o' feather bonnets on the deck we were carryin' for the Territorials. My boat was shaved clean doon to the water-line till she looked like wan o' them timber-ponds at the Port[6] — not an article left standin'! A crank-shaft

4. *Gourock railway station, built by the Caledonian Railway Coy. opened to passenger traffic in June 1889.*

5. *Old or experienced sailors*

6. *Along the Renfrewshire side of the Clyde, including the Port Glasgow area (the 'Port' of Para's description) were a series of timberponds, areas of shallow water enclosed by wooden palisades where logs lay seasoning.*

smashed on us, and the helm wass jammed. The enchineer — a man Macphail belongin' to Motherwell — had a couple of ribs stove in, and the mate got a pair o' broken legs; at least there's wan o' them broken and the other's a nesty stave. I kept her on her coorse mysel' for five hours, and the watter up to my very muddle. Every sea was smashin' on me, but I never mudged. My George, no! Macfarlane never mudged!'

The Paisley passengers were intensely moved, and produced a consoling bottle.

'Best respects, chentlemen!' said Para Handy. 'It's me that would give a lot for the like o' that at three o'clock this mornin'. I'm sittin' here withoot a rag but what I have on me. A fine sea-kist, split new, wi' fancy grommets, all my clothes, my whole month's wages, and presents for the wife in't — it's lyin' yonder somewhere off Innellan . . . It's a terrible thing the sea.'

At Greenock two other passengers came into the compartment, brimful of admiration for a storm they seemed to think peculiarly British in its devastating character — a kind of vindication of the island's imperial pride.

'They've naething like it on the Continent,' said one of them. 'They're a' richt there wi' their volcanic eruptions and earthquakes and the like, but when it comes to the naitural elements —' he was incapable of expressing exactly what he thought of British dominance in respect of the natural elements.

'Here's a poor chap that was oot in his ship in the worst o't,' said the Paisly passengers. Para Handy ducked his head in polite acknowledgement of the newcomers' flattering scrutiny, and was induced to repeat his story, to which he added some fresh sensational details.

He gave a vivid picture of the *Vital Spark* wallowing helplessly on the very edge of the Gantock rocks; of the fallen mast beating against the vesel's side and driving holes in her; of the funnel flying through the air, with cases of feather bonnets ('cost ten pounds apiece, chentlemen, to the War Office'); of Sunny Jim incessantly toiling at the pump; the engineer unconscious and delirious; himself, tenacious and unconquered, at the wheel, lashed to it with innumerable strands of the best Manilla cordage.

'I have seen storms in every part of the world,' he said; 'I have even seen yon terrible monsoons that's namely oot about Australia, but never in my born life did I come through what I came through last night.'

Another application of the consolatory bottle seemed to brighten his recollection of details.

'I had a lot o' sky-rockets,' he explained. 'We always have them on the best ships, and I fired them off wi' the wan hand, holdin' the wheel wi' the other. Signals o' distress, chentlemen. Some use cannons, but I aye believe in the sky-rockets; you can both hear and see them. It makes a dufference.'

'I kent a chap that did that for a day and a nicht aff the Mull o' Kintyre, and it never brung oot a single lifeboat,' said one of the Paisley men.

It was obvious to Para Handy that his tragedy of the sea was pitched on too low a key to stir some people; he breathed deeply and shook a melancholy head.

'You'll never get lifeboats when you want them, chentlemen,' he remarked. 'They keep them aal laid up in Gleska for them Lifeboat Setturday processions. But it was too late for the lifeboat anyway for the *Fital Spark*. The smertest boat in the tred, too.'

'Good Lord! She didna sink?' said the Paisley men, unprepared for such a *dénouement*.

'Nothing above the water at three o'clock this mornin' but the winch,' said the Captain. 'We managed to make our way ashore on a couple o' herrin'-boxes . . . Poor Macphail! A great man for perusin' them novelles, but still-and-on a fellow of much agility. The very last words he said when he heaved his breath — and him, poor sowl, withoot a word o' Gaelic in his heid — waas, "There's nobody can say but what you did your duty, Peter." That wass me.'

'Do ye mean say he was drooned?' asked the Paisley men with genuine emotion.

'Not drooned,' said Para Handy; 'he simply passed away.'

'Isn't that deplorable! And whit came over the mate?'

'His name wass Dougald,' said the Captain sadly, 'a native of Lochaline, and ass cheery a man ass ever you met across a dram. Chust that very mornin' he said to me, "The 5th of November, Peter; this hass been a terrible New Year, and the next wan will be on us in a chiffy."'

By the time the consolatory bottle was finished the loss of the *Vital Spark* had assumed the importance of the loss of the *Royal George*,[7] and the Paisley men suggested that the obvious thing to do was to start a small subscription for the sole survivor.

For a moment the conscience-stricken Captain hesitated. He had scarcely thought his story quite so moving, but a moment of reflection found him quite incapable of recalling what was true and what imaginary of the tale he told them. With seven-and-sixpence in his pocket, wrung by

7. *The* Royal George, *a hundred gun ship of the line, capsized while under repair at Spithead in 1772 with the loss of 900 lives.*

the charm of pure imagination from his fellow-passengers, he arrived in Glasgow and went home.

He went in with a haggard countenance.

'What's the matter wi' ye, Peter?' asked his wife.

'Desperate news for you, Mery. Desperate news! The *Fital Spark* is sunk.'

'As long's the crew o' her are right that doesna matter,' said the plucky little woman.

'Every mortal man o' them drooned except mysel',' said Para Handy, and the tears streaming down his cheeks. 'Nothing but her winch above the water. They died like Brutain's hardy sons.'

'And what are you doing here?' said his indignant wife. 'As lang as the winch is standin' there ye should be on her. Call yoursel' a sailor and a Hielan' man!'

For a moment he was staggered.

'Perhaps there's no' a word o' truth in it,' he suggested. 'Maybe the thing's exaggerated. Anything could hapen in such a desperate storm.'

'Whether it's exaggerated or no' ye'll go back the night and stick beside the boat. I'll make a cup o' tea and boil an egg for ye. A bonny-like thing for me to go up and tell Dougie's wife her husband's deid and my man snug at home at a tousy tea! . . . Forbye, they'll maybe salve the boat, and she'll be needin' a captain.'

With a train that left the Central some hours later Para Handy returned in great anxiety to Gourock. The tragedy of his imagination was now exceedingly real to him. He took a boat and rowed out to the *Vital Spark,* which he was astonished to see intact at anchor, not a feature of her changed.

Dougie was on deck to receive him.

'Holy smoke, Dougie, iss that yoursel'?' the Captain asked incredulusly. 'What way are you keepin'?'

'Fine,' said Dougie. 'What way's the mistress?'

The Captain seized him by the arm and felt it carefully.

'Chust yoursel', Dougie, and nobody else. It's me that's prood to see you. I hope there's nothing wrong wi' your legs?'

'Not a drop,' said Dougie.

'And what way's Macphail?' inquired the Captain anxiously.

'He's in his bed wi' "Lady Audley" [8],' said the mate.

'Still deleerious?' said the Captain with apprehension.

8. *Not a case for concern or reflection on the engineer's morals—Lady Audley is of course the heroine of one of Macphail's beloved 'penny novelles'.*

'The duvvle was never anything else,' said Dougie.

'Did we lose anything in the storm last night?' asked Para Handy.

'A jar, and a bucket, and your own sou'-wester,' answered Dougie.

'My Chove!' said Para Handy, much relieved. 'Things iss terribly exaggerated up in Gleska.'

Gourock Pier *Argyll & Bute District Libraries*

34 INITIATION

THERE was absolutely nothing to do to pass the time till six o'clock, and Hurricane Jack, whose capacity for sleep under any circumstances and at any hour of the day or night was the envy of his shipmates, stretched himself out on the hatches with a fragment of tarpaulin over him. In about two seconds he was apparently dreaming of old days in the China clipper trade, and giving a most realistic imitation of a regular snorter of a gale off the Ramariz.

'There's some people iss born lucky,' remarked the Captain pathetically. 'Jeck could go to sleep inside a pair o' bagpipes and a man playin' on them. It's the innocent mind o' him.'

'It's no' the innocent mind o' him, whatever it iss,' retorted Dougie with some acidity. 'It's chust fair laziness; he canna be bothered standin' up and keepin' his eyes open. Ye're chust spoilin' him. That's what I'm tellin' ye!

Para Handy flushed with annoyance. 'Ye think I'm slack,' he remarked; 'but I'm firm enough wi' Jeck when there's any occasion. I sent him pretty smert for the milk this mornin', and him wantin' me to go mysel'. I let him see who wass skipper on this boat. A body would think you wass brocht up on a man-o'-war; ye would like to see me aye bullyin' the fellow. There's no herm in Jeck Maclachlan, and there iss not a nimbler sailor under the cope and canopy,[1] in any shape or form!'

Dougie made no reply. He sat on an upturned bucket sewing a patch on the salient part of a pair of trousers with a sail-maker's needle.

'There ye are!' resumed the Captain. 'Darnin' away at your clothes and them beyond redemption! Ye're losin' all taste o' yoursel'; what ye're needin's new garments aalthegither. Could ye no', for goodness sake, buy a web o' homespun somewhere in the islands and make a bargain wi' a tyler?'

'Tylers!' exclaimed Dougie. 'I might as weel put mysel' in the hands o' Rob Roy Macgregor![2] They're askin' £6. 10s. the suit, and it's extra for the trooser linin'.'

Para Handy was staggered. He had bought no clothes himself since his

1. *Popular poetic terms for the over-arching vault of heaven. Compare with "This most excellent Canopy the Ayre . . ." Shakespeare: Hamlet Act 2, Sc.2. or "Without any other cover than the cope of heaven" Tobias Smollett: Humphrey Clinker.*

2. *Rob Roy Macgregor (1671-1734) was a notorious Highland outlaw and freebooter. He figures prominently in the novel Rob Roy by Sir Walter Scott.*

marriage, and had failed to observe the extraordinary elevation in the cost of men's apparel.

'Holy Frost!' he cried. 'That's a rent in itsel'! If that's the way o't, keep you on plyin' the needle, Dougie. It's terrible the price o' everything nooadays. I think, mysel', it's a sign o' something goin' to happen. It runs in my mind there wass something aboot that in the Book o' Revelations. I only paid £2 10s. for a capital pilot suit the year I joined the Rechabites.'

The mate suspended his sewing, and looked up suspiciously at the skipper.

'It's the first time ever I heard ye were in the Rechabites,' he remarked significantly. 'Hoo long were ye in them?'

'Nearly a week,' replied Para Handy, 'and I came oot o' them wi' flyin' colours at the start o' the Tarbert Fair. It was aal a mistake, Dougie; the tyler at the time in Tarbert took advantage o' me. A fisherman by the name o' Colin Macleod from Minard and me wass very chief [2] at that time, and he wass a Freemason. He would aye be givin' grips and makin' signs to ye. By his way o't a sailor that had the grip could trevel the world and find good company wherever he went, even if he didna ken the language.

'Colin was high up in the Freemasons; when he had all his medals and brooches on he looked like a champion Hielan' dancer.

'He was keen, keen for me to join the craft and be a reg'lar chentleman, and at last I thocht to mysel' it would be a great advantage.

'"Where will I join?" I asked him.

'"Ye'll join in Tarbert; there's no' a lodge in the realm o' Scotland more complete," says Colin. "And the first thing ye'll do, ye'll go up and see my cousin the tyler; he'll gie ye a lot o' preliminary instruction."

'The very next time I wass in Tarbert I went to the tyler right enough for the preluminaries.

'"I wass thinkin' o' joinin' the Lodge," I says to him, "and Colin Macleod iss tellin' me ye're in a poseetion to gie me a lot o' tips to start wi'. What clothes will I need the night o' the meetin'?"

'He wass a big soft-lookin' lump o' a man, the tyler, wi' a smell o' singed cloth aboot him, and the front o' his jecket aal stuck over wi' pins; and I'll assure ye he gave me the he'rty welcome.

'"Ye couldna come to a better quarter!" he says to me, "and it'll no' take me long to put ye through your facin's. There's a Lodge on Friday, and by that time ye'll be perfect. Of course, ye'll have the proper garments?"

'"What kind o' garments?" says I. "I have nothing at aal but what I'm

3. *Very friendly*

wearin'; my Sabbath clothes iss all in Gleska."

"'Tut! tut!' says he, quite vexed. 'Ye couldna get into a Lodge wi' clothes like that; ye'll need a wise-like suit if ye're to join the brethren in Tarbert. But I can put ye right in half a jiffy."

'He jumped the counter like a hare, made a grab at a pile o' cloth that wass behind me, hauled oot a web o' blue-pilot stuff, and slapped it on a chair.

"There's the very ticket for ye!" he says, triumphant. 'Wi' a suit o' that ye'll be the perfect chentleman!'

'I wassna needin clothes at aal, but before I could open my mouth to say Jeck Robe'son he had the tape on me. Noo there's something aboot a tyler's tape that aye puts me in a commotion, and I lose my wits.

'He had the measure o' my chest in the time ye wud gut a herrin', and wass roond at my back before I could turn mysel' to see what he wass up to. "Forty-two; twenty-three," he bawls, and puts it in a ledger.

'He wass on to me again wi' his tape, like a flash o' lightnin'; pulled the jecket nearly off my back and took the length o' my waistcoat, and oh! my goodness, but he smelt o' Harris tweed, and it damp, singein'!

"'Hold up your arm!" says he, and he took the sleeve-length wi' a flourish, and aal the time he wass tellin' me what a capital Lodge wass the Tarbert one, and aboot the staunchness o' the brethren.

"'Ye'll find us a lot o' cheery chaps," he says; "there's often singin'. But ye'll have to come at first deid sober, for they're duvvelish particular."

'By this time he wass doon aboot my legs, and the tape wass whippin' aal aboot me like an Irish halyard. I wass that vexed I had entered his shop withoot a dram, for if I had a dram it wasna a tyler's tape that Peter Macfarlane would flinch for.

'By the time he had aal my dimensions, fore and aft, in his wee bit ledger, I wass in a perspiration, and I didna care if he measured me for a lady's dolman.[4]

"'Do ye need to do this every time?" I asked him, put aboot tremendous.

"'Do what?" says the tyler.

"'Go over me wi' a tape," says I.

"'Not at aal," he says, quite he'rty, laughin'. "It's only for the first initiation that ye need consider your appearance. Later on, no doot, ye'll need regalia, and I can put ye richt there too."

"'It's only the first degree I'm wantin' to start wi'," I says to him; "I want to see if my health'll stand it."

4. *A type of cloak with large cape-like sleeves.*

"'Tach!' says the tyler; "ye'll get aal that's goin' at the wan go-off. There's no shilly-shallyin' aboot oor Lodge in Tarbert. Come up to the shop tomorrow, and I'll gie the first fit on."

'I went to him next day in the afternoon, and ye never in all your life saw such a performance! The tape wass nothin' to't! He put on me bits o' jeckets and weskits tacked thegither, withoot any sign o' sleeves or buttons on them; filled his mooth to the brim wi' pins, and started jaggin' them into me.

"'Mind it's only the first degree!' I cried to him. "Ye maybe think I'm strong, but I'm no' that strong!"

'Him bein' full o' pins, I couldna make oot wan word he wass mumblin', but I gaithered he wass tellin' me something aboot the grips and password. And then he fair lost his heid! He took a lump of chalk and began to make a regular cod o' my jecket and weskit.

"'Stop! Stop!' I cries to him. "I wass aye kind o' dubious aboot Freemasons, and if I'm to wear a parapharnalia o' this kind, all made up o' patches pinned thegither, and chalked all o'er like the start o' a game o' peever, I'm no goin' to join!"

'The tyler gave a start. "My goodness!" he says, "it's no' the Freemasons ye were wantin' to join?"

"That wass my intention," I told him. "And Colin said his cousin the tyler in Tarbert wass the very man to help me. That's the way I'm here."

"'Isn't that chust deplorable!' says the tyler, scratchin' his heid. "Ye're in the wrong shop aalthegither! The tyler o' the Mason's Lodge in Tarbert's another man aalthegither, that stands at the door o' his Lodge to get the password. I'm no' a Mason at aal; I'm the treasurer o' the Rechabites."

"'The Rechabites!' says I, horror-struck. "Aren't they teetotal?"

"'Strict!' he says. "Ye canna get over that — to start wi'. And ye're chust ass good ass a full-blown Rechabite noo, for I've given ye aal I ken in the way o' secrets."

'So that's the way I wass a Rechabite, Dougie, I wass staunch to the brethren for seven days, and then I fair put an end to't. I never went near their Lodge, but the suit o' clothes came doon to the vessel for me, wi' a wee boy for the money. It wass £2 10s., and I have the weskit yet.'

'£2 10s. And aal that sport!' said Dougie ruefully. 'them wass the happy days!'

35 AN IDEAL JOB

As the *Vital Spark,* outrageously belching sparks and cinders from fuel eked out by wood purloined some days before from a cargo of pit-props, swept round the point of Row,[1] Para Handy gazed with wonder and admiration at the Gareloch, full of idle ships.[2]

'My word!' he exclaimed, 'isn't that the splendid sight! Puts ye in mind o' a Royal Review!'

'I don't see onything Royal aboot it,' growled the misanthropic engineer, Macphail. 'It's a sign o' the terrible times we're livin' in. If there was freights for them boats, they wouldna be there, but dashin' roond the Horn and makin' work for people.'

'Of course! Of course! You must aye be contrary,' said the Captain peevishly. 'Nothing on earth'll please you; ye're that parteecular. It's the way they chenerally make work for people that spoils ships for me. I like them best when they're at their moorin's. What more could ye want in the way o' a bonny spectacle than the sight o' aal them gallant vessels and them no' sailin'?'

Macphail snorted as he ducked his head and withdrew among his engines. 'There's enough bonny spectacles on board this boat to do me for my lifetime,' he said in a parting shot before he disappeared.

Para Handy turned sadly to the mate. 'Macphail must aye have the last word,' he said. 'The man's no' worth payin' heed to. Greasin' bits o' enchines every day o' your life makes ye awful' coorse. I'm sure that's a fine sight, them ships, Dougie?' There must be nearly half a hundred there, and no' a lum reekin'.'

'They're no bad,' answered Dougie cautiously. 'But some o' them's terrible in need o' a stroke o' paint. Will there be anybody stayin' on them?'

'Ye may depend on that!' the Captain assured him. 'There iss a man or two in cherge o' every vessel, and maybe a wife and femily. The British Mercantile Marine iss no' leavin' ocean liners lyin' aboot Garelochheid wi' nobody watchin' them. A chentleman's life! It would suit me fine, instead o' plowterin' up and doon Loch Fyne wi' coals and timber. Did I no' tell ye the way Hurricane Jeck spent a twelvemonth on a boat laid up

---

1. *Row (a village on the Gareloch) was officially re-named Rhu in 1927 to avoid mispronunciation and to get closer to the original Gaelic source of the village's name—rudha—a promontory.*

2. *In the depressed trade conditions which prevailed after the First World War the sheltered waters of the Gareloch were used as moorings for surplus shipping.*

in the Gareloch when tred was dull aboot twenty years ago?'

'Ye did not!' said Dougie.

'She wass a great big whupper o' a barquenteen[3] caaled the *Jean and Mary,* wi' a caibin the size o' a Wee Free Church, and fitted up like a pleesure yacht. She had even a pianna.'

'God bless me!' gasped the mate, half incredulous.

'Jeck had the influence in them days, and he got the job to look efter her in the Gareloch till the times got better. The times wass good enough the way they were for Jeck, wance he had his dunnage on board. "Never had a job to bate it!" he says; "I wouldna swap wi' the polisman in the Kelvingrove Museum."[4]

'I would think he would be lonely,' said Dougie dubiously. 'A great big boat wi' nobody but yoursel' in it at night would be awfu' eerie.'

The Captain laughed uproariously. 'Eerie!' he repeated. 'There iss nothin' eerie any place where Hurricane Jeck iss; he had the time o' his life in the *Jean and Mary.*

'Wance they got their boat clapped doon in the Gareloch and Jeck in charge o' her, the chentlemen in Cardiff she belonged to forgot aal aboot her. At least they never bothered Jeck except wi' a postal-order every now and then for wages.

'The wages wassna desperate big, and Jeck put his brains in steep to think oot some contrivance for makin' a wee bit extra money.

'It came near the Gleska Fair, and there wassna a but-and-ben in Garelochheid that wassna packed wi' ludgers like a herrin'-firkin. When Jeck would be ashore for paraffin-oil or anything, he would aye be comin' on poor craturs wantin' ludgin's, so he filled the *Jean and Mary* wi' a fine selection. For three or four weeks the barquenteen wass like an hotel, or wan o' them hydropathics.[5] Jeck swithered aboot puttin' up a sign to save him from goin' ashore to look for customers.

'Ye never saw a ship like it in all your life! It wass hung from end to end wi' washin's aal July, and Jeck gave ludgin's free to a man wi' a cornacopia that he played on the deck from mornin' till night.'

'Wass it no' a terrible risk?' asked Dougie.

3. *Barquentine—a sailing vessel with square sails on the fore-mast and the main and mizzen rigged with fore and aft sails.*

4. *Glasgow's Museum and Art Gallery in Kelvingrove Park was opened in 1901.*

5. *A spa hotel specialising in the treatment of minor disorders by one form or another of water treatment—sea bathing, medicinal springs etc. One of the Clyde's leading establishments of this type—Shandon Hydro on Garelochside—was in sight of Para as he tells this tale.*

'No risk o' any kind, at aal, at aal. The owners wass in Cardiff spendin' their money, and they never saw the Gareloch in their lifes but in the map. Jeck kent he wass doin' a noble work for the health o' the community — far better than the Fresh Air Fortnight![6]

'When the Fair wass feenished, and his ludgers went away, I'll assure ye they left a bonny penny wi' the landlord o' the *Jean and Mary*. He thocht the season wass done, but it wasna a week till he wass throng[7] again wi' a lot o' genteel young divinity students that came from Edinburgh wi' a banjo.

'"Gie me a bottle o' beer and a banjo playin', and it's wonderful the way the time slips by," says Jeck. He learned them a lot o' sailor songs like "Ranza Boys!" and "Rollin' doon to Rio", and the folk in Garelochheid that couldna get their night's sleep came oot at last in a fury to the ship and asked him who she belonged to.

'"Ye can look Lloyd's List," says Jeck to them, quite the chentleman, "and ye'll see the name o' the owners. But she's under charter wi' a man that's aal for high jinks, and the cheneral hilarity — and his name iss John Maclachlan. If there iss any o' ye needin' ludgin's, say the word and I'll put past a fine wee caibin for ye, wi' a southern exposure."

'They went away wi' their heids in the air. "I ken what's wrong wi' them," says Jeck. "Oh, man! If I chust had the spirit licence!"

'That wass his only tribulation: he had ass good an hotel below his feet ass any in the country, but he daurna open a bar.

'The summer slipped by like a night at a weddin'; the cornacopia man went back to his work, but Jeck fell in wi' an old pianna-tuner that could play the pianna like a minister's wife, and aal the autumn Jeck gave smokin' concerts on the *Jean and Mary,* where all the folk in cherge o' the other vessels paid sixpence apiece and got a lot o' pleasure.

'"If I had chust a brass band!' says Jeck, "and a wise-like[8] man I could trust for a purser, I would run moonlight trips. But it would be an awful bother liftin' the anchor; perhaps I'm better the way I am; there's no' the responsibility wi' a boat at moorin's."

'But the time he showed the best agility wass when he had a weddin' on the ship. The mate o' another vessel wass gettin' spliced in his good-mother's[9] hoose in Clynder, where there wassna room for dancin'.

6. *A movement to give city dwellers holidays by the sea or in the countryside.*

7. *Full, busy.*

8. *Sensible, reliable*

9. *Mother-in-law*

'Jeck hired the *Jean and Mary* to them; the company came oot in boats from aal ends o' the Gareloch, wi' a couple o' pipers and that many roasted hens ye couldna get eggs in the shire for months efter it. They kept it up till the followin' efternoon, wi' the anchor lamp still burnin' and aal the buntin' in the vessel flyin'.

'A well-put-on[10] young Englishman from Cardiff came alongside in a motor-lench in an awfu' fury, and bawled at Jeck what aal this carry-on meant. There wass sixty people on board if there wass a dozen.

'"Some frien's o' my own," says Jeck, quite nimble, and aye the chentleman. "I have chust come into a lot o' money, and I'm givin' them a trate."

'But that was the last o' Jeck's command in the *Jean and Mary;* the poor duvvle had to go back and work at sailorin'.'

10. *Well spoken, of good manner*

Shandon Hydro *Authors' Collection*

36 PARA HANDY'S SHIPWRECK

(This previously uncollected story was published in the Glasgow Evening News of 21st August 1905)

ONE of Para Handy's favourite stories is about the wreck of the *Sarah*. It is only to be got from him under certain circumstances. First of all the audience must be congenial; then Dougie must be present for purposes of corroboration, and the Captain himself must be in trum. If you show the slightest glint of incredulity in your eye as the story progresses, the narrator will miss out all the most thrilling details, and give you a story with no more excitement in it than there is in a temperance tract; if Dougie is absent the Captain's story completely fails him; if he is not in trum, he prefers to borrow your tobacco and listen quietly to any lies you yourself may have to tell.

I never heard him tell it with such dramatic effect as on the night they put in the cries for Dougie's wedding.[1] Two very innocent drovers were in the company at the Ferry House, and at nine o'clock Para Handy buttoned his pea-jacket tightly, tied a firm knot in his muffler, and announced that he was in the best of trum.

'I'm feeling chust sublime,' he said. 'If I had my old ear for music I would sing aalmost anything, and then you would see the fun. It's not drink, mind ye; it's chust youth. Youth! youth! man, there's nothing like it! If I wass on board of the boat I would put the peter on that silly cratur, Macphail the enchineer.'

'You have as fine an ear for music ass any man ever I heard at your time of life,' said Dougie.

'Well, I'll alloo I'm consudered not bad at times, but I have wan of them ears that comes and goes, and this iss one of the nights I would be going off the tune here and there.'

'It's me that would like fine to hear you singin', Captain Macfarlane,' said one of the drovers. 'If another dram wass — eh — what do you say yoursel?'

'Och, there's no occasion for another dram,' said the Captain. 'I'm no' needin' it; but maybe Dougie would be none the worse, poor fellow.'

Dougie graciously signified his acceptance of the drover's further hospitality on behalf of the company, and then proposed that, as the

1. *Made arrangements for calling the banns for Dougie's wedding. The attentive reader will have noted that in Chapter 16 'Dougie's Family' the mate had ten children. The time of this re-telling of the tale of Para's shipwreck must therefore be set at an early period.*

Captain was not prepared to sing, he might tell about the wreck of the *Sarah*.

'It's not every place I would tell it,' said the Captain, clearing his throat, 'for I'm wan of these men that hates to be taalkin' and braggin' aboot themsels, but seein' we're all together, and it's a solemn occaasion for Dougie, I'll tell you.'

'It wass a kind of gabbard I had called the *Sarah* before I got command of the *Fital Spark;* she wass the smertest gabbard ever you saw, built by a man of the name of Macnab, and his with one eye, that's mairried to a cousin of my own. Here rale name was the *Sarah Elizabeth,* but och! we chust called her *Sarah* for a short cut. Dougie and me wass six years on her together, were we no', Dougie?'

'We were that!' said Dougie. 'Go on, Captain, fine, Captain!'

'I canna stand bouncin', but as sure as daith the *Sarah,* when she had a wind on her quarter and her sails mended, would go like a man-o'-war, and I made passages between Bowling and Campbeltown that was the taalk of the country at the time. We were that smert with her there wass some notion of us carryin' the mails; you'll mind of that yoursel', Dougie?'

'Fine,' said Dougie.

'The place where the *Sarah* wass wrecked wass up aboot Loch Hourn way;[2] if I had wan of them maps I would show you. We were carryin' a cargo of salt for the herrin'-curers. It wass blowin' a gale of wind that would frighten any man but a Macfarlane, but I kept her at it in a way that was chust sublime. I forgot to tell you I wass the smertest sailor sailin' oot of the Clyde at that time, though I wass only three-over-twenty years of age. Isn't that so, Dougie?'

'Quite right, Captain.' said the mate, promptly. 'You were splendid aalthegither.'

'It would be aboot half-past ten o'clock in the forenoon, or maybe twenty-five meenutes to eleven, when Dougie, my friend here, wass struck on the small of the back by a nasty kind of a wave, and washed over the side. He made a duvvle of a splash! There wass me left in the boat mysel', for there wass only the two of us to start with; I can tell you it wass a sore predicament! I put her nose roond into the wind and brought here to, and threw off my boots and jumped over the side efter Dougie. I forgot to tell you I was acknowledged the best swimmer in Scotland at that time.

2. *A sea loch on the northern side of the Knoydart peninsula. This was presumably one of the times Para was '. . . wrecked in the North at places that's not on the maps' ('A Night Alarm').*

I think you'll guarantee that, Dougie.?'

'Ay, or England, too," said Dougie. 'You could sweem like a dooker.' [3]

'Well, Dougie would be two-and-a-half miles, or maybe two and three-quarters, from the *Sarah* when I came up to him, and aal he had to keep him afloat wass a match-box. He wass ass wet ass he could be. I kept him up with the wan hand, and swam with the other back to the vessel, and he wass that exhausted he had to go to his bunk. But that wass only the start of our tribulation, for when we were sweemin' back to the *Sarah* she gybed hersel', and the mast wass blown over the side. I wassna mich put aboot for the mast, for it wass an old wan anyway, but she wass driftin' ass hard ass she wass able in the direction of some terrible rocks yonder, and if she wass to be saved at aal I had to do something pretty slippy. I forgot to tell you I wass the strongest man in Britain at the time. Donald Dinnie [4] wass chust a child to me; are ye hearin', Dougie?'

'You were a terrible strong man,' said the mate, 'Sampson wass a mudge compared to you.'

'Well, I wouldna say Sampson mysel',' said the Captain with modest depreciation: 'I hate bouncin', so I'll no' say I wass stronger than Sampson, but I wass pretty vigorous. So what did I do but get oot the oars and keep her from going ashore on the rocks. I wass rowing yonder the best part of six oors, and got her past the worst of it, but wan of the oars broke, and she went on a rock that wass not marked on the chart aboot sixty fathoms from the shore. She gave an awful dunt!

'I forgot to tell you that at that time I wass the best jumper in the world. I wass truly sublime ass a jumper; Dougie 'll tell you himsel'.'

'There was nothing to touch you at the jumping,' said the mate. 'It's my belief you could have jumped higher than Ben Nevis at that time.'

'Not at aal, not at aal; but I wass a bonny jumper at the same time. So what did I do when the *Sarah* went aground on the rock, but jump ashore with my mate here on my back, and we were not two meenutes off the *Sarah* when she went to bits no' the size of waistcoat buttons. So there wass me and Dougie in a strange country where they havena the right Gaalic at aal, and live on nothing but herring and potatoes. We lost everything; aal except tuppence ha'penny I had in my pocket. It wass the day of a cattle market. "If we have oor wits aboot us, we'll maybe make something to be going on with" I said to Dougie, and we made a bit of a plan. If Dougie had his trump it wouldna be so bad, but the trump went

3. *Tautology. Swim like a swimmer.*

4. *A noted Highland strong man.*

doon in the vessel, and so we had to fall back on mysel'. I wass to go into the middle of the market and sing, and Dougie was to come up in a wee while among the crood, the same ass if he didn't know me, and put roond the hat for a collection for a poor ship-wrecked mariner, efter puttin' in the tuppence ha'penny I had. Wassn't that the way of it, Dougie?'

'That wass exactly the way of it, ass sure ass I'm sittin' here,' said Dougie. 'You're doin' beautiful, Peter, go on.'

'I forgot to tell you that there wass not a better singer in Scotland than myself at that time. I wass namely everywhere. When I started singin' at the market, the folk gathered roond in hundreds and listened. I wass doing tremendously fine at

> "Up the back and doon the muddle,
> te deedlum, te tadalum."

but there wass no word of Dougie wi' the hat and the tuppence ha'penny. At last I saw him comin' oot of the inn, and I at that time I knew I wass a stupid man to trust him with so mich money aal at once. But fortunately he did not spend more than the tuppence; he came up and stood wi' the crood, and efter a while he said, ass smert ass you like. "Is that you, Peter Macfarlane?" "It's me, sure enough," said I, "who are you?" "Do you no' mind your old shipmate?" said Dougie, winkin' at me. Then we shook hands, and Dougie told the crood that I wass the Captain of an Atlantic liner that went ashore, and the only wan saved. "Let us make up a collection for the poor fellow," said Dougie, "and I'll be the first to put something in the hat." Wi' that he put the ha'penny and the tin top of a lemonade bottle in his kep, and went roond the crood wavin' the kep in front of them. There wassna a man there that didn't come to the rescue of the poor shipwrecked mariner, and some of them, thinking the tin top of a lemonade bottle wass a shillin', put in silver and — hoo mich did we make, Dougie?'

'Hoo mich do you say yoursel'?' asked Dougie, cautiously.

'Fifteen shillings and eightpence.'

'That wass it exactly,' agreed the mate. 'It was a good thing I had the sense to go into the inn, for it wass there I got the tin top of the lemonade bottle.'

'It wass salt wass the cargo,' said Para Handy, reflectively. 'I sometimes think I have it in my system yet; I'm that thirsty.'

37 THE *VITAL SPARK'S* COLLISION

(This previously uncollected story appeared in the Glasgow Evening News of 20th November 1905)

THERE was a haze, that almost amounted to a fog, on the river. The long, unending wharves on either hand, and the crane-jibs, derricks, masts, hulls, and sheds looked as if they had all been painted in various tones of smoky grey. From the vague banks came the sound of rivet-hammers, the rumble of wheels, and once, quite distinctly, from out of the reek that hung about a tar-boiler at the foot of Finnieston Street, The Tar, who was standing by the Captain at the wheel, heard a gigantic voice cry, 'Awa', or I'll put my finger in your e'e!'

'We'll soon be home noo,' said The Tar. 'Man, it's a fine cheery place, Gleska, too.'

Para Handy gave one knock as a signal to the engineer, then bent down and said to that functionary, who was really within whispering distance, 'I think you can give her another kick ahead, Macphail, there iss nothing in the road, and I would be aawful sorry if you lost the wife's tea-pairty.'

'There's no' another kick in the old tinker,' said Macphail, viciously, wiping his perspiring brow with a wad of waste, and spitting on his engine.

'"Tinker" 's no' a name for any boat under my cherge.' said Para Handy, indignantly 'She's the smertest in the tred, if she chust had a wise-like enchineer that kent the way to coax her.'

As he spoke there loomed out of the haze ahead the big hull of a steamer going much more cautiously in the same direction up the river, and threatening to block, for a little at least, the progress of the *Vital Spark*.

'Keep on her port and you'll clear her,' said Dougie.

'Do you think yoursel' we can risk it?' asked the Captain, dubiously.

'We'll chust have to risk it,' said Dougie, 'if Macphail's going to get to his wife's tea-pairty this night.'

And so the accident happened.

The case was tried at the Marine Court[1] before River Bailie Weir, the charge being that, on the afternoon of the 3rd inst., Captain Peter Macfarlane, of the steam lighter *Vital Spark,* had, between Lancefield Quay and Anderston Quay, while going in the same direction as the

1. *Scottish burghs and cities appointed senior councillors to the office of Bailie to act as local magistrates. In addition to the other local courts Glasgow also had a River Bailie Court sitting daily in McAlpine Street to try minor cases originating on the river.*

steamer *Dolores,* of Havre, and at a greater rate of speed (1) caused the *Vital Spark* to pass the *Dolores* on the port side; (2) failed to signal to the master of the Dolores that he was approaching; and (3) attempting to cause the *Vital Spark* to pass the *Dolores* before she had given the *Vital Spark* sufficient room to pass.

The Captain of the French boat, who gave his evidence through an interpreter, said, in the course of it, that the *Vital Spark* was steering very badly.

Para Handy, the accused, interrupting — 'Holy smoke! and me at the wheel mysel'!'

Witness, resuming, testified that he saw the skipper of the *Vital Spark* once leaving the wheel altogether, with the result that she took a sheer away and could not recover herself. More than once the crew of the *Vital Spark* shouted to him, and gesticulated wildly, but he did not understand their language. So far as he could guess, it was not English.

Para Handy, violently — 'Not English! There iss not a man on my boat that hass wan word of any other language than English.'

The Magistrate — 'with a Scotch or Hielan' accent, of course.' (Laughter.)

Para Handy — 'Hielan' or Scotch is chust a kind of superior English.'

Witness went on to say he told accused to come up on the starboard side, and he would try to make room for him to pass. But the *Vital Spark* came in on the port quarter and kept there, boring in under the *Dolores'* belting, with the result that there was a collision, and the *Dolores* had a plate bent, some stanchions broken at the aft port gangway, and pipes damaged.

The first witness for the defence was the mate of the *Vital Spark,* Dugald Cameron.[2] On being requested by the agent for the defence to tell his story in his own way, Dougie coughed, cleared his throat, took in his waist-belt two holes, rubbed the palms of his hands together till they creaked, and said — 'We were comin' up the ruver at a medium speed, not

---

2. *A salutary reminder to us not to trust the court reporting of even such a reliable journal as the Glasgow Evening News. All our other evidence points to Dougie's surname being Campbell. His testimonial to the benefits of the Petroloid Lotion (see 'The Hair Lotion' in the complete edition) is signed 'Dougald Campbell'. This is not however the only vexed issue affecting Dougie. Just like his skipper his very place of birth is a mystery. In 'A New Cook' (no. 22 in this edition) he is described as 'a Cowal laad' while later in 'An Ocean Tragedy' (no. 33 in this edition) Para tells his audience that the mate was 'a native of Lochaline'. Lochaline is in Morvern on the Sound of Mull and many miles north of Cowal - the area around Dunoon on the Firth of Clyde.*

sayin' a word to nobody, and the Captain himsel' at the wheel, when the French boat backed doon on the top of us and twisted two of her port-holes against the bow of oor boat. I cried to the French boat —'

The Magistrate — 'What did you cry?'

Witness, addressing the accused — 'What wass it I cried, Peter?' (Laughter.)

The Magistrate — 'You must answer the question yourself.'

Witness — 'Ay, but the Captain helped me at the crying.'

The Magistrate — 'Never mind if he did; what did you shout to the *Dolores*?'

Witness, bashfully — 'I would rather no' say; would it do to write it on a piece of paper?' (Renewed Laughter.)

The witness, being allowed to proceed without the question being pressed, said — 'The *Fital Spark* at the time wass going with consuderable caaution, not more than three knots or maybe two-and-a-half, and everybody on board keeping a smert look-oot.'

The Assessor — 'Did the Captain leave the wheel at any time before the collision occurred?'

'Iss it Peter? Not him! he wass doing splendid where he wass if it wass a Chrustian he had to do with in front and not wan of them foreigners.'

'Did you blow your steam-whistle?'

'Hoo could we blow the steam-whustle and the Captain's jecket hanging on it? Forby, there wass no time, and Macphail needed aal his steam for his enchines anyway. There wass not mich need for a whustle wi' The Tar and me roarin' to them to keep oot of the road. Anybody would think to see them that they owned the whole ruver, and them makin' a collusion without wan word of English! They chust made a breenge down[3] on the top of us.'

Colin Dewar (The Tar) was the next witness for the defence. He deponed[4] that he was standing close beside the Captain of the *Vital Spark* when the collision took place. The *Vital Spark* was hardly more than moving when the French steamer suddenly canted to the left and came up against the lighter's bow. She gave a good hard knock. Just before the collision the Captain and the Mate cried out to the Frenchman.

The Magistrate — 'What did they cry?'

3. *A precipitate descent*

4. *Declared on oath. One may compare The Tar's not entirely credible evidence with Munro's comment in 'The Clyde, River and Firth' about 'the loyal lies of witnesses in a Board of Trade examination'!*

The Tar, after a moment's deliberation, 'I don't mind very weel, but I think they said, "Please, will you kindly let us past?"'

The accused — 'Holy smoke! Colin; the chentleman that's tryin' the case will think we're a bonny lot of dummies.' (Great laughter.)

The Tar, continuing his evidence, said there was a sort of fog on the river at the time. They had come up from Greenock to Govan at a pretty fair speed for the *Vital Spark* because the engineer was particularly anxious to get to his house early in the evening, but above Govan they slowed down a good deal. Could not say what rate of speed they were travelling at when the collision with the *Dolores* took place. Might be six knots; on the other hand, might be two or three knots; he was not a good counter, and would not care to say.

The Assessor — 'Do you know the rules of the road at sea?'

The Tar — 'What? Beg pardon, eh?'

'The rules of the road at sea?'

'It wass not in my depairtment; I am only the cook and the winch; the Captain and Dougie attends to the fancy work. It iss likely the Captain would know aal aboot rules of the road.'

The accused — 'I ken them fine —
Green to green and rud to rud
Perfect safety, go aheid!'

The Magistrate — 'Did the Captain of the *Dolores* say anything when he found you butting under his port quarter?'

The Tar — 'He jabbered away at us in French the same ass if we were pickpockets.'

'You're sure it wass French?'

'Yes. If you don't believe me, ask Captain Macfarlane. And the very worst kind of French.'

The Assessor, humorously — 'What was he saying in French?'

The Tar — 'Excuse me. I wouldna care to repeat it. I wish you saw his jaw workin'.'

The charge was found not proven,[5] and the accused was dismissed from the bar. The crew of the *Vital Spark* promptly transferred themselves to a judicious hostelry near the police court, and in the gratitude of his heart at having got off so well, Para Handy sent The Tar out to look for the French captain to invite him to a little mild refreshment. 'There's no doot,' he said, 'we damaged the poor fellow's boat, and it wass aal Macphail's fault

---

5. *The unique third verdict available to Scottish courts in addition to guilty or not guilty.*

177

cracking on speed to get up in time for his wife's tea-pairty.'

Macphail, looking very uncomfortable in his Sunday shore clothes, sat gloomily apart, contemplating a schooner[6] of beer.

'It's a waarnin',' said Para Handy, 'no' to obleege onybody, far less an enchineer. All the thanks I got for it wass a bad name for the *Vital Spark*. She'll be namely aal over the country now.'

'Ach! it wass only a — Frenchman!' said Dougie.

'Still and on a Frenchman hass feelings chust the same's a Chrustian,' said Para Handy. 'Here's The Tar; did you get him, Colin?'

'He wouldna come,' said The Tar, 'and I gave him every chance in the two languages.'

'Weel, chust let him stay then,' said the Captain. 'Seein' we got Macphail into Gleska in time for his wife's tea-pairty at the cost o' the *Vital Spark*'s good name in the shipping world, perhaps he'll stand us another round.'

Whereupon Macphail looked gloomier than ever, and contributed the first remark he had made all day.

'To the mischief wi' the tea-pairty,' he said. 'I was a' wrang wi' the date; it's no till the next Friday, and when I got hame my wife was in the middle o' a washin'.'

6. *A tall glass containing 14 fluid ounces.*

38   PARA HANDY AT THE POLL

[This previously uncollected story was published in the Glasgow Evening Newson 22nd January 1906, just days after the General Election which had resulted in the victory of the Liberal party.]

A LIBERAL canvasser, with two red rosettes displayed on his person, came down Campbeltown quay on Friday, and, with a hand on the standing rigging of the *Vital Spark,* asked which of the men on deck was Captain Macfarlane.

'That's the man they put the blame on,' said the engineer Macphail, nastily, indicating Para Handy. 'Him wi' the no' waistcoat.'

'What is't? asked the Captain, suspiciously eyeing the canvasser. His mother's house in Campbeltown[1] was rented in his name, and he was a voter, though the fact had quite escaped his attention. He feared the man with the rosettes might be a committee man of some sort wanting to sell him tickets for a soiree, concert, and ball. Either that or a Rechabite looking for converts.

'I called about this election,'[2] said the canvasser, stepping on board. 'Bein' a kind of a workin' man, I suppose ye'll be votin' for Mr. Dobbie?'[3]

'Holy smoke! have I a vote?' asked the Captain, really surprised.

'You have that,' said the canvasser, briskly producing a burgh register, and sticking the stump of a lead pencil in his mouth preparatory to chalking off another adherent of Campbell-Bannerman's[4] and the cause of Chinese liberty.[5] 'Here's your name as nate's ye like in print — "Peter

---

1. *Universal male suffrage was only introduced with the 1918 Reform Act. The provisions of the series of Reform Acts culminating in that of 1884/5 had extended the franchise to a widening range of householders. Thus Para enjoyed the right to vote by virtue of his mother's home being registered in his name.*

2. *Campbeltown, with Ayr, Irvine, Inveraray and Oban, formed part of the Ayr Burghs constituency. The total electorate, on the limited franchise of the period, was only 8031.*

3. *Joseph Dobbie, an Edinburgh solicitor, was, in reality as well as in Munro's story, the Liberal candidate at the 1906 election. He was indeed the sitting member, having won the seat at a by-election in 1904*

4. *Henry Campbell-Bannerman (1836-1908). Leader of the Liberal Party from 1899. Prime Minister from 1905 until his death. Knighted 1895. Born Glasgow. M.P. for Stirling Burghs 1868-1908.*

5. *The importation of indentured Chinese labourers into the Transvaal and the support of Balfour's Conservative Government for this measure was bitterly attacked by Campbell-Bannerman and the Liberals as the reintroduction of slavery.*

179

Macfarlane, Master Mariner''; and it's lucky you're here anyway the day
to put in your vote.'

'I'm not much of a scholar,' said Para Handy, scratching his head.

'It doesn't matter about that,' said the canvasser. It's only a scart[6] of a
pen, but the whole nation's dependin' on't. It's men like you that's the —
the bulwark of Britain —'

'You said it!' agreed the Captain: 'Brutain's hardy son; that's what I
am; am I no', Dougie?'

'Whiles,' said Dougie.

'Ye ken what the Tories is?' proceeded the canvasser. 'Livin' on the fat
o' the land, and the like o' you and me workin' our fingers to the bone for
poor wages.'

'I wouldna say but you're right,' said the Captain.

'Then you're game for Dobbie?' said the canvasser, who was in a hurry
to secure his man and pass on to the next on his list.

'Dobbie,' said Para Handy, reflectively, 'what way do you spell
Dobbie?'

'Ye don't need to spell anything about it,' said the canvasser. 'It's spelt
for ye; all ye have to do is to put a cross in front of his name, and that'll be
all right.'

'What's the other man's name?' asked the Captain.

'It's — it's — let me seen now — oh, aye, it's Younger,[7] but, tuts! never
mind about him; he's all wrong. He's no use for the life o' you and me. If
it's a cheap loaf[8] ye're wantin' and a Bill for the workin'-man,[9] stick you
by Dobbie.'

'That's what I wass thinkin' myself.' said Para Handy, who as a matter
of fact had never given the subject a thought before this moment. 'He's
no' in the shuppin' tred, Dobbie, is he? There's a lot o' new boats buildin'
that skippers iss needed for.'

---

6. *Scratch*

7. *George Younger was in fact the Conservative candidate for Ayr Burghs in 1906
and had stood against Dobbie at the 1904 by-election—when he had been defeated
by the narrow margin of 44 votes.*

8. *Free trade, protectionism and the implications of these policies on prices were
key issues in the 1906 election.*

9. *Universal manhood suffrage. Campbell-Bannerman was also an advocate of
female suffrage.*

'No,' said the canvasser, diplomatically, 'but he's acquent wi' a whole jing-bang o' folk that's in that line. It's the Liberal party that keeps up the shippin' trade. Give the chaps a chance; the Tories had it all their own way for nearly twenty years. And now what are they wantin'? To put up the price o' the loaf —'

'It's seldom I eat it,' said Para Handy; 'there's nothing like cakes and scones.'

'It comes to the same thing,' explained the canvasser. 'They're goin' to tax everything. And just look at what they're doin' wi' the poor Chinese.'

'What are they doin' wi' them?' asked Para Handy, who was determined even at the last hour to bring himself up-to-date with modern politics.

'They're — they're — makin' them work in mines and wash themselves every day,' said the canvasser, who was a little vague on this subject himself.

'Holy smoke!' said Para Handy. 'Poor craturs!'

'That'll be all right, then; you'll come up to the pollin'-booth as soon as ye can and back Dobbie?' said the canvasser, shutting up his book.

'Och, aye,' said the Captain; 'it's likely I'll take a daunder up and do the best I can.'

The Liberal canvasser had scarcely reached the end of the quay when a gentleman with two blue rosettes swung himself airily on board the *Vital Spark* and button-holed her commander.

'Captain Macfarlane,' he said, 'I knew you at once. There's no smarter steam lighter comes into Campbeltown Loch than the *Vital Spark,* and I always said it. How's trade? Well, well, I suppose you're for the old flag. Not a word! Pity about Dobbie, isn't it? — nice sort of chap and all that, but on the wrong side, the wrong side completely. You're for Younger, of course?' And he whipped out his section of the register, and damped his stump of lead pencil as the other man had done.

'Younger,' said the Captain, agreeably. 'A smert chap. I hope and trust he's keepin' fine?'

'Oh, splendid!' said the canvasser. 'Game for anything. By Jove, and he'll show them! Just fancy the way the Liberals are letting trade slip out of our hands! They say, you know, that what we import has to be paid for by what we export.'

'What I said myself; if you don't believe me, ask Dougie,' said the Captain.

'Of course. Well, it's like this — there's the Irish; you don't want Home Rule for Ireland?'[10]

'The Irish!' said Para Handy. 'They're aal wrong except Divverty, him that keeps the shippin' box at Greenock, and he's wan of the best. Divverty's chust sublime.'

'Then look at the herring trade,' said the canvasser. 'The Norwegians dump their cheap herring on us and spoil the real Loch Fyne — that's Free Trade for you!'

'Ye're quite right,' said Para Handy. 'What sort of a man iss he this Mr. Dobbie I hear them speakin' aboot?'

'I could tell you lots about him,' said the canvasser, darkly, 'but I'm not the man to carry stories. Stick you by Mr. Younger and you'll be all right. It means bigger wages, and the Union, and a whole lot of other things you know as well as I do without my telling you. It's on the like of you the country's depending to — to — to see things put right. Will you come away up and vote now?'

'I'll be up efter my dinner,' said Para Handy.

The Captain washed himself after dinner, put on his hard-felt hat, and went to do his duty as a citizen. When he returned more than an hour later he told the Mate all about it.

'It's no' an easy job yon,' said he, 'and ye get no thanks for it, not wan drop. You would think at a time like this there would be something goin', but it's a good thing we can do withoot it.'

'Who did ye vote for?' asked the Mate.

'When I went up,' said Para Handy, paying no attention to the question, 'the polis sercheant showed me into a room where there wass two or three men and wan black tin box. "What's your name?" said wan of the chaps. "Peter Macfarlane," said I, and he handed me a ticket. I wass goin' to put it in my pocket and come away when the sercheant lifts up a screen[11] and pushes me into a kind of a cell with no furniture in it but a bit of lead pencil, and it chained. I waited in for a while, thinkin' he was goin' to bring something, and at last he pulled the screen, and said, "Hurry up, Peter; what's keepin' ye?"

'"Nothing's keepin' me," said I; "it wass yoursel' put me here."'

10. *Irish Home Rule had been a dominant issue in British politics from the 1870's. The Liberal party split on the issue in 1885 with the so-called Liberal Unionists voting against Gladstone. Campbell- Bannerman favoured granting Home Rule at a suitable time.*

11. *The Ballot Act of 1872 introduced the secret ballot into British Parliamentary elections*

'"Tuts! he said, "it's in there ye vote. Put your cross on the paper ye got, and then come oot here and put the paper in this box," and then he drew the screen again.

'I took oot the paper and looked at it, and, faith, it didna give me much help, for there wass chust two names on it. "Peter," says I to mysel' "this iss a great responsibility. Ye must pause and consuder, and no' put in the wrong man."

'I was thinkin' away to mysel' ass hard ass I could when the sercheant tugged back the screen again, and said, "For the love of Moses, are ye sleepin' in there, Peter, or writin' a book, or what? Mind there's a lot o' other voters oot here waitin' a chance o' the keelivine (lead pencil). Finish the chob, and come away oot."

'"Campbell," said I to him, "it's not every day Peter Macfarlane puts a man in Parliament and he's not goin' to be hurried over the chob by you or anybody else."

'"I'll have to bring the Sheriff to ye if ye don't come oot pretty sherp," said the sercheant quite nesty, and went away.

'I started thinkin' again of what a responsibility it wass, and whether I would give the chob to Dobbie or Younger, and in other ten meenutes back comes the polis sercheant wi' a chentleman.

'"Come, come." said the chentleman, "what's all this aboot? It's no' a bathin-machine ye're in, my good man. If you have filled up your paper, come out and put it into the ballot-box, and give others a chance. If ye're not ready in three minutes, oot ye come, whether ye vote or no'."

'I saw there wass no use puttin' off any longer, so I made my mark on the paper and came oot and put it in the box and settled the thing.'

'But who did ye vote for?' asked Dougie.

'The right man, of course,' said Para Handy, cautiously.

'And who is the right man?' asked the Mate.

'The man I voted for,'[12] said Para Handy, and went below to hang up his hard hat.

12. *Whether with Para's help or not the Conservative candidate, George Younger, won Ayr Burghs with a majority of 261 votes against the Liberal tide and continued to represent the constituency until 1922. A member of the well-known brewing family, Younger received a Baronetcy in 1911 and was created Viscount Younger of Leckie in 1928. He died in 1929.*

Neil Munro 1907 *The Baillie*